Introduction to the Sociology of Language

Introduction
to the
Sociology
of
Language

Fernando Peñalosa
California State University, Long Beach

Newbury House Publishers, Inc. / Rowley / Massachusetts / 01969
ROWLEY • LONDON • TOKYO

1981

Library of Congress Cataloging in Publication Data

Peñalosa, Fernando.
    Introduction to the sociology of language.

    Bibliography: p.
    Includes index.
    1. Sociolinguistics.   I. Title.
P40.P4   401'.9   80-29329
ISBN 0-88377-183-7

Cover design by Barbara Frake

NEWBURY HOUSE PUBLISHERS, INC.

Language Science
Language Teaching
Language Learning

ROWLEY, MASSACHUSETTS 01969
ROWLEY ● LONDON ● TOKYO

First printing: April 1981

Printed in the U.S.A.   5   4

**To the memory of
my grandfather,
Lic. Sebastián Peñalosa Cosío
and my father,
Sr. Fernando Peñalosa Casanova**

who bequeathed to me the following humorous
verse, illustrative of the layperson's amazement at
the miracle of first language acquisition

> Asombróse un portugués
> al ver que en su tierna infancia
> todos los niños en Francia
> pudieran hablar francés.
> —Arte diabólico es,—
> dijo torciendo el mostacho,
> pues para hablar el "gabacho"
> un fidalgo en Portugal,
> llega a viejo y lo habla mal,
> ¡y aquí lo "parla" un muchacho!

Acknowledgments

The author would like to thank the following publishers and authors for permission to quote from their works:

Academic Press and William G. Lockwood: *European Moslems*, by William G. Lockwood, p. 53.

American Folklore Society: "Playing the Dozens" by Roger G. Abrahams, *Journal of American Folklore*, v. 75, p. 210.

Marjorie Boulton: *Zamenhof, Creator of Esperanto*, by Marjorie Boulton, pp. 6–7.

Cambridge University Press: book review by Ralph Fasold, *Language in Society*, v. 4, pp. 202–203; *Speech Acts*, by John R. Searle, p. 25; book review by Joel Sherzer, *Language in Society*, v. 2, p. 273.

ECO-Logos: "Esperanto and the Ideology of Constructed Languages," *International Language Reporter*, v. 16, p. 4.

Harper and Row Publishers: *Language in Culture*, Dell Hymes ed., pp. 229–230; *Language and Woman's Place*, by Robin Lakoff, p. 42.

Harcourt, Brace, Jovanovich, Inc.: *The Meaning of Meaning* by C. K. Ogden and I. A. Richards, pp. 299–300.

Holt, Rinehart and Winston: *Language*, by Leonard Bloomfield, p. 497. Copyright 1933 by Holt, Rinehart and Winston, Inc. Copyright renewed © 1961 by Leonard Bloomfield.

Massachusetts Institute of Technology: *Aspects of the Theory of Syntax*, by Noam Chomsky, p. 3.

Claudia Mitchell-Kernan: *Language in a Black Urban Community*, pp. 106–107.

Mouton Publishers: *Sociolinguistics*, William Bright, ed., p. 88; *Advances in Language Planning*, Joshua A. Fishman, ed., pp. 427–428; *Readings in the Sociology of Language*, Joshua A. Fishman, ed., p. 534; *Man, Language and Society*, Samir Ghosh, ed., p. 215; *Language in the Crib*, by Ruth Weir, *passim*.

Newbury House Publishers: *Attitudes and Motivation in Second Language Learning*, by Robert G. Gardner and Wallace Lambert, p. 3.

Oxford University Press: *The Tongues of Men and Speech*, by J. R. Firth, p. 99.

Penguin Books Ltd.: David Crystal, *Linguistics* (Pelican Books 1971), p. 61. Copyright © David Crystal, 1971; "Introduction" by Pier Paolo Giglioli from *Language and Social Context*, ed. Pier Paolo Giglioli (Penguin Education, 1972), p. 16. Selection © Pier Paolo Giglioli 1972. Reprinted by permission of Penguin Books Ltd.

Routledge & Kegan Paul Ltd.: *A Question of Answers*, by William P. Robinson and S. J. Rackstraw, v. 1, pp. 11–12.

Scarecrow Press and Mary Ritchie Key: *Paralanguage and Kinesics*, by Mary Ritchie Key, pp. 116–117.

Society for the Psychological Study of Social Issues: "The Bilingual's Perform-ance: a Psychological Overview" by John Macnamara, *Journal of Social Issues*, v. 23, no. 2, p. 64.

University of Pennsylvania Press: *Foundations in Sociolinguistics*, by Dell Hymes, p. 75.

Preface

This volume is an attempt to summarize what is currently known concerning the relationships between social behavior and language behavior. The sociology of language is the interdisciplinary field which studies such relationships, and this text constitutes an introduction to the field. The book is intended both for graduate and advanced undergraduate students and for interested laypersons who have no extensive knowledge of either sociology or linguistics. Thus, students of linguistics will find much that is familiar to them in Chapter 2, and social science students will in Chapter 4. In both of these chapters, however, I have tried regularly to show the relevance of linguistic data for social data and vice versa.

It is hoped that the book will stimulate the reader to go on and investigate the subject further by following up bibliographic references which interest him or her. The problem is not a dearth of material but rather, a super abundance. Books and articles are coming out at such a rate that it is virtually impossible for any single person to keep up with the field as a whole. Thus, it is hoped that the overview presented here will help orient the reader to the main areas and issues and stimulate him or her to further exploration.

Any book, especially one dealing with an ill-defined and far-flung field, necessarily reflects the personal orientation of its author. While I have tried to present material in as objective fashion as possible, still my biases should be clear to the reader: my strong feeling for and support of minority rights and cultural pluralism.

While the shortcomings of the work are solely my own, whatever merit it may have is entirely to the credit of the many authors upon whose research I have drawn. In this connection, I would like to pay special tribute to the amazingly productive Joshua A. Fishman, to whom all students of the subject are enormously indebted. It was his *Readings in the Sociology of Language* (1968) which first inspired me to take up the study of this field.

I am also grateful to California State University, Long Beach, for a sabbatical leave for the 1975–76 academic year, during which much of the research for this book was completed. I would also like to thank the anonymous reviewers of the manuscript, who made extremely useful suggestions and criticisms, as well as Martha Castleman, Karen Fawson, Lorraine Michael, and Judy Penley, who typed various portions of the manuscript. Finally, I am deeply grateful to my wife Doris for the love and understanding which makes my work immeasurably easier.

Fernando Peñalosa

Rancho Palos Verdes, California
April 1980

Contents

Introduction to the Sociology of Language

1

Introduction

1.1 The sociology of language

Ever since people began consciously to analyze their surroundings, they could not help but notice ways in which language and other human activities were interrelated. Since ancient times, scholars have recorded their observations and speculations on language in society. In more recent centuries we have the classical statements of Wilhelm von Humboldt on the relationships between language and world view; Émile Durkheim's theorizing about the influence of social structure on cultural configurations, including language; and George H. Mead's discussions of the role of communication in the socialization process, including the development of the self. These scholars clearly saw the enormous significance of language for the emergence and survival of human societies (Luckmann 1975:19).

More recently, anthropologists such as Bronislaw Malinowski (1956) and linguists such as J. R. Firth (1970), Uriel Weinreich (1953a), and Charles Ferguson (1959) have understood and investigated the relationships of linguistic data and social phenomena. Nevertheless, the sociology of language as a defined, labeled and self-conscious field of study is a very recent phenomenon, developing only since the beginning of the 1960s. (See the historical account by Grimshaw [1971]). The earliest textbooks and specialized journals are scarcely a decade old. The journals *Language in Society* and the *International Journal of the Sociology of Language* commenced in 1972 and 1974 respectively. The first two important collections of readings on the subject were Hymes' (1964) *Language and Culture in Society* and Fishman's (1968) *Readings in the Sociology of Language*. The first textbook was Fishman's *Sociolinguistics* (1970). Spearheading the development of the field were the now defunct Committee on Sociolinguistics of the Social Science Research Council, founded in 1964, and the Research Committee on Sociolinguistics of the International Sociological Association, founded in 1967. Outside the mainstream of these developments were the pioneering works of J. O. Hertzler (1953, 1965).

1

The growing interest of linguists in the relationship between language forms and social meaning has resulted from a number of different motivating factors, such as the need for a sounder empirical base for linguistic theory, the belief that linguists should investigate the social factors influencing language use, and the belief that sociolinguistic knowledge should be applied to urgent educational problems, with particular reference to ethnic minorities.

These factors have been particularly important in the United States. In other areas of the world, interest has been stimulated by the need for language planning and development in the former colonial areas of the Third World, widespread bilingualism and migration in Europe, the problems of integration of indigenous populations into the national society in various Latin American countries, and widespread illiteracy in most of the world. In addition in the multiethnic Soviet Union, there has long been an interest in the relationship between language and society. The People's Republic of China has its own unique sociolinguistic problems and challenges.

Because the most commonplace, ubiquitous, and most important of all man's characteristics is undoubtedly his use of language, social scientists of all varieties have long acknowledged its importance and its indispensability. At the same time, they proceeded to ignore it as an object of study. Therein lies one of the strangest paradoxes in the history of the social sciences. As Giglioli (1972:7) expresses it, "Just because they viewed language as a necessary prerequisite of every human group, sociologists thought that it was of no consequence in differentiating social behavior and therefore neglected its study."

It is true that language-related variables have been utilized in sociological research (for example, in studies of bilingual populations), but the structure of language or of language use itself had not been taken account of. Sociological theory in general has paid almost no serious attention to language. Thus, for example, the index to Cohen's *Modern Social Theory* (1968) does not contain even a single reference to language, and the index to Turner's *The Structure of Sociological Theory* (1974) has but a single reference, namely to a brief mention of language as a basic "resource" for interaction to occur. A half dozen or so other textbooks or collections in sociological theory taken at random will ordinarily reveal a complete lack of discussion of language. The same is not generally true of textbooks in social psychology which take language seriously, although they do not necessarily incorporate the views of contemporary linguistics, psycholinguistics, or sociolinguistics.

Sociologists have neglected the interrelationship between the regularities of social behavior and linguistic data for a number of reasons. In the first place, exceedingly few sociologists have received any extensive training in linguistics and, hence, are not aware of the nature and importance of linguistic facts and how to analyze them. Furthermore, sociologists have always emphasized the overwhelming importance of language as a criterion of humanity, as being absolutely essential for human communication, and for the existence of culture, social interaction, and societal continuity. Its pervasiveness, universality, and crucial importance was acknowledged, but language as a variable was rarely examined by sociologists. Conversely, linguists have in the past typically studied

languages as self-contained systems. If they did take social factors into consideration, they either utilized anecdotal, impressionistic evidence or collected social
data without observing even minimal standards of good sociological data gathering and analysis. Fortunately, this is becoming less true as younger linguists
trained in sociological and statistical methodology have done sociologically
sophisticated research. Scholars such as Labov, Bailey, Wolfram, Cedergren, and
the Sankoffs are only a few of these.

Some of the interrelationships between the structure of language and the
social contexts in which it is used are of a universal nature, that is, they are found
in all human societies and might be considered sociolinguistic universals. The
vast majority of the relationships, however, are variable because of the enormous
variability of both linguistic and social structures among and within human
societies.

The most fundamental assumption of any sociology is that human behavior is
not entirely random or erratic. It is, within certain limits, predictable, that is,
patterned. In language, as in other human phenomena, one searches for
patterned regularities and finds that language is rule-governed. The formulation
of such rules or norms constitutes much of the work of linguists. The fact that such
rules are affected by social context is one of the postulates of sociolinguistics.

Human beings interact directly with each other in a variety of social contexts or
settings and likewise influence each other in more indirect ways through the
mediation of political, economic, educational, and other institutional structures.
What people say to each other and how they say it is a salient component of all
such interaction and influence. The "how" includes such phenomena as the use
of particular languages, dialects, or styles, as well as characteristics of language
itself, that is, choice of words (lexicon), aspects of meaning (semantics), the
sounds employed (phonology), and the way elements have been sorted and
combined to form sentences (syntax). Furthermore, a pervasive characteristic of
human beings is that they not only act and observe the actions of themselves and
others, but they also have attitudes and emotions about such acts. Man is an
evaluating animal and an emotive animal. Man not only talks, he talks about how
people talk, and such talk reflects his attitudes and emotions about language.

The discussion so far has been largely in abstract terms. To make the above
points more concrete, I will list by way of illustration a number of situations or
phenomena which have been, or could be, subject to analysis within the framework of the sociology of language. In each case, the issue will be phrased in the
form of a question posed for the investigator. The number of the section of this
book which discusses each is indicated.

> How does the structure of the nuclear family affect the way in which language
> is acquired by the child? (4.2)
> How can one analyze what goes on during a conversation? (5.5)
> How do judgments regarding correct or incorrect grammar arise, and what are
> the social consequences of such judgments? (6.1)
> Why are boys more likely than girls to say *fishin'* for *fishing*? (8.2)
> How is social status signified and acknowledged by the way people use
> language? (8.3)

formal register

What are some of the ways in which language is used to promote group identity? (9.1)   *Ghana*

How do language similarities and differences contribute to the growth of nationalism? (10.1)

What happens when two populations speaking different languages come into contact with each other? (10.4)

Under what conditions does a population give up its own language and adopt another? (10.6)

What social factors promote or discourage bilingualism in an immigrant population? (7.1)

How is language utilized by some people to control others? (11.2)

What kinds of criteria are likely to be operative when a formerly colonized country sets about choosing a national language or languages? (11.3)

The leading figure in the development and characterization of the sociology of language as an identifiable discipline, Joshua A. Fishman, has defined the field as follows:

"The sociology of language examines the interaction between these two aspects of human behavior: the use of language and the social organization of behavior. Briefly put, the sociology of language focuses upon the entire gamut of topics related to the social organization of language behavior, including not only language usage per se, but also language attitudes and overt behaviors toward language and toward language users" (Fishman 1972b:1). This approach focuses on linguistically related social problems such as linguistic minorities, bilingualism, language planning, conflict, and standardization.

The field is also just as often conceptualized as *sociolinguistics*, the study of the distribution of specific features of linguistic structure by identifiable social categories. Emphasis has been placed on the fact that the variability of linguistic forms reflects human social diversity. Wherever we find different kinds of people, we find different kinds of language.

Another important version of the field is referred to as the *ethnography of communication*, which begins with an examination of the functions which language might carry out in human societies and then studies the ways in which people, in fact, use language to fulfill these functions. This approach involves a detailed study of human, small-group interaction. It should be noted that this contemporary development stresses all the dimensions of speech, emphasizing that it is not a matter of haphazard individual choice but is patterned and largely predictable. These differences of emphasis between the sociology of language, sociolinguistics, and the ethnography of communication will be ignored here, and all three approaches will be included under *Sociology of Language* and *Sociolinguistics*, used interchangeably and characterized by the adjective *sociolinguistic.*.

Sociolinguistic work ordinarily focuses on either interaction in small groups (*microsociolinguistics*) or on the relations between language use and the major institutions of society (*macrosociolinguistics*). The first often emphasizes social-psychological factors, the second politico-economic factors. Crosscutting the division of the field into its macro and micro aspects is the distinction between the *synchronic* (studies at a given point in time) and *diachronic* (historical perspectives on sociolinguistic phenomena).

1.2 Relation to other fields

The sociology of language is an outgrowth of the interests of a number of separate academic disciplines which have focused on the convergence of linguistic and sociocultural factors. It is instructive to consider how the sociology of language relates to these other fields and how it differs from them in general orientation, theory, and methodology.

Anthropologists have perhaps contributed more to the sociology of language than members of any other discipline except linguistics itself. In anthropology, the field generally known as "language and culture" has long emphasized the notions that the functions of language vary from community to community and that a repertoire of language codes or varieties is used within a single community. These notions paved the way for some of the most important contemporary concerns of the sociology of language. The anthropologists have also concentrated on such topics as the relationships among grammatical structure, world view, and semantic categories, as well as the influence of language on human interaction.

Perhaps the keynote of sociolinguistics has been its emphasis on variability. Anthropologists have emphasized that languages, like human populations, are inherently heterogeneous and variable and that different kinds of people use different kinds of language for different kinds of purposes. Linguistics and even the commonsense views of language encountered in other disciplines have tended to look at a given language as if it were a uniform, monolithic whole. Psychology traditionally has studied language out of social context, in contrived experimental situations. Educational psychology has typically accepted laymen's notions of "correctness" and stereotyped the children of the poor and minorities as "verbally deprived" or even as "alingual." Sociology typically has utilized commonsense concepts in looking at language and has viewed it as homogeneous, rather than as a means of creating and expressing social differences. In contrast to the parent disciplines, the sociology of language considers natural language behavior as heterogeneous, variable, and influenced by context, that is, by real-life language-use situations. Sociolinguistics prefers to consider social and linguistic norms as problematic and to be determined by empirical inquiry. Thus, for example, multilingual individuals are not necessarily to be considered "abnormal" or "unstable."

Readers who come to this book with some background in sociology are undoubtedly interested in what kind of contribution the study of language can make to sociology. Some aspects of sociolinguistics have more relevance for sociology than others. For example, the sociology of knowledge depends on the analysis of language but has not made much progress (except in the area of ideological criticism) because of insufficient grounding in the sociology of language. The sociology of religion for the most part naively accepts the linguistic basis of the socially molded symbolic words utilized by religious systems. Questions raised by the sociology of language likewise are obviously relevant for the sociology of literature. The sociology of language similarly has much to offer to opinion research and the sociological analysis of mass media and propaganda analysis. The sociology of the family (in the analysis of socialization processes, marital adjustment, and interaction) sorely needs sociolinguistic insights. Other

obvious areas of application are the theory of social control and social stratification, political sociology (especially nationalism), and sociologically oriented
psychiatry.

The sociological analyst is constantly trying to establish a fit between his own
scientific language and the language used by his respondents. The analyst does
not simply take data; he creates them by means of his procedures of classification and ordering. He should be acutely aware of how the rules of his own
language direct and shape his observations. The sociologist's assumptions and
presuppositions cannot be viewed apart from the language in which he does his
theorizing and research. Sociological language must be clarified because linguistic structure and use affect the way people interpret and describe the world.

The ethnography of communication can make a contribution toward the
understanding of interrogative behavior in various human groups, an understanding which is vital to the interests of sociologists who design and administer
questionnaires and interviews that are taken for granted in the sociologist's own
subculture. The sociologist needs to avoid questions or types of questioning that
may appear insulting, boorish, threatening, or meaningless to respondents.
Certain types of questions can be asked or answered only by certain persons or in
certain defined contexts. All these the sociologist must learn about (Grimshaw
1969:17–18).

The problem of meaning in sociological research is one which can be clarified
by sociolinguistic theory and research. The social researcher necessarily must be
concerned with the structure of meaning, whether he is studying face-to-face
interaction or survey research data. He must be especially sensitive to the social
meaning carried by linguistic forms above and beyond their obvious referential
meaning. But the sociology of language can make and has made a contribution
not only to the methodology of sociology but also to its substance. The bulk of this
book deals with these substantive contributions.

As the practical and ideological implications of sociolinguistic topics are
pursued, the sociology of language impinges on the terrain of political science,
philosophy, education, economics, and other fields. Perhaps because sociologists have for the most part de-emphasized the political and economic aspects of
social life and focused on more general types of social processes, the political and
economic aspects of language do not loom importantly in the available literature
of the sociology of language. Most sociologists have focused on microsociolinguistic topics, whereas scholars working in the field such as historians, political
scientists or educationists have been more sensitive to political issues. Perhaps
what is needed is a more sharply focused field of politicolinguistics, that is, a field
where linguistic behavior and attitudes can be viewed in terms of the power relations extant in a given society. Aristotle said that "Man is a political animal." All
social relationships have a power dimension, and man is *especially* a political
animal when he is involved in the act of speaking.

The field of philosophy impinges upon linguistics at a number of important
points, such as the logical foundations of syntactic structure and in the mutual
interest of both fields in semantics. The concern of the ordinary-language
philosophers with the speech act (section 5.6) is an interest more directly

concerned with sociolinguistics. There has long been a debate between two philosophical positions known as rationalism, which claims that at least some human knowledge comes from the mind or reason, and empiricism, which claims that all human knowledge derives from experience. Until recently the empiricist position held undisputed sway in both linguistics and sociology, but the theories of Chomsky in linguistics and the growth of ethnomethodology in sociology have surely weakened this position. Scholars are now not so much concerned with the discovery of structures as they are in studying how the human mind uses its logical capacity to create and construct its own linguistic and sociocultural systems and its own natural and social reality.

Psychology has had a long-standing interest in language and has undertaken experimental and observational studies directly concerned with the perception and acquisition of language. Unfortunately, the older studies were based on the concepts of structural linguistics (when they had any linguistic sophistication at all) and, hence, were using a model of language much simpler than what we have come to accept as a result of the influence of generative transformational grammar. As a consequence of the latter there has been a tremendous growth of activity in the field which has come to be known as psycholinguistics. This field overlaps somewhat with sociolinguistics, to their mutual benefit. Its major contributions have been in the study of first language acquisition, that is, the psychological processes involved in the child's learning his native language. New insights have also been obtained in questions of meaning and perception, language-processing, and bilingualism. The psycholinguists have been concerned also with the psychological reality of deep structure and other linguistic theoretical constructs. They have ventured into the study of nonverbal communication and language attitudes. Studies focusing on the functioning of the human brain as related to language, on the other hand, have come to be known as neurolinguistics.

To the extent that psychology becomes social psychology, the perspective more closely approximates that of sociology. The sociology and social psychology of mass communication, public opinion, and collective behavior is interested in how language is used by the few to influence the behavior of the many. The focus here is on the content of language, rather than its form. It is, of course, not always possible to separate content and form, even in analysis, hence such studies overlap with, and potentially contribute to, the sociology of language and vice versa.

Paradoxically, sociologists have made relatively little contribution to sociolinguistics except in limited areas of microsociolinguistics, especially the analysis of conversation. The macrosociolinguistic studies reported in this book are the work primarily of linguists, anthropologists, and political scientists.

1.3 Theory and methodology

If the sociology of language is to be more than the pedantic or rhetorical rephrasing of the tribal wisdom, it must proceed as any other academic discipline. Any work undertaken within its frame of reference ought to proceed in the manner generally identified as scholarly activity. The sociology of language collects and analyzes empirical data, utilizes theories as frames of reference for the conduct of research, and revises such theories in the light of the results of research. The methodology used has generally been that of the academic disciplines with which the practitioners are affiliated. Some of the theories, on the other hand, because of the very special nature of the field, are somewhat distinctive.

The basis of any serious study must be some sort of empirical data and not mere conjectures, opinions, speculations, or prejudices. One observes what people do and say, including their opinions. We may also utilize the observations of others, including those in written form. The validity of such second-hand observations must, of course, be carefully evaluated to ascertain the extent to which they conform to acceptable canons of methodology and theory. One's own empirical observations, likewise, must pass scrutiny by qualified others.

By knowing the methodology employed, that is, the actual steps employed in obtaining and analyzing the data, one can make judgments as to their validity. By knowing the theoretical frame of reference utilized, one can better understand why particular data were obtained rather than others. All theory is selective. It focuses one's attention on certain phenomena rather than others because one cannot simultaneously observe "everything" in any given situation. Some things are considered irrelevant or as simply given ("Constants"), while attention is focused elsewhere, that is, on those variables which presumably relate to each other in ways predicted by the theory employed. Thus, the nature of data, methodology, and theory are intricately interrelated.

Because the sociology of language has been interdisciplinary in nature, a wide variety of methods have been employed in securing data for analysis: structured and informal observations, surveys and censuses, experimentation, intensive interviews, and documentary and historical analysis. Adequate sampling methods are needed to study a cross-section of the speech of large heterogeneous urban populations. Failure to do this has given false pictures of the speech of cities, for example. And now through sampling we can make rigorous statements about differences between the speech of men and women, rather than just providing impressionistic descriptions or case studies. Another problem is securing samples of the way people talk in natural situations. As Bloomfield (1933:497) has observed, "Diffidence as to one's speech is an almost universal trait. The observer who sets out to study a strange language or a local dialect, often gets data from his informants only to find them using entirely different forms when they speak among themselves. They count these latter forms inferior and are ashamed to give them to the observer. An observer may thus record a language entirely unrelated to the one he is looking for." Thus, the dilemma is presented of how to get samples of natural speech. We must observe without being observed. Labov has devised a number of ingenious methods for solving this problem. For example, in his study of r deletion (i.e., "dropping" r except when followed by a vowel) in New York City, he went up to sales clerks in various department stores, asking them where ladies' shoes were or some other articles which he knew were on the fourth floor. After the clerk answered, he would say, "I beg your pardon?" to get the clerk to repeat herself, thus getting a sample of four possiblities for r deletion. That is, clerks would answer "fourth floor," "fawth floah," "fourth floah," or "fawth floor," and he would go from the scene and tabulate the answers. (For results, see section 8.4.) Another technique is to get people used to a tape recorder's being on so that they will talk (more or less) naturally even in its presence. Door-to-door surveys can not only collect people's responses to questions about social characteristics and linguistic behavior but also collect data directly from the way they speak, although they are likely to pay more attention than usual to their speech in the presence of the interviewer. Interaction sequences can be recorded on videotape. This procedure is especially successful with small children in the classroom, as they quickly adapt to microphones and the presence of a videotape recorder.

Sociolinguistic data gathering has not always conformed to the strict canons of what is ordinarily considered to be sociological research methodology. This is not in itself necessarily a bad thing. Too precise a methodology can be too limiting and restricting in a new area where the precise nature of the variables involved is not always clearly understood.

Methods used by the researcher will, of course, depend on the subject to be studied, as well as his own disciplinary and theoretical orientation. Scholars with microsociolinguistic, macrosociolinguistic, and ethnography of communication interests use a wide variety of different methodologies. Those with macrosocio-linguistic interests will depend heavily on already published statistical and historical data, as well as sometimes surveys. Students of social dialects, for example, will have to familiarize themselves with sampling methods and interview techniques. They have to be able to calculate measures of social status, a task made simpler if sociological surveys have been carried out recently in the area under study. Those carrying out sociolinguistic surveys must familiarize themselves with census data so as to ensure an appropriate representation in the sample of the subject population by age, sex, ethnic group, socioeconomic status, or other variables important to the research.

Once persons have been selected for study, methods for the elicitation of data have to be decided upon. One can use informal conversation, structured inter-views, or ask the respondent to read paragraphs or word lists, to take certain tests, or to listen to recorded materials and make comments on them.

Data can also be collected by less rigorous means, such as the researcher's having the students in his classes fill out questionnaires or react to recorded samples of speech. One may also utilize the group interview, particularly when the group is a natural one, such as a boys' gang, family group, or party situation. Here one is able to observe language in actual use, as well as the social interac-tion which accompanies it.

A number of researchers, particularly anthropologists, have used the method of participant observation. The researcher participates in the life of the com-munity and observes their linguistic and other behavior as unobtrusively as possible. None of these methods are mutually exclusive, of course, and potentially all of them could be used in the same research project to obtain a good picture of the linguistic behavior of a particular population or group. (Some research techniques are discussed in this volume in connection with particular topics, e.g., the matched guise technique for studying language attitudes in section 7.5.)

Sociolinguistic data are so ubiquitous that one can collect them almost anywhere. We must insist, however, that they be gathered carefully, systematically, and with awareness of precisely how one is doing it. What kind of methodology one uses is predicated on assumptions regarding the nature of the phenomena being studied—in this case, the nature of language, the nature of society, and the nature of the interrelationships between the two. Theory constitutes a systematic explanation of observed data and makes sense out of data.

To the extent that a theory adequately accounts for the facts, it will predict future events. In other words, we predict that under certain stated conditions, the presence of certain variables (quantified, if possible) will produce given results. For example, if the theory states that certain linguistic phenomena are to be explained by certain social configurations or processes, then whenever we find the latter, we should expect to find the same linguistic phenomena. A fairly safe prediction, for example, would be that differences in relative social status will be lexically, grammatically, or phonologically marked.

Being able to predict what will happen under given conditions is prerequisite to any application of the findings to practical purposes. Human speech is involved in virtually all other human activities, and so conceivably all problematic situations have a linguistic dimension which may be relevant to the solution of the problem. The main reason for the recent burgeoning of the sociology of language has been the great interest in a number of language-related problems, so that applied sociolinguistics is one of the major divisions of the field. So many social problems cry for solution that there are those who claim that we cannot afford the luxury of theoretical research, that is, research to test theories, and that all research ought to be aimed at the solution of pressing practical problems. A sense of social responsibility can demand no less. But because of the intimate interdependence of theoretical and applied research, it would be foolhardy to insist on one at the expense of the other. At the same time, it is reasonable to insist that theoretical research be developed primarily in those areas where there is likely to be some benefit for the solution of pressing practical problems.

Whereas theory reflects judgments as to what is, ideology reflects judgments about what should be. Ideologies enshrine value judgments as to what is right and wrong, good and bad, important and unimportant. A social ideology passes judgment on existing imperfect social orders and defines, if only by implication, the perfect society. Of all the considerations involved in scholarly study, perhaps the ideological dimension of sociolinguistic work has been the most neglected. Underlying ideological positions are not always made explicit, nor have they generally been subjected to scrutiny by others. Some ideological position necessarily underlies all theoretical statements, as well as the planning, execution, and reporting of empirical research. In the social area, in sociolinguistics as elsewhere, such ideological positions usually involve assumptions regarding at least two very important matters, namely power relationships and ethnic/class values.

While all of us have our own personal positions on these matters, it is our professional ethical responsibility to make our value judgments, our political positions clear, so that others may judge our work in the full knowledge of the presuppositions and assumptions which underlie it. If we are in favor of the forced assimilation of minorities into the dominant society, or if we believe, on the other hand, in cultural pluralism or Chicano nationalism, or whatever, we ought to make our positions clear. In sociolinguistic work, as in most, if not all, spheres of life, honesty is the best policy.

Discussion questions

1. How does the sociology of language relate to your own special field of interest? What do you expect to gain from studying the sociology of language?
2. How does the sociology of language differ from sociolinguistics? Do you feel this is a valid distinction?
3. What are the different branches of the sociology of language? Which one of these interests you the most, and why?
4. How does the perspective on language offered by the sociology of language differ from that of other disciplines?
5. Distinguish macrosociolinguistics from microsociolinguistics, identifying the topics dealt with in each.
6. Discuss the relationship between theory and methodology in the sociology of language.
7. What are some of the methods sociolinguists use in collecting data? Explain which methods seem most congenial to your interests and needs.

2

The nature of language

2.1 Models of language

There seems to be fairly general agreement among linguists that language is a system which relates meaning to sound, whether in the action of speaker or hearer. Presumably the speaker has some meaning which he wishes to convey. He utters certain appropriate sounds. The other person hears these sounds and attempts to derive the meaning expressed by the speaker. How this actually occurs is the object of theoretical disputes. Contemporary linguistic science is, in the simplest terms, trying to find out what happens when people speak and when they listen. The principal focus of linguistic research has been on the grammar. Within grammar the emphasis may be on one of its three main areas or levels: *phonology,* the system of speech sounds; *syntax,* the means by which words and other grammatical units are combined to form sentences (nowadays usually taken to include morphology, the study of patterns of word formation); and *semantics,* the meaning system. In practice, it is not only impossible but also undesirable to keep these levels separate. Every language (and every speaker) also has a *lexicon,* or dictionary (in an abstract, not physical sense) which contains the words, grammatical forms, idioms, etc., and the rules for their use. In practice, it is often difficult to tell where lexicon ends and grammar begins. This question, and the way in which the grammar does relate sound and meaning, are matters of great theoretical importance in linguistics, and a wide variety of positions have been taken. The most productive ones, however, can be grouped under the general heading of *generative-transformational grammar,* an approach publicly launched by Chomsky's *Syntactic Structures* (1957).

One of the most important assertions of generative-transformational grammar is the recognition of universal grammar, i.e., that certain features are present in all human languages, presumably as a consequence of pan-human structures of cognition. Besides its insistence on making all grammatical explanations complete and *explicit,* transformational grammar generally assumes the existence of a more abstract level of representation ("deep" or "underlying" structure) below that of actually uttered forms ("surface" structure), and more closely tied into the meaning of the sentence. Consider these simple examples of different surface structure (but which presumably have the same underlying structure) from three different areas of the grammar.

Syntax   1. David gave Manuel a fish.
             2. David gave a fish to Manuel.
             3. Manuel was given a fish by David.
Phonology 4. What did you eat?
             5. Wha' did ya eat?
             6. Whadya eat?
             7. Whajeat?
Semantics 8. eye doctor
             9. ophthalmologist

This is not the occasion to get into the nature of the underlying abstract syntactic, phonological, and semantic representations in these examples, except to point out that the surface forms 2, 4, and 8 are probably the surface structures in each case which are closest in form to the more abstract underlying representations.

Transformational grammar is particularly interested in the processes by which various types of sentences are derived through a series of transformations from basic underlying declarative sentences. Thus, for example, if we consider 2 the basic sentence, then 1 could have been derived through a "dative" transformation and 3 through both "dative" and "passive" transformations. *Did David give a fish to Manuel?* would be derived via a "question" transformation from the same underlying structure.

In speaking about linguistic behavior, we thus cannot talk about "language" in vague, generalized terms but must focus on specific phonological, syntactic, or semantic phenomena. Because our frame of reference is generally a "scientific" one, we will describe how people speak, without praise or condemnation. Our approach, in other words, is descriptive rather than prescriptive.

Consider the following sentences:
    10(a) Carlos nunca ha estado en Oaxaca
    10(b) Carlos has never been in Oaxaca
    11(a) Dame el reloj
    11(b) Give me the watch

From sentences 10, we clearly understand that Carlos is still alive, for the present perfect tense in both Spanish and English carries the connotation that the subject is still alive at the time the statement is made. Relating the meaning of sentences to the relevant features of the "real world" constitutes the study of *pragmatics,* a necessary adjunct to sentence grammar. On the other hand, it is clear from the use of the definite article in sentence 11 that the desired watch has already been referred to, i.e., the meaning of the sentence is partially derived from the discourse in which it is embedded. Therefore, another necessary part of linguistics is *discourse analysis.* Closely allied to this is *conversational analysis,* in other words, the study of the use as well as of the structure of language. Conversation is only one, although undoubtedly the most important one, type of speech event, a category which also includes speeches, joke telling, therapeutic interviews, etc. Speech events are considered to consist of smaller units referred to as speech acts, such as statements, questions, promises, insults, etc. How speakers do all these things in different societies is the subject of a most fertile and promising field of research, the ethnography of communication.

Universals

The concept of universals is relatively new in both sociology and linguistics, that is, the idea that certain characteristics are found in all human societies or in all human languages. The assumption in the latter case is that fundamentally all languages are at base the same because the human brain is everywhere the same. All humans, therefore, live in the same world, and experience is directly translatable from one culture to another and from one language to another. What then are some of the features all human languages share?

All languages use both consonants and vowels. The order of sounds is meaningful, that is, for example, pin and nip do not mean the same thing. The order of words and other sentence elements also convey meaning. A limited set of consonants and vowels in any language can be combined to produce an infinite number of different sentences.

As a result of the development of generative transformational grammar, much of the search for universals has concentrated on syntax. One position is that every grammar requires such categories as noun, predicate, and sentence but that other grammatical categories and features may be differently arranged in different languages.

All languages have some sets of two or more words which mean the same or almost the same thing, such as English skunk and pole cat. Likewise, every language has at least some words each of which means more than one thing, such as English bank or fair. All languages have means of negating statements and asking questions.

A number of language universals seem particularly relevant to social factors and may reflect sociocultural universals. For example, all languages have lexical items that shift their meaning depending on elementary features of the speech situation. That is, every language has what are known as deictic elements, such as personal or demonstrative pronouns or words like "here" or "there." Every language has an element that denotes the speaker and one that denotes the addressee, that is, the first and second person singular pronouns, and so on. Furthermore, every human language has proper names (Hockett 1966:21).

With increasing attention paid to what many feminist critics are calling our "sexist language," it is interesting to consider the nature of grammatical gender, one alleged source of sexism (see also section 8.2). Gender (masculine and feminine) is a matter not only of grammatical relationships but also of social convention, as contrasted with sex (male and female) which is a biological distinction. It is universally true that if a language has gender categories in the noun, it will have gender categories in the pronoun. Furthermore, if a language makes distinctions of gender in the first person, it will always have gender distinctions in the second and/or third person. Also, when we find gender distinctions in the plural of the pronoun, we will find gender distinctions in the singular (Greenberg 1966:96). The search for universals is one of the most active areas of current linguistic research (cf. the four-volume collection on the subject edited by Greenberg 1978).

Animal and human communication

A major theoretical issue in the human sciences is whether the differences between animal and human communication systems are discrete or form a continuum, whether they represent two different orders of phenomena. Chomsky (1972:70), although noting that the two types of systems share some properties, asserts that human language is based on entirely different principles. Humans are not simply more intelligent but possess a specific type of mental organization. Human language is not just a more complex form of the type of communication utilized by other animals. One of the most important characteristics of animal communication systems is that they ordinarily consist of a limited number of signals, each of which has its own behavioral or emotional referent. Even the most elemental stages of human speech seem to be quite beyond any nonhuman species.

Animals not only do not have language in the human sense but also have been singularly unsuccessful in learning human language when given an opportunity to do so. The problem is not so much the inability to reproduce human sounds or to learn to associate words with their referents. The latter they learn with relative ease, at least with a limited number of concepts. The major stumbling block appears to be their inability to deal with human syntax. Their ability to combine signs is very limited.

Attempts to teach gestures have been more successful than attempts to teach vocalization, as shown by the work of the Gardners with a chimpanzee they have raised as a human infant. They taught their chimpanzee, Washoe, to "speak" by means of deaf-mute sign language. Washoe had a vocabulary of some 30 words at 25 months of age, a figure which compares favorably to the number of words human children use at that chronological age. Three years later she had two or three times as many. Washoe is addressed in and responds in sentences but with a difference: Washoe combines words without restriction, something human children do not do. There are no constraints on the way she combines signs. Thus, the concept of a sentence must be an innate human possession and not the product of learning (McNeill 1971:533; Gardner and Gardner 1969; Kess 1976).

Rumbaugh (1977) and his colleagues on the Lana Project devised a computer-based training system for teaching a chimpanzee to "read" and "write" using ideographs and to perform simple arithmetic computations. Messages were in the form of strings of ideographs which could be typed on a keyboard and read from a visual display. Lana's conceptual system appears to be prelinguistic; that is, rather than thinking in words, she uses language as a means of creating a symbolic map of those ideas which are already in her mind. The same conclusion is suggested by Premack's (1976) study of another chimpanzee, Sarah, who learned to "read" and "write" using a system of plastic symbols stuck to a board.

As in the case of Washoe, both Sarah and Lana were taught to communicate with humans by using a visual language. The ability manifested by all three was remarkable. Since human language is the product of human culture, we see that in the case of those humans, deprived of human culture, as in the case of the feral and isolated children (see section 4.2), that they are very incompetent communicators, and the gap between humans and apes no longer seems so extensive.

Hoijer (1969) has identified four characteristics of human language, unique to human communication systems, which he calls productivity, displacement, duality of patterning, and traditional transmission. The productivity of language refers to the fact that it is an open system capable of producing an almost infinite number of utterances. Man's language enables him both to utter and to understand sentences that are completely novel, that no one has ever spoken or heard before. As a matter of fact, almost every sentence is uttered for the first time. The productivity of human language is perhaps the most-oft repeated fact in contemporary linguistics.

Displacement refers to the fact that humans can talk about things and events that are remote in time or space or, in fact, may never have existed. Duality of patterning refers to the fact that, with a very limited set of consonants and vowels, seldom more than fifty, many thousands of words can be formed, whereas in animal call systems, each call differs from the rest, both in sound and in meaning. Traditional transmission refers to the fact that language is not biologically transmitted by genes, as are call systems, but is socially taught and learned. Duality of patterning appears to be the key to the origin of language. Hoijer (1969:58–59) suggests that this was created only once in one place because its development is so far-reaching, so revolutionary, and so fruitful. It then must have spread to all hominids, so that all humans are linguistic, as well as cultural and biological, brethren. In fact, Swadesh (1972) using the comparative method, has tried to prove that all languages are descended from a single original human language.

In trying to explain the origin of language, De Laguna (1927:41) notes "... it is to the great superiority of speech over animal cries as a means of social control that we must look for the chief cause of its evolutionary origin and development." Given the discontinuity between animal call systems and human language structure, how is it possible that the latter could have evolved out of the former? Well known are the ideas of G. H. Mead, who supposed that social gesture preceded vocal gesture. Other theorists believed that the former developed along with the latter to reinforce vocabulary and supplement voice intonation. Firth, on the other hand, believed that voice developed in the trees but gesture developed on the ground (Firth 1970:143). Actually, there are three interrelated controversial issues involving the relationship between gestural and vocal communication systems. There are the questions of whether human speech originated in gestures or vocal cries; the matter of whether nonhumans, such as chimpanzees, can have language; and the dispute as to whether such languages, such as American Sign Language (Ameslan), are "true" languages.

Although agreement is far from complete, a consensus appears to be emerging from the research results of scholars from diverse disciplines studying these issues. (For a history of the theories of the origin of language, see Stam 1976).

It now appears to be the case that human gestural language, developed originally from primate gestures, could have become relatively complex and efficient before the emergence of vocal language some 50,000 years ago or so, at the beginning of the Upper Paleolithic period (Hewes 1978). Such a silent gestural language could have been particularly useful in the tracking and hunting of game animals. The development of vocal language did not abolish the need for gestural language. People resort to gestures to supplement vocal language, to communicate in the absence of a common language, and to communicate with the deaf. Deaf people automatically devise their own sign language to communicate with each other, unless they have been taught some relatively standardized variety such as American Sign Language. Such languages as Ameslan or American Indian Sign Language are not simply translations of the language of hearing persons into hand signals. Ameslan is not English; it is a language of gestures with its own lexicon and syntax, which are quite different from those of English. Despite the lack of grammatical inflections, word-order constraints are minimal. Apparently ambiguities are resolved by the accompanying kinesic features. Sign language should not be confused with finger spelling, which is language twice removed, as it is a representation of writing, which is a representation of speech. However, the two are often combined, as a person may spell grammatical endings and particles, proper names, etc. Introduction of many spelled words, plus stricter conformity to the rules of English syntax, produces a "high" variety of Ameslan which has higher prestige than the "lower" variety of "pure" Ameslan. According to Stokoe (1972), this parallels precisely the concept of diglossia as described by Ferguson (1959) (see section 7.3).

There is much bilingual "interference" between Ameslan and English, as practically all American deaf persons either speak, lip read, read or write English and, hence, are bilingual. But since most deaf children learn Ameslan in school, if they learn it at all, it is in effect a second language for most of them, unless they learned it from deaf parents. Although deaf people live in a world of hearing people, they, in fact, form a community with its own repertoire of language varieties.

While linguists have been willing to grant language status to the gestural systems of the deaf, they have been more reluctant to grant language competence to nonhumans. Chimpanzees have been quite clever in responding to human speech, in manipulating symbolic tokens, and especially in learning human sign language. In the latter case, Washoe was said to be unable to comprehend the principles of order, that is syntax. However, order of elements does not appear to be the crucial variable in determining whether we are dealing with a true language or not, for deep structure may not be ordered. Furthermore, some order has now been observed in Washoe's signing, while it is, in fact, minimal in Ameslan users. Also, a number of chimpanzees have learned to sign. Experimenters at the Institute for Primate Studies in Oklahoma are now trying to get the animals to use sign language to communicate with each other and are interested in whether mothers will pass it on to their offspring. But an important point must not be lost sight of. While subhumans may be taught to use true language, no such animals have, in fact, devised their own. Assuming that the higher primates have the intellectual capacity for language, then the question arises as to why they did not develop it while the hominids did. We may reasonably speculate that the more complex society of hominids required a true linguistic system for communication purposes. Whatever the cause-and-effect relationship may have been, it is certain that the complexity of human society and the complexity of human language evolved hand in hand.

Paralanguage and kinesics

Nonlinguistic communication is a normal part of the communication process and is integrated with linguistic communication. Under the name "body language," it has become of considerable popular interest in recent years. The terms "kinesics" and "paralanguage" are used among social scientists.

Paralanguage is defined by Key as "some kind of articulation of the vocal apparatus or significant lack of it, i.e., hesitation between segments of vocal articulation." This can include all sorts of noises such as hissing, shushing, and whistling, as well as speed, quality, and pitch of voice. According to Key, *kinesics* includes all body movement which communicates meaning such as physical or physiological action, automatic reflexes, posture, facial expression, and gesture (Key 1975b:10).

"Body language" is not to be confused with nonverbal communication which is a much broader concept. Thus, one can communicate by the composition or placement of objects, as well as by pictures and graphs, pictorial signs, etc. (Ruesch and Kees 1961). Body language, however, is used in interpersonal interaction either as a substitute for or as an accompaniment of verbal communication (most often vocal but also signed or written).

In order to fully understand what is really happening in human interaction as far as the communication process is concerned, one has to examine kinesics and paralanguage, as well as verbal signs. Paralanguage, kinesics, and verbal communication together form a definable system. Nonverbal behavior is structured, as is other linguistic and nonlinguistic behavior. Because of its complexity and magnitude, no one can systematically describe the structure of his own nonverbal behavioral pattern without concerted analytical effort. Nonverbal competence is for the most part below the level of consciousness and culturally patterned. As an instance of the cultural patterning of nonverbal communication, the case of Mayor Fiorello La Guardia of New York City may be cited. He was trilingual, tricultural, and trikinesic. This famous politician spoke English, Italian, and Yiddish, and with each shift of language, he also shifted his kinesic and paralinguistic behavior (Efron 1972:196).

In a wide range of informally reported studies, Goffman (e.g., 1959, 1967, 1971, 1978) has called our attention to the ways in which people manage the impressions they give to the people with whom they interact in various kinds of encounters. Paralinguistic and kinesic movements play a great part in such interpersonal interaction, as in the use of different vocalizations, glances, gestures, and positionings.

Birdwhistell (1970) analyzes the communication process as one in which interacting parties contribute messages along one or more channels, such as language, movement, or smell. These elements are viewed as culturally patterned. He has produced many detailed analyses of motions, especially those of Americans, using special transcription systems for recording body movement. Birdwhistell utilizes a motion picture camera and a slow-motion projector. He is convinced that body motion is a learned form of communication which can be broken down into an ordered system of isolatable elements. Sensitive to the cultural setting in each case, his detailed kinesic analyses provide ample verification of his viewpoint.

Hall (1959) has emphasized the ways in which people in different cultures use time and space to communicate. These different ways of utilizing time and space frequently cause problems in cross-cultural communication. Persons unaware of these differences may be offended or feel threatened. For example, being twenty minutes late for a business appointment carries quite different meaning in Latin America as contrasted with the United States. In the latter, there appears to be a scale of lateness in which different lengths or periods of lateness have different social implications and behavior patterns associated with them. Hall identifies the shortest periods as "mumble something" periods and slight apology periods, followed by mildly insulting periods requiring full apology, then rude periods and finally downright insulting periods. We would expect evaluation of the period of lateness also to be related to the relative social statuses of the two individuals. In some cases, status may be validated by the amount of lateness, as at a party in the United States where generally higher status people arrive later and leave earlier. Hall also points out that much difficulty in interpersonal communication may arise from the different uses of space by people from different cultures, for example, the different position of the bodies of people in conversation. The close proximity of speakers in a friendly conversation of Arabs, for example, is felt to be uncomfortable by an American, who ascribes hostility or sexual interest to a position so close that each person can feel the other's breath on his face (Hall 1969:159–160).

Competence and performance

One distinction that is frequently made is that between *language* and *speech* or *langue* and *parole* (de Saussure) or *competence* and *performance* (Chomsky), that is, between the idealized or abstracted patterns of the language and the way people actually speak. The former is, of course, not directly observable but is inferred from the latter. The former is what it is that the native speaker knows how to do with his language. The methods de Saussure (1962:321) urged to study these two aspects are somewhat paradoxical. He conceived of the social aspect of language, *langue,* as so general that it is in the possession of every speaker so that one can investigate *langue* by asking anyone about it, even oneself. On the other hand, the details of the individual's use of *parole* can be ascertained only through a survey of the population (Labov 1972b:105).

Chomsky rejects, or at least postpones, the study of performance as a proper concern of linguists. Therefore, in a real sense his theory is a theory of grammar rather than a theory of human language. Chomsky (1965:3) has expressed his goals in a statement that has become classic:

"Linguistic theory is concerned primarily with an ideal speaker-listener, in a completely homogeneous speech community, who knows its language perfectly and is unaffected by such grammatically irrelevant conditions as memory limitations, distractions, shifts of attention and interest, and errors (random or characteristic) in applying his knowledge of the language in actual performance." This viewpoint is contradicted by the central concern of sociolinguistics, namely the inherent variability found within any given language and its attention to the social contexts within which real live people, not abstractions, are actually speaking.

2.2 Prescriptive grammar

The type of grammar which is most familiar to the reader is undoubtedly the prescriptive type, that is, one which tells you what you should say if you want to speak and write your own language or some foreign language correctly. Do's and don't's are given, with examples of bad, good and better usage. Such books are used by people who wish to "improve" their speech and tend to emphasize two things, that is, good style (clear and/or elegant speech) and the avoidance of bad grammar (that is, the way speakers of lesser educational and/or socioeconomic status speak). Such grammars contain a great deal of descriptive material, for example, paradigms such as declensions or conjugations. Unfortunately, much traditional grammar in the past was based on the framework of Latin grammar, quite different from that of, say, English, rather than on a strictly independent analysis of the language itself. Hence, even the descriptive parts were faulty and unrealistic. Thus, for example, it fostered the "logical" notion that two negatives make a positive, and *I don't have no money* "really" means *I have money*. This deviation from "standard" usage is a dialect difference and is found throughout the English-speaking world. Such usage is often looked down upon by educated people but is nonetheless "logical," for double or multiple negatives with negative meaning are the rule in standard Russian and Spanish and many other languages. Take, say, the following sentence in standard Serbo-Croatian:

Nisam nikada nikome rekao o tome ni riječi. "I haven't ever said a single word about that to anybody."

The literal translation is "I haven't never to no one said about that not even a word." (Partridge 1972:121).

Thus, such judgments of "incorrectness" are judgments based upon social considerations, not logic. Yet people are more likely to be convinced by an argument which purports to be based on logic rather than one which is patently derived from social prejudice.

The study of prescriptive grammars, who makes them, who uses them for what purposes, what kinds of social conditions promote their use, and who benefits are all questions of potential sociological and political interest. One studies the activities and effects of the prescriptivists; one does not necessarily accept their judgments as to how a particular language actually works.

Robert A. Hall (1960) has been one of the most vigorous polemicists attacking prescriptive notions of language. A structural linguist, he insists on the notion that if a certain form of expression comes naturally to a given individual, it's all right to say it. Among the most important of Hall's arguments is that there is no such thing as good and bad (or correct and incorrect, grammatical and ungrammatical, right and wrong) in language. "Correct" can only mean "socially acceptable." He believes that there is no such thing as "written language." He regards speech as basic in human life and writing as a reflection of speech. To change the writing is not to change the language. The way a person speaks is more an authority for his own speech than any dictionary or grammar. Hall maintains that words do not have any "real" meaning as opposed to other "false" meanings. The meaning which people give to a word is its *real* meaning in that particular situation. No language or dialect has more merit than any other, and language change is not "decay" or "corruption," so that a later stage of a language is not necessarily worth either more or less than an earlier stage. According to Hall, "good" language is language which gets the desired effect with the least friction and difficulty for its user, whereas "good" style is simply that style of speaking or writing which is most effective under any given set of circumstances.

It is possible that Hall's position is an extreme one. As a matter of fact, in the light of generative theory, it does occur that a person can make "mistakes," that is, produce sentences that are not generated according to the rules of an identifiable dialect, even his own personal idiolect. A person might say, for example, by mistake, *I didn't wrote that letter yesterday,* or a nonnative speaker might say *For three years now I am speaking English every day.* These two sentences are *unacceptable* to native speakers of English. That is, there *is* such a thing as an ungrammatical or unacceptable sentence. It is necessary, however, to distinguish between the concepts of grammatically incorrect and socially inappropriate. Formal language is inappropriate in an informal situation, and informal language is inappropriate in a formal situation. To find out how a language "actually" works, one must attempt to describe the language without any preconceptions as to correctness or incorrectness from a logical or any other standpoint. Although modern linguistics has emphasized this point, it goes back at least as far as Noah Webster who wrote that "Grammar is built solely on the structure of language. That which is not found in the practice of speaking a language can have no place in a grammar of that language. . . . Grammars are made to show the student of language what a language is—not, how it ought to be" (quoted by Haugen 1966a:12). In more recent times, the excesses of the prescriptivists have been caricatured in the fictional character of Miss Fidditch (originally named by Henry Lee Smith, Jr.), the English teacher who relentlessly pursues the goal of "correct" English with her young charges (Joos 1962:xiv).

2.3 The study of language

The preferred point of departure of most linguists for the study of language is grammar; indeed, for many linguists, grammatical theory is synonymous with linguistic theory. When the linguist attempts to write a grammar of a language, or of some specific part of it, what he is trying to do is to devise a theory of the language, that is, to generalize about how the language works (or how language in general works if he is dealing with universal grammar or linguistic universals). As a theory, a grammar attempts to predict what people will or will not say. The ability of a grammar to do this explicitly, fully, accurately, and parsimoniously is the measure of its validity.

Grammars are ordinarily stated in the form of rules, that is, generalizations regarding certain forms or categories of forms. A rule specifies to what forms the rule applies and then says what happens to these forms.

Labov has distinguished *categorical* rules, rules which must be followed in all circumstances (for example, the "reflexive" transformation, so that you must say "I wash myself," not "I wash me"); *optional* rules, where the grammar permits a choice (for example, the "dative movement" transformation which gives "I gave Sam the lizard," as well as "I gave the lizard to Sam"); and *variable* rules, such as the phonological variation between "fishing" and "fishin." These are rules which respond systematically to such phenomena as dialect, speaking style, social setting, age, sex, etc.

The competence of the native speaker presumably includes a knowledge of which rules are categorical, which are optional, which variable, and under which conditions they are used. Frequently foreigners reveal their nonnative status by turning a variable rule into an obligatory one. Thus, for example, no matter how often a native speaker of English says *dese, dem* and *dose,* he does not use these forms exclusively. He always uses enough standard *these, them* and *those* to show that he can produce *th-* words. He does not confuse *dose* "those" with *doze* "to sleep." (Labov 1971a:50)

Although no strong case has been made for the psychological reality or unreality of rules, it must certainly be the case that they have *social* reality in that they are frequently the object of evaluation. Rules utilized more by the economically disadvantaged than by their more fortunate fellow citizens produce socially stigmatized forms, for example, the English "double-negatives" discussed above.

While rules are the form which grammars take, the latter are not the entire substance of language. The language itself consists both of lexicon (words, affixes, idioms, etc.) and rules for their use, as well as grammar, the latter consisting in turn of phonology, syntax, and semantics.

2.4 Semantics

Sociologists have long been concerned, directly or indirectly, with questions of meaning; hence, it is understandable that sociologists find it easier to develop an interest in linguistics which stresses semantic questions rather than linguistics based on models of syntax of a very abstract nature. This is particularly true if the models account for social, as well as referential, meaning. We are particularly interested in meaning as it is expressed in language in actual social situations. For each speech event to be examined, there is an immediate social context to be considered, as well as the social conditions obtaining in the broader society which affect the specific situation. In any case, it is always necessary to keep in mind pragmatic considerations of the "real world" as related to the linguistic facts of the case. What semantic systems do, evidently, is to relate linguistic to nonlinguistic phenomena, so that when we give the meaning of some linguistic event, we are stating rules for its use in terms of nonlinguistic events.

The ways in which people use language are meaningful in themselves. By exercising the options (grammatical, referential, situational and personal) within domains of his competence, the speaker expresses his meaning. Perhaps most fundamental of all is _referential meaning_: the speaker wishes to talk about something; in other words, he refers to things, persons, concepts, and makes comments about them (the subject-predicate phenomenon). He utilizes the syntactical and phonological resources of the language to express his meaning, exercising his options in the choice of specific pronunciations, vocabulary items and grammatical constructions. It is not quite the same thing socially to say _Kindly refrain from attempting to deceive me with your false words_ as to say _Don't give me none of that jive, Please don't lie to me,_ or _Cut out the B.S.,_ although referentially the meanings are very similar. Choice of variants will, of course, be affected not only by the situation, as perceived by the speaker, but they will also reflect personal characteristics of the speaker—his own linguistic style, as well as his emotional and psychological state at the moment. It is his selection of a synonymous variant from among those available which conveys _social meaning_.

Linguistic creativity extends to the construction of semantic oddities as a form of word play. Take, for example, this nonsense verse which the author recalls as being popular in his childhood:

One bright day in the middle of the night,
Two dead boys got up to fight.
Back to back they faced each other,
Drew their swords and shot each other.
A deaf policeman downstairs heard the noise,
Came up and killed the two dead boys.

It is both from a knowledge of the language and from a knowledge of the real world that a person is able to identify sense and nonsense, contradiction and plausibility.

For a number of scholars, often referred to as the London School, meaning of an utterance was derived from the context in which it occurred. For Malinowski, for example, the notion of context of situation originally referred to the context of human activity concurrent with, immediately preceding, and following the speech act, whereas Firth considered "context of situation" to be the whole cultural setting in which the speech act is located.

Malinowski later came to the same view, pointing out that in order to understand speech, one must be a participant in the activity in which the speech is involved. In explaining the difficulty of translating words from very different cultures, Malinowski (1956:299–300) noted that "All words which describe the native social order, all expressions referring to native beliefs, to specific customs, ceremonies, magical rites—all such words are obviously absent from English as from any European language. Such words can only be translated into English, not by giving their imaginary equivalent—a real one obviously cannot be found—but by explaining the meaning of each of them through an exact ethnographic account of the sociology, culture and tradition of that native community." Above all, one must be informed about the situation in which the words are spoken. We must also know the knowledge shared by speaker and hearer, as well as all culturally standardized assumptions and presuppositions relevant to the speech situation being studied. Of course, rarely if ever do we have all the necessary information for this kind of interpretation.

In more recent years, that school of sociologists calling themselves ethnomethodologists has developed some conceptions of meaning different from those of linguists or anthropologists. Ethnomethodology emphasizes the interpretative work involved in making sense out of social situations, including the speech used therein. Ethnomethodologists emphasize the situational nature of meaning and that the interpretative procedures for extracting meaning are largely below the level of members' (their word for persons) consciousness, which can be discovered by tenacious, often tedious analysis (cf. Cicourel 1974; Turner, ed. 1974).

One particularly relevant concept in this connection is that of *presupposition*. In other words, while sentences make certain assertions about the real world, or request information or action on the part of the listener, they also contain within themselves still other assertions about the real world which are assumed to be true by the speaker (or, at least, he wishes the hearer to believe that he, the speaker, assumes them to be true), but which are not embodied in the subject and predicate of the sentence. This point of view has been stressed by Sherzer (1973), who says: "Some of the things which have been called presuppositions are intimately related to the social and cultural beliefs of the members of the speech community, so much so that one could easily argue, on the basis of some sorts of presuppositions, that linguistic analysis is impossible without prior or concomitant social and cultural analysis."

Consider the following two sentences:

1. John insulted Mary, and then she insulted *him*.
2. John called Mary a virgin, and then she insulted *him*.

In a now famous argument, George Lakoff has asserted that "him" in sentence 2 can be stressed only if it is presupposed that to call someone a virgin is to insult that person. Otherwise, "insulted" is stressed. What is considered an insult is determined by the cultural beliefs of the community or of some segment thereof (Sherzer 1973:279–280). Thus, linguistic analysis even in the narrow sense (stress placement) requires us to study the social life of the community. And, needless to say, social analysis requires a profound knowledge of the semantics of the language or languages used in the community.

2.5 Language phylogeny and typology

Languages can be classified genetically, that is, in terms of common origin; typologically, that is, in terms of type of structure; and arealy, that is, by particular geographical areas where languages, because of long-term mutual influence, share significant common features—for example, the Balkan Peninsula or India. With reference to the genetic relationships of languages, those known or thought to be derived from some common ancestral tongue form what are known as language families. Presumably the later languages were all once dialects of some earlier language. Thus, for example, most of the languages of Europe belong to the Indo-European family, which besides English and other Germanic languages (German, Dutch, Swedish, Danish, etc.) includes Latin (and its daughters French, Spanish, Italian, Romanian, etc.), Greek, Slavic (Russian, Polish, Czech, Serbo-Croatian, etc.), languages of India such as Hindi-Urdu, Bengali, Marathi, etc. and many others from northwest Europe to southern Asia, whose speakers encompass a broad spectrum of cultural and racial types.

Another important language family is the Semitic, including Babylonian (Akkadian), Hebrew, Phoenician, Arabic, Aramaic, and Amharic, the national language of Ethiopia. Speakers of Arabic range from central Asia to Central Africa and likewise include speakers of many different racial and cultural types. The Indo-European family has sometimes been referred to as *Aryan,* that is, "Iranian," as the ancient Indo-European speaking invaders of India presumably originated in Iran. Hitler's racial theories notwithstanding, it is, of course, nonsensical to speak of an "Aryan" race or of a "Semitic" race. There are only speakers of Aryan languages or Semitic languages. But, one might ask, don't those who speak related languages have something in common besides linguistic structure? Some of the people speaking related languages obviously share a common (not necessarily unmixed) ancestry; the ancestors of the others certainly must have had some historical connection in the past (see sections 10.4 and 10.5). A language cannot be shared in a vacuum; such sharing must be mediated by social relationships. We can only speculate about the nature of these relationships in the past, in the absence, that is, of any archaeological or historical evidence. But what we can be sure of is that these relationships were basically of the same nature as those we observe today where languages are being adopted or mixed: military conquest followed by subjugation, colonization, and acculturation; trade relations; religious and cultural conversion; border and neighboring tribal relations; and the "prestige" or practical advantages to be gained by adopting the language of a society which is thought to be "superior" militarily, politically, economically, or culturally. Thus, for example, in the case of persons of African ancestry in the Americas presently speaking English, Spanish, French, or Portuguese, we have historical evidence of the institution of slavery to account for this wholesale case of linguistic dislocation and acculturation. Similarly, in the Ottoman Empire, young boys from Balkan families were transported to Anatolia where they learned Turkish and became fiercely loyal Janissary soldiers or officials in the administration, in effect ceasing to be Serbs, Greeks, etc., and becoming Turks. Similar institutions undoubtedly have had a long, if inglorious, history in other times and places. On the other hand, linguistic affiliation may become the basis of nationalistic political movements, as in the case of the nineteenth century pan-German, pan-Slavic, and pan-Turkic movements (see section 10.1).

Among nineteenth and some early twentieth century scholars, even in the work of Malinowski, there was a tendency to equate a child's language with a so-called primitive language, and both with early language—all of them being considered simple and inaccurate modes of expression used for practical purposes, especially magical ones. Such characterizations were based on an ethnocentric view of culture and language that failed to take into account the complex nature of all language.

The point that there is no necessary correlation among race, language, and culture was perhaps made most forcefully by Franz Boas (1911); that is, people speaking related languages do not necessarily have similar cultures, and persons sharing the same or similar culture do not necessarily speak languages with similar structures. Furthermore, "advanced" nations do not necessarily have "advanced" linguistic structures. While technology may be a criterion of "advanced" culture, there are no criteria for "advanced" linguistic structures, although technologically advanced societies generally have much more extensive lexicons. As Sapir (1921:234) so aptly put it, "When it comes to linguistic structure, Plato walks with the Macedonian swineherd, Confucius with the head-hunting savage of Assam." It was once thought that the so-called language types, namely isolating, agglutinative and flexional, could be put on a scale from lower to higher forms. An "isolating" language was one like Chinese, in which words do not take any kind of grammatical prefixes or suffixes but are invariable. Words, generally one syllable, cannot be analyzed into separable meaningful components or "morphemes." An "agglutinative" language was one like Turkish in which a whole series of morphemes were "glued" together, without any of them undergoing modification; each morpheme clearly retains its own meaning and shape. The equivalent of a whole English phrase, clause, or sentence may be expressed in a single word, e.g., *sokaktakiler* from *sokak* "street," *ta* "in," *ki* "which" and *ler* "plural," that is, "The people in the street." A "flexional" language was characterized as one in which the grammatical suffixes were often fused and lost their separate character. For example, in Latin *amo* "I love," *am-* is the root meaning "love," while the suffix -*o* conveys the meaning of both "I" and "present indicative active." Compare the Turkish equivalent *severim*, where *sev-* is the root meaning "love," -*er* is "present," and -*im* is "I."

Some nineteenth century scholars like Müller and Whitney even went so far as to correlate the three types of language structure with three stages of social organization. They thought that the isolating languages were associated with a family stage of social development, the agglutinative languages with nomadic society, and the flexional with Western European type societies (Firth 1970:78).

While we may smile at the naïveté of these precultural relativity linguistic scholars of the nineteenth century, some correlation between language type and level of technological or sociocultural development must not be rejected out of hand. The differences, however, lie more in the areas of lexicon and style than in morphology. Hymes (1972b) has forcefully claimed that evolutionary advance can be clearly seen with reference not to linguistic form but to linguistic function. Certain types of syntactic development make certain kinds of arguments and analysis available for scientific discourse, as does an expanded lexicon for naming everything in the world. Languages such as English and Japanese, for example, have developed in this fashion. But all languages are probably equal for other functions, such as interpersonal relations, aesthetic play, poetry, religious insight, and expression.

2.6 Writing systems or orthographies

Writing is important as a medium of communication in its own right and as materialization of speech, so that language can be transmitted over space and time. What people have said and thought is rescued from the passing nature of oral communication. Writing affects the social organization of practically all human institutions. But the potentialities of writing depend on the particular kind of writing system utilized in any given society, as well as on its institutions.

There was no writing before about 8,000 years ago. It was well developed in Mesopotamia and Egypt about 6,000 years ago, in China about 4,000 years ago, and among the Mayas of Yucatan over 2,000 years ago. Our own writing system, in fact all known alphabets, trace back to that of ancient Egypt. Writing has existed for at most 1/100 of the time that language has existed. The majority of the world's population is still illiterate.

In ancient Egypt and Sumeria, writing was used primarily for recording sacred texts and business transactions and for the same purposes when it spread to the peoples of the eastern Mediterranean. In Greece, writing began to be used for general literature. In China, writing was used for literary and practical uses from the start, while the Mayas used writing for astronomical and other priestly purposes.

Writing is not language but a representation of language. The two are inter-dependent, and there are a number of different possibilities for change, for example, writing systems may change, or people speaking a particular language may switch over to a new writing system. Similarly a language may change, but the written representation may remain fixed. A writing system may be adapted or invented for a language which previously had none. Thus, there are a number of different types of change which can occur in the relationship between languages and writing systems (see discussion in section 11.2).

Writing systems may vary from the alphabetic, where the ideal is a one-to-one correspondence of sound and letter, through the syllabic, where each character represents a single syllable, to the ideographic or logographic where each character represents a single word, concept, or grammatical morpheme. Some writing systems incorporate more than one of these principles, as, for example, Japanese, which utilizes both logographic and syllabic characters in ordinary writing.

There are many variations in the degree of correspondence between letter and sound in alphabetic writing. For example, the spelling of English or French is largely historical, that is, it reflects the pronunciation of earlier periods. Semitic writing, such as that of Hebrew or Arabic, normally indicates consonants and long vowels only.

Writing systems may help emphasize an ethnic or linguistic distinction. Thus, Serbo-Croatian, which is essentially one language, is written with Roman characters by the Croats but with Cyrillic characters by the Serbs. Similarly, Hindi and Urdu are essentially the same language, but ordinarily Hindi is written in Devanagari (Sanskrit) characters by Hindu speakers and Urdu in Arabic script by Muslim speakers. Further to emphasize the difference, there has been a policy of incorporating large numbers of Arabic and Persian words into written Urdu and Sanskrit words into written Hindi, in each case drawing on a linguistic, cultural and religious heritage largely unknown to the members of the other, often hostile, ethnic community.

The relationships between writing and speech have varied historically according to the socioeconomic basis of different societies. Thus, the preliterate society has no writing; in the preindustrialized civilized society, writing was confined to a small urban upper class. In such societies, the script is usually complex, and the priestly group makes up a large proportion of the *literati*. The elite has a common language that facilitates communication over wide distances, covering many local languages and dialects, for example, Sanskrit, Arabic, or Chinese.

As industrialization with its scientifically based technology has appeared, modern elites have been concerned with maximizing communication within and among complex organizations, democratizing the class system, secularizing religious systems, and uniting speech and writing. The scientific orientation of the industrialized society has also led to the development and spread of modern linguistics.

Transitional societies, that is, those in the process of industrializing, have generally tended to engage in language and script reform. Their leaders have been much concerned with developing means of teaching people to read in their own vernacular. Until recently, whenever elites were interested at all in promoting literacy, they would impose their own writing system upon the language of the nonliterate peoples under their control. They rarely took into consideration such questions as efficiency, economy, and consistency of the script, or whether it was appropriate for the languages upon which they were being imposed. To cite one of the most flagrant examples, as Sjoberg (1966) notes: "When Turkic peoples in Central Asia came under the dominance of Muslim culture, the Perso-Arabic script was as a matter of course accepted as the medium of writing for these languages. But this script, with its general neglect of short vowels, was a poor fit for languages in the Turkic group, some of which have nine or more vowel phonemes. Of course, the propagation of mass literacy was not the intent. The purpose was to disseminate the dominant culture, to achieve and maintain communication between the rulers and the ruled, and thus to facilitate matters of government, particularly the collection of taxes or tribute and the suppression of rebellion."

Possession of a writing system does not mean necessarily that the language will be used for all written purposes. For example, at one extreme the language may be used for writing personal letters, ranging through its use in popular magazines and newspapers, writing and publishing books in the language, through use of the language for regular publication of original scientific research. At the highest level, it is a language in which translations and abstracts of scientific work in other languages are regularly published. Ferguson (1971:52–53) has identified four such levels by which we can measure the degree of graphization:

W0 — not used for normal written purposes (modern Aramaic)
W1 — used for normal written purposes (letters, newspapers, books) (Amharic, Thai, Slovenian)
W2 — original research regularly published (Hebrew, Arabic, Spanish)
W3 — translations and resumés of scientific work in other languages regularly published (English, Russian, German, French)

Discussion questions

1. Discuss the fundamental nature of language as outlined in this chapter. Does this differ from your previous conceptions and, if so, how?
2. What light does the existence of language universals throw on the question of the biological and psychological unity of the human race?
3. In what significant ways does human language differ from animal communication systems?
4. What is the relationship between vocal and nonvocal language? If you know someone who is bilingual in sign language and English, interview them about their experiences. (If the use of singular "them" and "their" bothers you, see section 8.2.)
5. During the next few days, observe other people's "body language." What do you think they are trying to communicate? What kinds of differences do you observe between, for example, older and younger people, men and women, people of different ethnic groups, occupations, etc.?
6. What is prescriptive grammar? What is the social motivation that lies behind its existence and enforcement? Examine your own attitudes about this topic.
7. Discuss the different kinds of meaning. What are some of the difficulties in studying meaning?
8. Explain how people confuse racial and linguistic categories. Do you, or your friends, or acquaintances, ever do this?
9. Discuss the relationship between writing and language, and how the relationship varies in different types of societies.

3

Social and linguistic change

Language and society are both typically in constant change. In noting the relationship between these two types of change, it is clear that any kind of linguistic change involves the interplay of universal linguistic forces and culture-specific social forces, although there may be some social change independent of language change and vice versa. However, certain types of language change considered "internal" by linguists, such as developments from Vulgar Latin to the Romance languages, will not be considered here.

Generally we may consider linguistic change as a complex response to many aspects of human behavior. There seem to be two principal types of dependence of linguistic on social change. In the first type, social change has resulted in linguistic change from culture contact, urbanization, industrialization, etc. (see Chapters 10 and 11). In the second type, the linguistic change is not the result of social change but is partially associated with certain social variables (see Chapters 8 and 9). For example, certain linguistic innovations may be more readily accepted by one social class than another. Conversely, social change may result from linguistic change. For example, linguistic assimilation may lead to disappearance of an ethnic group.

There are both linguistic and sociolinguistic changes; that is, either changes taking place in a single language or changes in how language varieties are being used for different purposes. A social psychological perspective also considers changes in linguistic attitudes as a form of sociolinguistic change. In order to establish the existence of linguistic change in the narrow sense, we must be able to observe two successive generations with comparable social characteristics in the same speech community.

Linguistic change may be conceived of as occurring in three stages as follows: 1) origin of the change in one of the variations already present in the speech of some people, (2) propagation of the change as it is adopted by more people and begins to compete with the old form, (3) completion of the change with the elimination of the competing variant (Sturtevant 1947). These variants are carriers of social values, so that the process of acceptance and rejection of variants takes place in the community's sociolinguistic structure) For example, in a number of areas in southern California, the contrast of the short vowels / ε / and /I/ before a final nasal consonant is being neutralized so that, for example *pin* and *pen* have become homophones. This vowel change is predominant among the younger speakers, though largely absent among their elders. Preadolescents coming into the area quickly adopt this change. On the other hand, most Chicano (Mexican American) youth, because of their relative isolation from the dominant society, continue to make this distinction. While this may also reflect influence from Spanish, the pronunciation may also be a mark of ethnic identity. Thus, this linguistic variable has social significance related to prestige, which is related in turn to age, geography, and ethnicity. The spread of the merger is dependent on these factors. We cannot account for the origin of this change in social terms, but we can account for its spread.

Because linguists have traditionally relied on psychology rather than on sociology in their consideration of extralinguistic factors, they have found it natural to rely on the mother-child relationship in the explanation of both language acquisition and linguistic change. They look at the child in his roles first as hearer and then as speaker. The transmission of language from one generation to the next is perceived as discontinuous, and change results from the recreation of the language by each child (cf. section 4.3 on language acquisition). According to one view (Halle 1962), the parent adds new rules to his grammar which the child incorporates into his own new simplified grammar. A major objection to this is that children do not speak like their parents but like their peers (Labov 1972g:304).

On the macrosociological level, European colonial expansion over the entire globe has brought about interrelated sociolinguistic changes, such as acculturation, bilingualism, linguistic nationalism, pidginization, standardization, construction of artificial languages and vernacular education (see Chapters 10 and 11). It must also be noted that some of this language change is purposive, that is, carried out by deliberate effort in language planning processes.

3.1 Social change

It must be stressed that widespread social change does not necessarily lead to widespread linguistic change, even under revolutionary conditions. For example, the Russian language did not fundamentally change after the Bolshevik Revolution. There is, however, more of a tendency for rapid linguistic change to take place under conditions of rapid rather than slower social change) Ordinarily linguistic change is much slower than social change, although we can only talk about relatively rapid or relatively slow change in either case.

The effect of Darwin's theory of biological evolution through natural selection on the development of evolutionary thought in the social sciences is a well-known chapter in the intellectual history of the past century or so. Despite the lack of scientific, completely "objective," criteria for what constitutes "primitive" versus "advanced," the notion dies hard that some peoples, art styles, languages, or family structures are higher on the evolutionary scale than others. There is then the basic question of whether in these fields evolution takes place at all. That is, is there a particular overall direction of development extending over a long time span, or is there no particular overall direction of change in the phenomenon being studied? On a limited scale, for example, in the change from Anglo-Saxon to English, we can see a direction of development.

Can we perceive any long-range sociocultural development associated with parallel linguistic development? For example, do we find a particular type of language structure in, say, highly industrialized societies as contrasted with, say, the type of language to be found in nomadic hunting societies? The people of the most highly industrialized countries in the world speak Indo-European languages, but the country which is perhaps coming to have the world's most productive economy, Japan, uses a language with a strikingly different structure. This is not to say that there is a complete lack of correlation. Industrialized countries do have larger lexicons because of the tremendous growth of specialized activities and products, although no syntactic or phonological associations can be established.

A further question is whether there is an adaptive function to linguistic evolution. It is hard to see, as Labov (1972d) points out, the benefit of our not being able to understand the French or the Chinese. The end result of linguistic evolution is the absence of communication between groups, which, however, promotes cultural pluralism. Perhaps cultural pluralism may be a necessary element in the human extension of biological evolution. Nevertheless, with isolation of cultures coming to an end in the modern world, we may expect more linguistic uniformation and less diversification in the future. Genetic diversification has pretty much ceased. What is happening now is the adaptation of languages and their varieties to new groups and new uses, for example, the spread of English around the world.

3.2   Factors stimulating change

Both culture contact and social isolation can influence the rate of linguistic change. When people from different cultures come into contact, each will at least, adopt a few words from the other language for new cultural items or concepts. The development of large-scale bilingualism will result in even more lexical borrowing, and perhaps in phonological and syntactic changes as well. Rapid technological change, whether indigenous or introduced from outside the society, will also necessarily result in large-scale expansion of the lexicon (see sections 11.1 and 11.2).

It is usually the case that social isolation leads to linguistic diversity and that the mixing of populations leads to linguistic uniformity, although these relationships do not necessarily hold under all conditions. Social and linguistic change may result from rural-urban migration or the arrival of colonists, immigrants, or slaves. What happens linguistically under conditions of culture contact greatly depends on the nature of the relationship between the two societies in question, that is, whether they are neighboring countries, colony and mother country, majority and minority groups, for example, and the degree of political and economic equality (cf. section 10.4).

Take, for example, the prestige of the culture of the other society. When the Seljuk Turks were Islamicized by the Arabs, they not only adopted the latter's alphabet for writing their language but also a great number of Arabic words in the religious, cultural, legal, commercial, and administrative areas. When the Seljuks subsequently overran the Persian Empire, they absorbed much of the rich Iranian culture and another vast influx of foreign words, this time from Persian. As a matter of fact, Seljuk Turkish was influenced in its grammar and phonology by both Persian and Arabic. The new language thus created was perpetuated (some critics would say "perpetrated") by their successors, the Ottomans, as Ottoman Turkish. The resultant written language (and the highly cultivated speech variety) was so strongly influenced by Arabic and Persian, that an effective diglossia (see section 7.3) existed between ordinary spoken Turkish and Ottoman proper. The more Arabic and Persian that was used in a sentence, the more elegant it was considered, so that almost any Arabic or Persian word could be used in any Ottoman sentence. Thus, in order to be proficient in the language, particularly in its more artificial written form, a person ordinarily had to know at least three words for every concept. For example, a reader had to know that the Turkish word *yürek,* the Arabic *qalb,* and the Persian *dil* all meant "heart," for the likelihood of encountering or using any of these in Ottoman was roughly equal. Perhaps the case of Ottoman Turkish is an extreme one, and when the sociopolitical conditions supporting this language collapsed with the overthrow of the Ottoman Empire after World War I, linguistic change was rapid.

Some types of social change are perhaps best described as demographic in nature, such as changes in size of population, or in relative size of its components, such as according to sex, age, ethnicity, social class, and, of course, numbers of speakers of languages and language varieties, as well as changes in the relative socioeconomic position of the various components of the population. Thus, the status of regional, occupational, or religious segments of the population of a nation or area may fluctuate, resulting in temporary over- or underevaluation of their respective speech habits.

Attitude is obviously a significant intervening variable. Attitudes toward language can have far-reaching historical consequences. Different social classes or groups may have strong opinions which may influence the development of a language or promote the rise of nationalism (see section 10.1).

Social and linguistic change may result from fluctuating conceptions of age and sex roles, with accompanying changes in speech fads, customs and habits, or from the influence of those social groups whose behavior is defined as deviant or divergent from the normal, and whose life styles give rise to slang, criminal argot, occupational jargons, etc.

Semantic changes may result from changes in the world of objects and historical accidents. Those involving euphemisms and metaphors may be due to psychological or social-psychological factors. A further source of linguistic change is the frequency of use of certain forms because of certain culturally determined forms of social interaction. Words frequently used suffer erosion (that is, become shorter); but frequency is not only a function of grammar but is also a function of social interaction which may require more frequent use of certain words or forms depending on the particular culture, subculture, or group. Frequent wear also occurs in greetings, titles, names, and basic vocabulary, such as the words for *come, go, be, can,* and *know* (Anttila 1972:187).

Linguistic change does not necessarily start with imitation of forms used by the more prestigious groups in the society. Linguistic innovation can begin with any group and spread outward, for example, the vowel shifts originating in working-class youth in large cities in the northern United States (Labov 1972g:286–287). Re-evaluation of prestige takes place, for example, the case of *r*-less pronunciation in New York City, which instead of being regarded as an international standard now symbolizes a regional peculiarity. Prestige must obviously be defined in terms of the people using the notion.

3.3 Invention, borrowing, diffusion

Traditional historical linguistics was much concerned with tracing the origin and spread of lexical items and phonological changes. It is obviously one thing to trace geographical spread and another to explain why certain changes are accepted in certain areas and others are not. Another drawback to this approach is that it is two-dimensional. A third dimension, the socioeconomic one (including ethnic, cultural, etc.) is lacking, for we must consider not only the changes spreading to a different geographical area but also spreading to different social groups within the same geographical area. That the two processes are interrelated would, furthermore, seem to be a reasonable hypothesis.

The most important consideration in the spread of innovation, whether linguistic or nonlinguistic, would appear to be prestige (but cf. Labov's *caveat* above). The latter is not easy to define, and the relationship between prestige and imitation may involve circular reasoning. That is, we may say that the fact that a particular group has prestige is proven by the fact that others imitate them (cf. the case of the Seljuks). We then turn around and postulate that people are more likely to imitate the speech and habits of prestigious people. Such reasoning involves what logicians call a tautology. In order to avoid this, we must establish some independent, if only indirect, criterion for prestige, such as socioeconomic status.

Linguistic innovation may spread by religious or class channels. Consider the two following instances.

As Hinduism and Buddhism spread east from India, many loan words of Indic origin were disseminated to the languages of south and east Asia but not the Indic languages themselves. The spread of Islam beyond the Middle East for the most part resulted in the spread of Arabic as a scholarly and ritual language but not vernacular, and all Islamic languages have adopted large numbers of Arabic words. Christian missionary activity, on the other hand, has promoted European languages as media of instruction all over the world. Graduates of mission schools often went abroad for further education and returned to become political leaders in their own countries (Le Page 1964:28–29).

The "guttural" sounding r of present day French, which is produced by vibrating a small projection of the soft palate, the uvula, apparently became fashionable in the upper classes of Paris in the seventeenth century and subsequently spread to most of France, Germany and Denmark, as well as to southern Sweden and Norway. It displaced the original tongue-tip trilled r, which is still used in Italian and Spanish, for example. The uvular r has also displaced the trilled r as the prestige norm in Israeli Hebrew. Thus has an innovation crossed not only class and geographical barriers but also linguistic ones. Lexical innovations, however, appear to be able to spread across much greater distances than either phonological or grammatical features (Trudgill 1974b:165).

3.4 Resistance to change

Why do some groups or individuals accept change and others just as readily resist it? Obviously tactors other than prestige are involved. Thus, for example, nationalism or xenophobia may conspire to resist any influence from other languages; as the need for new concepts arises, writers or scientists may prefer to coin words from pre-existing roots in their own language rather than adopt words from other languages) Witness the case of Icelandic, the language of a modern people, which has scarcely adopted a loanword during the last millennium, or modern Turkish or modern Hebrew which have both favored coining new words from indigenous roots over adoption of foreign words for new concepts. This is, of course, not resistance to change but rather resistance to a particular source of change.

A number of social psychological factors are ordinarily behind the normal widespread resistance to language change, such as the fear that new unstandardized verbal symbols might jeopardize understanding in the process of communication. Educated persons do not wish to sacrifice the advantages they have gained by displaying "incorrect" usage but rather prefer to speak "correctly" so as to validate their social status. Furthermore, conservatives may consider linguistic deviations as symptomatic of moral license or social disorganization. Statements by purists lamenting the "decay" of the English language appear frequently in daily newspapers and elsewhere in the mass media. Innovations such as the use of good as an adverb (He plays baseball real good), for example, instead of being looked at as simple linguistic changes (German gut underwent the same change long ago), are regarded as symptomatic of the decay of American civilization.

Discussion questions

1. What is the sequence of steps through which a linguistic change goes?
2. Some recent changes not yet completely accepted in American English are the change of pronunciation of processes from /prasɛsəz/ to /prasəsiyz/ or /prowsəsiyz/; I could care less instead of I couldn't care less; and a

phenomena or *a strata* instead of *a phenomenon* or *a stratum,* as well as *data* (pronounced /dædə/ rather than /deydə/ and used as a singular instead of a plural). Are you aware of these as recent changes in popular speech? Do you think they will become permanent changes? Why or why not? Can you think of some other recent changes, say, within the last five years or so?

3. How does social change bring about linguistic change? Can linguistic change bring about social change? Explain.

4. What factors help to slow down linguistic change?

4

Language, society and culture

The largest unit of analysis ordinarily considered by sociologists is the society, a unit not only larger than the community but much more, if not completely, self-sufficient. This concept is much more general and abstract than the one with which it is most often confused, namely the nation-state. The two may coincide, of course, but are not necessarily coterminous.

Traditionally, sociologists have concentrated on abstract social relations to the neglect of the political and economic aspects of society. To a considerable extent, this tendency is also manifested in much work in sociolinguistics and the sociology of language. This is particularly true of those who emphasize a microsociolinguistic focus in their work. Such work tends to focus on the formal aspects and to ignore the political and economic realities of the broader society.

Sociologists use the term *function* to refer to the consequences (whether intended or not and whether observed or not—that is, whether *manifest* or *latent*) of the actions of persons or groups. The consequences for society can be called social functions (or *macrofunctions*), that is, the impact on the social structure resulting from the carrying out of certain socially patterned activities. There are also individual functions (or *microfunctions*) such as the resulting impact on hearer and speaker of spoken language (see section 5.1). Some scholars believe we should use the ethnographic observation of communication to discover such functions. We cannot think of the functions of language as universal since they will necessarily vary from one cultural setting to another (Mathiot and Garvin 1975:1).

Both animal cries and human speech serve the basic functions of coordinating the activities of the members of the group so that they can attain their goals. As De Laguna (1927:19–20) notes, "Men do not speak simply to relieve their feelings or to air their views but to awaken a response in their fellows and to influence their attitudes and acts. It is further the means by which men are brought into a new and momentous relationship with the external world, the very relationship which makes for them an objective order."

Malinowski (1956:xii) suggested that the most fundamental function of speech was pragmatic, that is, to direct, control and correlate human activity. He believed all behavior must have a practical end; therefore, he emphasized the pragmatic functions at the expense of the symbolic.

It is reasonable to assume that the most fundamental, the most basic function of language is to control people's behavior. On a societal level, it might be hypothesized that the major function of language is social cooperation and control—promoting conformity to a society's norms. Language is a tool, a vehicle of the social order. It is a gross oversimplification either to identify language with communication, or to view its sole function as communication. In many instances it serves for the reflection, clarification, consolidation, or alteration of interpersonal relationships and sociocultural values. The major effect of language has been the creation of a system that made integration, social coordination and cooperation, as well as cultural cumulation and transmission, possible.

Culture is an adaptive device by which man survives in his various environments and so is language, the most obvious purpose of which is the conveying of information, including information about the situation and the speakers. This is a function which it serves in all societies. But other functions are served as well, such as to mark social identities and social statuses, establish and maintain social relationships, and to serve the expressive needs of individuals. A function performed by language in one society may be performed by a different social institution in another society. Not all societies use language or focus on it to the same extent, value it equally, or use it for the same purposes. Similarly, some societies have only one language, and some have more than one. One language might, thus, be assigned a number of different functions in one society, which are divided among more than one language in some other society. Not all languages or language varieties are capable to the same extent of fulfilling any given function. In a multilingual state, different languages may serve different functions, such as wider communication (national and international), education at different levels, and religion.

The relationships between social and linguistic variables are at the very heart of the concerns of the sociology of language. How this relationship is conceptualized bears directly on the theories that are generated and the research which is conducted in the field. Some scholars like Wolfram (1971:96) assume a direct causal relationship between social differences and linguistic differences. This is not the only conceptualization possible. There are, in fact, four different possible perspectives on this issue, that is, that social structure is dependent on language; that language is dependent upon social structure; that each is codetermining; and that both are dependent upon some third factor such as world view, the organization of the human brain, or the fundamental nature of humanity. Grimshaw (1971) has indicated that the fourth alternative is untestable and that the first two are incomplete and can be subsumed under the third and most reasonable perspective, that of mutual codetermination or mutual embeddedness. Until proven otherwise, it seems reasonable and safe to take as our basic assumption the notion that language and society influence and determine each other.

4.1 Human groups and language

Groups, of whatever size, tend to have their own special languages, codes, or styles, whether this consists of a few unique words shared by an intimate couple or a language which is the national patrimony of a people. Likewise, human groups usually have names, and how they are called is reflective of the linguistic system in use.

Some occupations are characterized by specialized knowledge of a particular language, as in the case of medical doctors or pharmacists who are required to know Latin or musicians Italian. Knowledge of a sacred language may be shared by religious functionaries or scholars. Knowledge of the written language may be confined to a special class of scribes, as among the ancient Egyptians or Baby-lonians. For other occupations, language itself is the focus of activity, as in the case of interpreters, translators, language teachers, and of course, linguists.

Many religious groups utilize a sacred language or languages for liturgy and prayer, and for the reading and study of sacred texts in that language, such as the use of Latin in Catholicism, Hebrew and Aramaic in Judaism, Arabic in Islam, Sanskrit in Hinduism, Pali in Buddhism, Coptic in the Egyptian church, and so forth. It is important to recognize that in many cases like these, people ascribe a sacred character not only to their scriptures and liturgy but frequently to the language itself. Thus, for example, ultra-orthodox Jews in Palestine in the 1880s opposed Eliezer Ben Yehuda's efforts to revive Hebrew as a spoken language, asserting that Hebrew was too sacred to be used for secular purposes. It was unthinkable, they believed, that the sacred tongue could be used to curse a dog or to tell an off-color joke. Yet Ben Yehuda's point won the day, and Hebrew eventually became the principal daily vernacular of Jewish Palestine and later Israel's national language. To this day, however, members of certain ultra-orthodox sects refuse to speak Hebrew.

A few years ago, the Catholic Church abandoned its centuries-old policy of requiring the Mass to be said in Latin. For long, this move was opposed because some leaders of the Church felt that separate national churches would emerge if Latin were abandoned as the common language of the Church. They preferred a situation where the vast majority of Church members did not understand the words of the Mass which they were required to hear. Whether the Church will become more strengthened or more divided as a result of this move is a moot point, but what is apparent is the great importance given by many institutions to a common language for purposes of continuing solidarity.

Sociologists make a distinction between primary groups (those which are of primary importance in the formation of personality and enculturation to society's norms, such as family, friendship groups, etc.) and secondary groups (those in which people have a less intimate, less personal involvement, such as work or organizational groups and whose influence on the development of the individual is secondary or minimal). This distinction is obviously pertinent to a discussion of language.

It is in primary groups, particularly the family, where we learn our first language or languages and the rules for their use. Primary group, socialization, and language acquisition are all closely tied in together. At least partially because of the close, warm intimacy of the primary group, the language we learn in the context of such a group (our "mother" tongue) tends to have particularly warm associations, such that our deepest, strongest personal feelings often can be expressed adequately only in that language, in the particular variety learned in the home. Special feelings likewise may be felt for the language itself.

It is furthermore typical that if an additional language or language variety is learned, it is likely to be acquired in the context of secondary group relations: in school, army, or marketplace. The formality of the language variety will bear some relation to the formality of personal relations prevailing in the group in which the particular language variety is being used. Thus, the sociolinguist is particularly interested in the relationship between the structure and nature of groups on the one hand, and the nature and use of the linguistic varieties utilized by such groups on the other.

Studies of language acquisition have been done mainly within the confines of the nuclear family, particularly in its isolated American middle-class form. Results coming in from studies of language acquisition in various cultures, however, show remarkable consistency in the linguistic data. We know much less about the sociolinguistic rules and their use. Form of family structure would appear to be pertinent to such processes, as Bernstein claims (see 8.4 below).

One of the areas of particular concern to anthropologists for three or four decades now has been the nature of the relationship between language and the nonlinguistic aspects of the culture. The reader has undoubtedly heard, for example, that the Eskimos have many different words for kinds of snow because snow is so important to their way of life. Language and culture are very intimately related (see section 4.5).

Language has often been used as a theoretical model for culture, particularly as both phenomena are largely unconsciously patterned, though the patterning of language is easier to perceive and conceptualize. As indicated above, nonverbal language is also patterned and largely hidden from the consciousness of its users.

Sociologists appear to be content not just to ascertain cultural norms but also in a sense to establish them, as they identify various kinds of behavior as deviant from the norm. Just as the "normal" society visualized by many American social scientists is the conservative, small town, "WASP" society of the turn-of-the-century, so the linguist's labeling of a particular speech variety as "standard" and the other, related, varieties as "nonstandard" may sometimes be related to the same kind of thinking.

What is especially interesting in this connection is the relationship between "deviant" linguistic and "deviant" nonlinguistic behavior. An observer is likely to notice that "bad" children are using "bad" language, especially "bad" boys. One of the traditional reasons for avoiding "bad" language, for example, the English "four letter words," is to avoid the suspicion that the speaker might have deviant morals, as well as colorful language. Formerly a person might be greatly shocked to hear a woman use any kind of a word having sexual connotations, as supposedly reflective of something less than a perfectly chaste style of life.

Contrariwise, traditionally (and in many societies still) extremely polite language was supposedly reflective of impeccable intentions and character, although, of course, most people knew better. The farthest to which this type of deceit is carried is in international diplomacy, where the most courteous of language frequently masks the vilest of intentions and the most debased of acts.

4.2 Linguistic socialization

Linguistic socialization refers not only to the linguistic competence acquired by children (lexicon and grammar) and communicative competence (the effective, suitable use of language) but also to the beliefs and attitudes acquired by children about language.

The acquisition of basic linguistic competence is completed at a relatively early age, say four or five years, whereas most linguistic attitudes and beliefs are probably acquired much later when the children can understand more subtle concepts such as, for example, social status. A clear picture of how language relates to social class differences is ordinarily evident to the child before he reaches early adolescence.

Until fairly recently, most discussions in sociological writings of socialization were very one-sided, that is, they emphasized the child as a fairly inactive, passive recipient of the socialization process. Now it is increasingly evident from ongoing research that far from being a blank slate, a passive recipient, the child is an active, creative fashioner of his own reality and of his own being. Children reject certain aspects of their socialization and refashion others to suit themselves. None of us are *just* creatures of our culture; we are its creators as well. Thus, the child, or rather children in groups (when left alone by adults), fashion their own original social structures, with their own norms, concepts, boundary maintenance mechanisms, and frequently secret languages. The child's creativity in devising special languages has been noted by a number of observers of children's behavior.

Children are skilled interactants; they develop skills in the social situations in which they daily find themselves. A very important part of the socialization process is the child's development of a self-concept. This development has linguistic correlates. The child will begin to use personal names or *mommy, daddy*, etc., which suggests that the child is growing aware of them. He must learn that his name refers to himself and that other people's names refer to them, if he is to be able to separate self from other. When pronouns such as *I* or *you* appear in the child's speech, it indicates that a sense of self is developing (Denzin 1972).

Social understanding develops in a prelinguistic stage. This prelinguistic social awareness encourages the child to attempt the acquisition of grammar because he already feels and understands the need to communicate. He acquires an awareness of what it is to accept a social world shared and known in common with others. It is now easier for him to avoid misunderstanding by others and frustration of his desires and wishes. He must express the latter in already existing ways. Because the child wishes to share his intentions with others and enter into a shared world, he accepts the norms of both syntax and vocabulary, for he realizes that the world is already shaped by others who have lived in it before.

Once the child has acquired the ideal of normative controls on a shared world, he will continue to know the world as a place that has a normative social structure. Since social rules do not have as clear detail as syntactic rules, it is only through the acquisition of the latter that the child gets the idea of the normative structure of the world shared and known with others. The first clear social norms the child becomes aware of thus are linguistic ones.

Cicourel (1970) noted that the central developmental question in childhood socialization is how adults routinely expose the child to the normative order. Adults are faced with unique communicative demands when interacting with young children. The adult employs specific simplified features of adult language to connect a specific interactive event with the child to more general notions of what is correct and possible in the adult world (Corsaro 1975). Both children and adults learn the social system at least partly because they try hard to find the significance of the linguistic variations they find. Both situations and statuses have linguistic correlates.

Piaget (1923) and Vygotsky (1962) both showed the close interrelation that exists between language, on the one hand, and the development of thought and the learning of logical categories, on the other. These two scholars, however, disagreed on the exact nature of this relationship. Piaget's fundamental thesis emphasized the idea of egocentrism dominating the language and thinking of the child. He took the stand that social life proper was nonexistent before about age seven or eight. Vygotsky takes the opposite view, having conducted experiments demonstrating that egocentric language has an organizing function in the child's social activity. It gradually changes into an inner speech which is, likewise, an organizer of behavior.

In socialization, the child not only acquires language within the social structure and through its mediation but also internalizes social reality by means of language, thus shaping both consciousness and personality structure. However, it is not language in general but a particular language and social dialect or other variety which is acquired by the child. The available linguistic repertoires are transmitted to the child by such specific social structures as institutionalized kinship systems, age groups, and educational institutions. The social reality which is internalized includes the acquisition and understanding of classification and interpretation schemes (including folk taxonomies), as well as concepts of space, time, causality, motivation, relevance, and value hierarchies. They learn what is taken for granted and what is considered to be problematic. All this is filtered and mediated through specific varieties of language.

Mackay (1973:184) believes that rather than use the term socialization, we should study adult-child interaction, which is substantively the study of cultural assimilation and theoretically the study of meaningful social interaction. Children clearly accomplish meaning through procedures of interpretation and analysis. Their interpretative competencies include the ability to reason, invent, and acquire knowledge.

The relative contribution of genetic endowment and environmental influences on linguistic development is still a matter of some controversy. Some light on this question is thrown by studies of the speech of humans who were reared with animals or in isolation, that is, devoid of human contact. These so-called feral and isolated children later learned to speak to varying degrees unless they were retarded to begin with or had a hearing problem. One other point is a crucial one, namely, the existence of a developmental period in the child for initial language acquisition. It is generally believed that if the child is not exposed to some language during this crucial period, he fails ever to develop any sort of normal speech. But if factors are favorable, special training can offset the effect of several, perhaps even eight, years of isolation from the human community (Brown 1958:192).

Part of the problem in understanding children isolated from human contact is the difficulty of ascertaining the extent to which the child's disabilities stem from the lack of human intercourse or from some original mental retardation of an organic nature. Although some of the so-called feral and isolated children were labeled as retarded by some experts who examined them, this was contested by others. Also the amount of time the child was isolated, and during which years of his life, was ordinarily not known. It is difficult to understand how an originally retarded child could have survived under difficult conditions in the forest or jungle. What is certain is that few, if any, learned to speak with any fluency at all. Victor, for example, who was found when he was about twelve, never learned to speak more than a couple of words (Itard 1962:xii).

Davis (1947:437) concluded from the case of Isabelle that isolation up to the age of six, with failure to acquire any language and thus to grasp cultural meaning, does not preclude the subsequent acquisition of either speech or cultural meaning. In fact, the child may go through the mental stages at a rate more rapid than normal. Another child, Anna, was possibly deficient to begin with and did not receive the best training available. Furthermore, she did not live long enough after being found. When she died at age ten, about two years later, her speech was at about the two-year-old level. She talked mainly in phrases but would repeat words and try to carry on a conversation.

Curtiss et al. (1974) have reported on the linguistic development of a child, "Genie," who had spent her entire life completely isolated in a small room, receiving only minimal care. She was physically punished if she made any sounds. Ever since the time she was discovered by authorities in 1970 at the age of 13, a team of psychologists, psychiatrists, neurologists, and linguists has been working with this unique case. She had no linguistic competence, beyond being able to respond to a few simple words. Although she was past age five, supposedly the critical age for learning a first language, Genie has made progress in learning to speak and understand. Compared with the development of other children, her vocabulary is much larger than that of children at the same stage of syntactic development. She learns new words rapidly, but her rate of syntactic development is much slower than normal, demonstrating the difference between storage of lists of elements and the rules of grammar.

Genie has remained an unsocialized person in many respects, and this is reflected in her limited knowledge of sociolinguistic rules. She is not sensitive to the range of social behavior which accompanies the actual spoken messages in the course of a conversation. She fails to acknowledge questions, statements, requests, summons, etc. much of the time, that is, appears to be conversationally incompetent. This is most probably a result of her social and psychological deprivation. As Curtiss (1977:233) indicates, "Genie grew up in an environment devoid of verbal interaction. Never or practically never having witnessed the performance of these sociolinguistic behaviors she did not develop them."

4.3 Language acquisition

Anyone who, as an adult, has struggled to master a foreign language is likely to be dismayed by the fluency displayed by four- or five-year-old native speakers of the language, a fluency one can scarcely hope to attain. How did these children learn this difficult language so fast and so well, one might ask oneself. The answer is, of course, the same way one learned one's own. What one takes for granted in one's own case seems like a minor miracle in the foreign setting. There is, of course, no necessary connection of language with race, and any normal human child can learn any language if he* is reared in a community where it is spoken.

Before the development of generative-transformational grammar, no one really had a clear idea of how complex a language really was and, hence, how difficult the task which the child has to accomplish. The older studies compiled lists of words which given children had learned by certain ages, as if language development could be judged by vocabulary alone. Furthermore, such an approach looked at the process as involving stimulus-response imitation and memorizing, whereas the more difficult task faced by the child is syntactic in nature and involves meaning and logic.

There is currently no one theory dominant in the area of language acquisition, but four factors previously largely neglected are now being emphasized: (1) language input to the child (2) patterns of verbal interaction (3) verbal routines (4) individual differences.

The child acquires a vast amount of learning as a result of a complex interaction among maturational factors, learning strategies, and the sociocultural environment. Not all scholars agree that grammar is necessarily the best place to examine such a process. Blount (1975:586), for example, suggests that semantics, rather than transformational syntax, provides better insight into child language. As we understand early semantic development, we will be better able to study the intriguing problem of how children eventually acquire syntax.

How is a child able to deal with the necessarily abstract nature of syntactic processes? Many psycholinguists today believe that the structure of cognition of the human brain is universally such that all normal children possess a knowledge of universal grammar which is innate and which enables them to process linguistic data. As they try to make sense out of what they hear from family, friends (and nowadays from television), children organize the data of language according to their own understanding of how the language works. In other words, they devise theories of their language which they are constantly testing and revising in the light of new input. Children create their own grammar or model of the

*Concerning my use of sex-indefinite "he," see page 130.

parental language, and as the children develop and their experiences broaden, this model increasingly comes to resemble the parental language.

In addition to semantic and syntactic operations, the child has to master morphology. In English, for example, this would include such things as past tense, participles, and plurals. Such items appear to be acquired in a fixed order, probably depending on semantic and/or transformational complexity, and clearly not from the frequency of their use by parents. McNeill (1970:84) has noted that, in any given society, children are not sent to public school until they have mastered the morphology of their language. Thus, in the case of English, with a relatively simple morphology, children begin school at five or six but Russian speaking children at age seven. Readiness for school is apparently judged by mastery of the morphology.

The child must also master the sound system. Jakobson (1968) argues that all children pass through the same steps of phonological development, though at different rates. The sequence of development is universal among the languages of the world. The child begins with those sounds which are common to the languages of the world, for example /p, t, k, a/. Sounds which distinguish the child's tongue from the other languages appear only later.

In stressing the innate capabilities of the child, the basically social nature of the acquisition process must not be lost sight of. Language is used by human beings in a social context. The child learns to speak to others before he learns to speak to himself egocentrically. Bruner (1975) claims that linguistic concepts are first realized in action. Children develop attention structures in interaction with parents, first developing the notion of predication from having their attention called to the characteristics or actions of objects. Basic case relations like agent, action, object, and recipient are first apprehended by children in observing and participating in action (especially play). They incorporate these relations and the accompanying parental comments into their language learning.

Parents simplify the phonology, syntax, and morphology used in speaking to children in certain regular ways. This makes it easier for children to figure out how the language works. This language used by parents is well designed to provide children with information about the world and about the social rules for the use of language (Gleason and Weintraub 1976).

Studies of language acquisition must pay attention to the part adults play in the process. Corsaro (1977) has identified the clarification request as a consistent feature of adult interactive styles used with children. The clarification request may consist of either a clarification marker (e.g., *what?*) or a partial repetition of the previous utterance. It may be used to clear up misunderstandings or to keep the conversation going. He records the following segment of conversation between a child (Buddy) and his father at home:

B-F: I got this (shoebox).
F-B: Oh, you want to buy some shoes, huh?
B-F: Yeah.
F-B: OK.
B-F: I'm gonna buy some sneakers.
F-B: Gonna buy some sneakers?
B-F: Yeah.

Such clarifications are often required because of an absence of shared cultural interpretations. They also help the adult control the flow of the interaction. The child begins to realize that what is obvious to him is not always as obvious to others. He learns how to resolve ambiguities and develop his communicative competence.

The focus of most child language acquisition studies so far has been on knowledge of grammar inferred from the child's performance, that is, from what the child says, the situations in which the sentences are spoken, and others' reactions to them. This kind of knowledge develops in an approximately invariant form, though not at an invariant rate for all children. The primary determinants of the order of learning are the relative semantic and grammatical complexity of constructions, rather than their frequency. Children learn the simpler structures first. This knowledge is somehow used in speaking and understanding sentences.

First language learning is not, in principle, necessarily different from learning to speak a second language as an adult, whether through formal study or anthropological linguistic field methods. In the first place, the dual nature of the speaker/hearer role must be acknowledged. In both instances it is the case that a person understands more than he is able to say, that is, a person's passive knowledge is always greater than his active knowledge of a language. It is undoubtedly the case that the child must understand a particular grammatical pattern before he can produce it (Miller and Ervin 1964).

Children go through a number of stages in their linguistic development. First, there is the earliest stage when the child makes all kinds of babbling and other sounds, some of which may resemble sounds of his own or some other language, while others are found in no human language. In any case, they are not used to signal anything. In the next stage, the child utilizes certain sounds to communicate, perhaps a dozen or so, but these sounds bear little or no resemblance to any words in the adult language. In other words, the child has created his own limited, short-lived, unique language (Halliday 1975).

In the following stage the child utters single words which are recognizably modeled after adult words, but each of which evidently is equivalent in meaning to a whole sentence. This is so-called holophrastic speech. Two things are clearly evident in this connection. One is that language acquisition could not take place as it does if the child did not have the concept of a sentence at the beginning of its language learning. The second consideration is that the child's initial hypothesis is everywhere exactly the same, namely, that sentences consist of single words (McNeill 1970:2). This stage is followed by one in which sentences consist of two words and which express a surprising variety of semantic relations between the pairs of words. This indicates that the child is developing complex abstract concepts, although he lacks control of a syntactic apparatus that would allow him to express himself in adult speech forms. For example, a sentence like *Mommy shoe* might mean "That's Mommy's shoe," "Mommy, put my shoe on," or "Mommy has a shoe," depending on context. Children thus have an understanding of the adult grammar but express themselves through their own. The one and two-word stages are apparently linguistic universals.

A much-cited piece of evidence for the notion that the child constructs his own constantly revised grammar is the acquisition of the irregular plurals and irregular past verbs in English. Along with the regular forms such as "knocked" and "cats," the child learns to say "came," "ran," and "did," as well as "feet," "mice," and "teeth." Only later does he say "comed," "runned," and "doed," as well as "foots," "mouses," and "tooths." The explanation seems to be that the child initially learns the irregular forms because they are among the most frequently appearing forms. Later on, he analyzes the regular noun plurals and past verbs as, for example, "dog+s" or "open+ed," then generalizes the rules to *all* nouns and verbs, giving "mouses," "doed," etc. Only later does he realize the rule has exceptions and that irregular verbs and nouns have to be marked in his lexicon as exceptions, together with the irregular shape they take in plural or past, as the case may be (McNeill 1970:85–86).

Further evidence against the imitative model of child language acquisition includes the frequent incapability of children to repeat an inflectional or syntactic change and correction after the parent. For example, if an adult says, "Say what I say: Where can I put them?" the child may respond, "Where I can put them?", processing the sentence through his own linguistic system (Slobin 1971:52). Likewise, parents frequently fail to perceive children's mistakes, or if they do, there is usually an apparent randomness of the correction of the child's speech. Furthermore, children normally fail to imitate parents' ungrammatical remarks.

There is also positive evidence for the child's active role. In a now famous study, Weir (1963) taped her infant's speech in its crib. The child spoke a great deal to itself, although there was no stimulus to provoke its response. These were monologues which the author's son addressed to himself before he went to sleep at night. The child was not imitating adult sentences but rather was experimenting with words, practicing vocabulary and grammatical paradigms. He corrected his own pronunciations and practiced substituting his small vocabulary into fixed sentence frames. Much of the material recorded by his mother bore a striking resemblance to the exercises in textbooks designed for the self-study of a foreign language. The child would utter such sequences of noun substitutions as:

What color, What color blanket, What color map, What color glass.

Noun-phrase substitutions:
    There's a hat, There's another. There's hat, There's another hat.

Adjective substitutions:
    Big Bob, Little Bob, Big and little, Little Bobby, Little Nancy, Big Nancy.

Verb substitutions:
    Listen to microphone, Go to microphone

Pronominal substitutions:
    Take the monkey, Take it, Don't take it off, Don't take the glasses off, Stop it, Stop the ball, Stop it, I go up there, I go, She go up there.

The child was practicing the language which he was learning from his parents and others.

An important source of learning for any child is the feedback from his every-day speech. If he demands or questions understandably and appropriately, the desired consequences will probably ensue. Apparently the parents' understanding is not dependent on the well-formedness of children's utterances. Reinforcement is not necessary for learning, though undoubtedly it does play some role. Much more important is the child's ability to generalize, hypothesize, and process information, which he does with or without parental guidance, and which many children do in the learning of a second language on the street. Parental approval depends on the truth value of the children's statements, not on their conformity to the norms of adult grammar. Brown (1973:410) asserts that parents probably do approve of well-formed utterances and disapprove or correct the ill-formed, but there is no available evidence yet to support these ideas. In any case, children appear to assume that they will be understood if they speak at all. This assumption is largely justified in that the context of speech is obvious and parents know what the child's experience has been, so that the child's utterances are often almost redundant. Yet the child has to learn to adapt the size and complexity of his sentences to different people and changing situations. At first, he is very narrowly adapted, linguistically and in all other ways, to a very particular kind of setting (Brown 1973:167–168). As the child moves out into different social settings, he not only expands his vocabulary but also adjusts his grammar increasingly in the direction of the adult model.

M. A. K. Halliday's approach to language acquisition is more sociolinguistic than previous studies, which have had a psycholinguistic orientation (Halliday 1975). He is concerned primarily with the development of the functions of language in the child. He focuses on interaction between parent and child. The child is able to mean before he adopts words for the realization of meaning. Halliday began the study of his son Nigel at age nine months, much earlier than previous studies. Nigel created his own system. For example, a vocalization like *nananana* meant something like "I want that thing now," which was always the way he expressed that idea at that age. It satisfied the child's material needs and was the earliest function to appear in Nigel's speech.

Scholars argue about the relative importance of the role of function in language acquisition. We are not sure whether "semantic and syntactic forms are somehow derived by the child from pragmatic acts, or whether the acquisition of formal structure entails separate cognitive processes for which communication function plays largely a motivational role," (Cazden 1977:418).

A sociological perspective demands close attention to the social circumstances surrounding language acquisition. Not only must we assume a priori the importance of such factors, but we must be sure that a biased sample of social situations will not lead us to declare as universal what might be culture bound or language specific. Extant studies of the child's acquisition of grammar are very limited in their social orientation. They have been mostly studies of middle-class, eldest children and have for the most part ignored any other social context than mother and child. (The studies by Bonifacio Contreras of the acquisition of Macedonian by preschoolers in Skopje, Yugoslavia are a notable exception.)

The study of the social environment in which children are learning language will eventually help us answer some important questions. For example, we don't know at what age children move outside the linguistic influence of their parents and fall under the dominant influence of their peer group. Most children acquire the dialect of their friends rather than their parents, but we don't know when this happens and to what extent and whether this linguistic puberty is biologically or culturally controlled (Labov 1971a:56).

As an example of the type of conclusions which can be reached by taking into account situational variables, we could mention a study of Edinburgh preschool children which showed that comparative expressions (*more, less, most,* etc.) occur much more frequently in "comparative" situations where several children are competing with each other in various tasks. It is obvious that the language of a single child at home would be less likely to show such structures (Campbell and Wales 1970:250).

Thus, as the child moves from one new situation to another, with new cultural items and new social relationships, he encounters new grammatical relationships or at least becomes increasingly aware of them. This leads the child to social circles of increasingly wider scope. He learns the way a particular vernacular is spoken in his particular family and neighborhood, then learns other varieties or styles. The middle-class child will not have to cross any social or linguistic boundaries when he goes to school, but the working-class child may have problems in this respect.

It is important not to confuse the child's version of the adult language with baby talk ("any special form of a language which is regarded by a speech community as being primarily appropriate for talking to young children and which is generally regarded as not the normal adult use of language" [Ferguson 1971:113]). Ferguson compared baby talk phenomena in Arabic, Marathi, Comanche, Gilyak, English, and Spanish and concluded that "Baby talk is a relatively stable, conventionalized part of a language, transmitted by 'natural' means of language transmission, much like the rest of the language; it is, in general, not a universal, instinctive creation of children everywhere, nor an ephemeral form of speech arising out of adult's imitation of child speech" (Ferguson 1971:114–115).

Baby-talk words most commonly refer to kin, body parts and functions, animals and basic qualities like "good," "bad," "little," and "dirty." Baby talk may be used because adults feel it is easier for the child or because they wish to foster nurturing and protective attitudes. Secondarily, such attitudes lead to speaking baby talk to animals or one's lover.

Historical records show that Arabic baby talk, for example, is today much like it was at the beginning of the nineteenth century and that the Latin baby-talk word for "food," *papa,* is still used in contemporary Spanish and Moroccan Arabic. Sometimes adults will adopt an item of child speech, or a baby-talk word may be accepted into common speech, as, for example, *peek-a-boo* (blouse), or the common usage in American English of *bye-bye* as a frequent form of leave-taking either face-to-face or on the telephone. Children, of course, learn baby talk from adults, adopt it as part of their own speech patterns, then drop it as they grow older and become aware of its age-graded nature.

Only after children have learned the grammatical rules and the rules for use of the language in different situations do they begin to play word games, to make nonsense rhymes, and to use "secret languages" like "Pig Latin," which show that they are now exploiting the alternatives within their internalized language system. They find that a few simple transformations will produce languages that outsiders find difficult to understand, at least at first. Children do this in many different societies, both simple and complex. Thus, both in their acquisition of their native language and in the creation of their own disguised languages, children show remarkable creativity.

4.4 Acquisition of communicative competence

Linguistic socialization includes not only language acquisition, and awareness of and attitudes toward language and language differences but also what has come to be known as the acquisition of communicative competence.

By communicative competence is meant the speaker's knowledge of what is appropriate to say, how it should be said, and when in the different social situations in which he finds himself. This may be the most important linguistic ability learned by the child, that is, the ability to produce utterances which are not only grammatical but also appropriate to the linguistic and situational context. As Hymes (1974b:75) has put it,

> A child from whom any and all of the grammatical sequences of a language might come with equal likelihood would be, of course, a social monster. Within the social matrix in which it acquires a system of grammar, a child acquires also a system of its use regarding persons, places, purposes, other modes of communication, etc.—all the components of communicative events, together with attitudes and beliefs regarding them. There also develop patterns of the sequential use of language in conversation, address, standard routines, and the like. In such acquisition resides the child's sociolinguistic competence (or, more broadly, communicative competence), its ability to participate in its society as not only a speaking but also a communicating member.

As soon as the child begins to talk, he begins to express himself differently depending on the person to whom he is speaking, what kind of a situation he is in, and whatever it is he wants to say. For example, children will speak differently to adults or to other children and will frequently simplify their language in talking to younger children. Depending on the child's social situation, he may have at his disposal different styles, dialects or languages which he uses for different purposes. As he matures, his repertoire will ordinarily become more varied, although in his lifetime some varieties may increase or decrease in importance or disappear altogether.

Thus, the child acquires linguistic and communicative competence, and likewise the person who would enter and participate in an alien culture, be he linguist or nonlinguist, must as a matter of course also acquire some degree of communicative as well as linguistic competence. In fact, a speaker often demonstrates his foreignness more vividly by gaps in his communicative than in his linguistic competence, as when he speaks to a bootblack as if he were addressing royalty.

An important part of the language socialization of the child is learning *routines* such as, for example, in the United States the appropriate use of *hi, bye-bye,* or the Halloween *trick or treat* routine: the child says, "Trick or treat," the adult responds verbally and by giving candy, and the child says, "Thank you." Parents instruct children by saying, "Say 'trick or treat,' " and "Don't forget to say 'Thank you' " (Gleason and Weintraub 1976). As Ferguson (1976) notes, "Routines are acquired differently from the rest of language in that they are explictly taught by parents, who prompt their use with the markers *Say,* and later *What do you say?* and who ask after the occasion *What did you say?*"

Part of the child's task is mastering register and style variation (see section 6.3). The child also learns to switch from one style to another or from one language to another if he is bilingual. Children even in nursery school, for example, may take on the roles and speech characteristics of doctors, cowboys, teachers, or mothers. They may use a telegraphic style when they assume that the other person does not speak their language, and they may simplify their language in addressing a younger child. As the child grows older it becomes more and more difficult for him to make major grammatical changes. This learning of social interactional and selectional rules begins at an early age and continues, depending on the child's opportunities for interacting with significant others of varying social character-istics and in various types of situations. Such opportunities are, of course, dependent on the child's location in the social structure with reference to such characteristics as family structure, social class, ethnicity, and residential area (Grimshaw and Holden 1976).

Societies differ in their conception of children as users and learners of language. Major socialization pressure is exerted at different stages of language development. Interest in speech and speech play may be encouraged or discouraged to varying degrees, and there is great variation in the extent to which speech is a mode of reward and punishment for children. Much research is needed along these lines. We need to focus on interaction sequences such as mother-child or child-child, as the child develops his language in response to the type of communicative tasks his life style requires. He has to acquire the ability to select appropriate words, styles, and codes, as well as the rules which govern the assignment of right to speak and the selection of appropriate content. There is some evidence that acquisition of these sociolinguistic rules is subject to over-generalization and the generation of structures different from those of adults (Cook 1973:324–325).

4.5 Cultural and linguistic relativity

The sociologist of knowledge studies how whatever passes for knowledge in a particular society or segment thereof has been produced by that society and the structures by means of which it is disseminated and controlled. By knowledge is meant not only received academic knowledge but also the common sense, everyday knowledge of the people. The sociologist strives to understand the social context of knowledge, not to evaluate its "truth" or "validity" except, of course, within its own sphere of activity. Ethnomethodologists studying how sociologists produce sociological knowledge have emphasized the great dependence of sociologists on the meaning of words—the interpretation of which, on questionnaires, for example, can vary fairly widely in a population. There may be differences in the interpretation of a particular question not immediately apparent to the linguistically unsophisticated. Thus, the sociologist is, or ought to be, interested in the principles underlying meaning in language, that is, semantics and their relation to cognition, the processes of knowing. Every sociologist should be concerned with meaning, and every sociologist of language ought to be especially concerned with the relationships between linguistic meaning and social meaning.

There are two different but related approaches to the study of the influence of language structure on cognitive processes and other symbolically mediated behavior. One approach deals with the *generic* function of language in shaping cognitive processes, while the other is concerned with the *comparative* problem of how lexical and grammatical differences among languages systematically relate to differences in the cognitive processes of their speakers. In other words, we must specify in what ways languages are alike, as well as how they differ. The notion of variation assumes some base from which phenomena vary. It is primarily the comparative problem that has held the attention of scholars.

Social scientists are in general agreement with the principle of cultural relativity, that is, the notion that cultures are to be understood in their own terms and that there are no standards by which one can evaluate some cultures as being better or worse, or higher or lower than others. An outgrowth of theories of cultural relativity is the idea of linguistic relativity—the claim that different language structures constrain the cognitive function of their speakers in different ways. The linguistic relativity view has come to be modified in recent years by the realization that not only do languages reflect more than they mold cultural values and orientation but also that the languages of the world share many more aspects of structure than was previously realized.

When we speak of cognitive organization as being constrained by linguistic structure, what we are referring to primarily is that certain aspects of the "real world" are obligatorily signalled by linguistic forms, whereas others are not. For example, some languages require that gender be marked in noun, verb, adjective, or pronoun, whereas others do not. Thus, in the former case one has to be continually on the alert to take into consideration the sex of the person speaking, spoken to or about, whereas in the other case speakers and hearers do not have their attention drawn to the fact of sexual differences. In some languages, tense may be important, that is, the verb automatically must indicate when an event took place—in the past, present, or future—and whether it happened at the same time as, or prior to, or after some other event. In other languages, time of occurrence is ignored, but the verb form indicates whether the person speaking actually witnessed the event or merely heard about it. Some languages, such as Turkish or Macedonian, make both kinds of distinction. Many analogies have been drawn between these kinds of grammatical distinctions and certain orientations in the culture of their speakers.

Generally known as the *Sapir-Whorf hypothesis*, the postulate that the structure of the languages we speak affects the way we perceive the world about us is ordinarily attributed to the American linguists Edward Sapir and Benjamin Lee Whorf, but the idea goes back at least as far as the nineteenth-century German linguist Wilhelm von Humboldt. As expressed by Sapir (1929:207), "Language is a guide to social reality . . . Human beings do not live in the objective world alone, nor alone in the world of social activity as ordinarily understood but are very much at the mercy of the particular language which has become the medium of expression for their society."

Whorf (1956) believed that languages with different structures conceptualized reality differently, for example, European languages in terms of space and time but a language like Hopi in terms of events. Many of his most important points were made comparing Hopi with what he called "Standard Average European" (SAE), on the assumption that European languages did not differ among themselves significantly enough to prevent their being considered as a group. The language gap between Hopi and SAE is indeed wide, and in each case the language is congruent with the culture. Determining the direction of causality is a different matter. A few pertinent plausible examples picked at random do not constitute proof. Furthermore, the differences concern surface morphology for the most part, and Whorf does not deal with deeper levels of syntax.

If the way a language is structured forms a kind of screen or filter through which its native speakers perceive, conceptualize, and categorize the objects of the natural land social world, then it must form or help to form a people's world view. Language would function, then, not just as a device for reporting experience but also as a way of defining experience. It must direct speakers' perceptions and supply their habitual modes of analyzing experience into significant categories. Significant and formidable barriers to cross-cultural communication would then arise from differences between languages, although intercultural communication is never impossible. Actually, it is just more or less difficult, depending on the degree of difference, not so much between the languages as between the cultures concerned.

Fishman (1960:333; 1972b:160–161) has identified four levels to the Sapir-Whorf hypothesis. The first level involves *codifiability* and asserts that people who speak languages making lexical distinctions not made by another language or languages are therefore better able to talk about certain things than the other speakers can. Obviously, codifiability differences are related to gross cultural differences. It is easier to remember and deal with things that have a high degree of codifiability. This is enhanced if the language typically uses a single word rather than a phrase for a particular object, e.g. *cirrus* rather than *wispy, horse-tail clouds* (Brown 1958:236–237).

The second level asserts that where a language makes certain lexical distinctions not made by others, it enables their speakers more easily to perceive differences in environment. Therefore, they can remember, perceive, or learn certain nonlinguistic tasks more rapidly or completely, such as Eskimos learning the different types of snow. The third level asserts that speakers of languages with particular grammatical features are predisposed to certain cultural styles or emphases, e.g. the European orientation toward clocks and calendars related to the verbal tense system. This level of analysis, which relates grammatical structure to worldview, has not normally sought nor supplied independent confirmation of the existence of whatever phenomena the grammatical data are supposed to indicate. This level of analysis is frequently argued for by picking and choosing grammatical forms, cultural values, and themes which happen to be congruent with each other. There is no attempt systematically to sample either. The fourth level asserts that grammatical features facilitate or make more difficult certain nonlinguistic behaviors such as in the cognitive and perceptual areas. With reference to this last point, the Sapir-Whorf controversy in part still rages because of its application to language differences between children of different social classes à la Bernstein (see section 8.4).

If there are significant connections between language and the rest of culture, they are difficult to validate, because it is impossible to generalize about entire cultures or social classes. Furthermore, we have to explain the fact that peoples very similar in culture speak languages completely unrelated (e.g. Germans and Hungarians) and that closely related languages are frequently spoken by peoples with a very different culture e.g. Finns and Samoyeds. Or consider Islamic societies which use such widely different languages as Arabic, Turkish, Persian and Indonesian. While languages may reflect cultural concerns, they do not cause them. As Fishman (1972b:155–158) has indicated, "Although many have tried to do so, no one has successfully predicted and demonstrated a cognitive difference between two populations on the basis of the grammatical or other structural differences between their languages alone." Another difficulty making it unfeasible to categorize or typologize entire languages or entire societies in any overall fashion is the widespread bilingualism and biculturalism in most of the societies of the world. In many cases where the structural differences in the linguistic system may be great, they may be utilized by speakers who share substantially the same culture or who may appropriately make different distinctions in different settings. Although different languages categorize experience differently, it is possible for a person speaking one language to understand the distinctions made by the other. Thus, while thought may be conditioned by language, it is not determined by it.

Perhaps ultimately the hypothesis that people speaking different languages perceive the world differently can only be decided by psychological experiments. It is not possible to extrapolate directly from linguistic to cognitive data. For example, because English uses the same words (long/short) for both time and space, it is not necessarily the case that we tend to view time in spatial terms, whereas a speaker of Hopi, who has different words to refer to time and space, does not perceive them in the same fashion, as Whorf asserts.

The view that each language is equally well adapted to its particular setting assumes that each language has only one setting, each setting only one language. The converse of the Sapir-Whorf hypothesis is that the social and natural environment is reflected in the language. This is largely a matter of vocabulary, for those features of social life and of the natural environment which are particularly important will be represented in the lexicon, whether different kinds of snow for the Eskimo, different aspects of the horse or camel among the Bedouin, or terms which pertain to the automobile in our own civilization. Sapir (1912:89) long ago noted that "... in actual society even the simplest environmental influence is either supported or transformed by social forces." Aspects of the environment will be reflected in the lexicon only if the people in that particular society have enough interest to make reference to it through the medium of language. It is not merely the physical environment which is reflected but the interest of the people in those environmental features.

The values current in a society may affect the language, especially by word taboos. But clearly the prohibition of the use of certain words in certain contexts is merely a special case of the notion that certain forms are appropriate in certain styles and registers and inappropriate in others. Taboo words, among others, are used for special effects. Their use in English may involve an effort very much akin to the use of magic in nonliterate societies (see section 4.7).

Since we cannot have a different word for each unique event or object, each word in a given language must necessarily refer to the range of events or objects. Some events or objects are always assigned to different terms, while others are classed together. Each language has its own unique way of grouping or distinguishing such entities. It must not be thought that the distinctions made by languages are all necessarily arbitrary and unique. For example, the notion that color distinctions are so has been recently discredited by the studies of Berlin and Kay (1969), who have shown that all languages place the foci of their color labels at very nearly the same spots on the color spectrum. In their original presentation, Berlin and Kay claimed that if five foci are identified, for example, they will always be white, black, red, green, yellow, and if there is a sixth, it will always be blue. While languages may have different numbers of basic terms, languages with the same number of basic terms will always have the same colors. Interestingly, the sequence is correlated with technological complexity, so languages with only two terms are spoken by technologically very primitive people (for example, in New Guinea), while languages with all eleven foci (including brown, grey, pink, orange, and purple) are confined to the complex cultures of East Asia and Europe. The basic color term theory has been revised more recently in some of its details, but the basic sequence and its implications appear to be supported by the research done since their original publication (Kay 1975).

4.6 Folk taxonomies

Other than the Sapir-Whorf hypothesis, perhaps the area that has received the most extensive attention of those interested in the relation between language and culture has been that of folk taxonomy. By taxonomy is meant some popularly accepted classification of plants, animals, colors, diseases, kinship terms, speech acts, or whatever. The investigator studies the principles behind the classifications which have been set up by people without regard to the principles of modern Western scientific systems. For example, in Baffin Land, Mackey

(1972b:135) was able to identify 21 distinctly different words for ice and snow in the local Eskimo language, some words requiring long sentences to translate into English.

All speech communities have folk taxonomies as part of their lexicons. These taxonomies are not necessarily reflections of either nature or the language but rather of locally accepted social conventions. While the native speakers may regard these taxonomies as the only possible ones for the phenomena in question and as reflecting certain self-evident truths, they are socially particularistic. Linguistic reflection of social reality, however, is likely to be only partial, as expansion, contraction, or change in the lexicon is likely to be slower than the related sociocultural changes.

Color and kinship terminologies have been the classical sources of relativist ideas. Kinship categories differ radically from one language to another, although analysis of kinship terminology is normally presented in terms of a universal or at least language-neutral set of symbols such as Fa="father," Mo="mother," Br="brother," Si="sister," So="son," Da="daughter," Hu="husband," Wi= "wife." If these can be considered semantic universals of kinship, then we imply that they are also cultural universals. The analyst identifies the components of meaning which distinguish the use of one term from that of another, such as sex, collaterality, generation, relative age, etc. These dimensions can be analyzed by a technique known as componential analysis, which studies the kinship semantics of each language in its own terms (Leech 1974:247–259). Thus, while the components may be universal, they are put together according to different principles in different languages and societies. These principles are then indicative of the social structure as well as the cognitive processes of the people who speak each of the languages. Thus, for example, in Spanish *tío* means not only "uncle" but also "father's or mother's first cousin." What in English is kept separate is socially and conceptually merged in Spanish. But English also merges what many other cultures keep separate, for *uncle* can refer to FaBr, MoBr, FaSiHu or MoSiHu. In many languages, there are separate terms for relatives by blood and relatives by marriage, as well as for distinguishing those on the mother's side from those on the father's, as these are important social distinctions.

4.7 Taboos and euphemisms

Words not only have referential meaning, that is, stand for certain things, persons or ideas but can evoke in themselves positive or negative attitudes. Thus, the uttering of certain words may be forbidden because they are deemed to be especially sacred, vulgar, obscene, or to refer to unpleasant matters, all as culturally defined. Of course, they are, in fact, used; otherwise they would be lost to the language.

Frazer (1922:284–305) pointed out that, in a wide range of nonliterate cultures, there is a reluctance or taboo against pronouncing a person's own name, the name of certain designated relatives, of the dead, or of royal and divine

personages. The taboo extends even to ordinary words which resemble the
tabooed name. Frazer believed that this taboo was a potent factor in lexical
change as many words dropped out of the local lexicon.

As cultures change, so do the linguistic taboos. Thus, note the following
observations made three decades ago and certainly obsolete in many, if not most,
segments of United States society, at least: "If you use the so-called 'four-letter' or
taboo words in mixed company except in the lowest classes of society, you will
immediately be subjected to extreme disapproval, condemnation and ostracism"
(Hall 1960:20).

Unpleasant associations are unavoidable in dealing with such subjects as
death, disease, crime, and punishment, as well as with the taboo-ridden subjects
of sex and excretion, so the process of euphemism inevitably influences our
speech. What we do is refer to something offensive or delicate in a way to make it
sound more pleasant or acceptable than it really is. We replace a word having
offensive connotations with another which does not overtly refer to the
unpleasantness being avoided. This linguistic device enables us to live with talk
about things that would otherwise shock or disturb us.

Euphemisms fall into two categories. In one, there is substitution of a word
phonetically similar to the disapproved one, for example, in English:

gee whiz	Jesus
aw shucks	aw shit
goldarn	God damned

or in Spanish:

caray	carajo
ay chihuahua	ay chingado
cilantro	culantro

In the last example, academic Spanish *culantro* ("coriander leaves") sounds
like *culo* ("rectum"), so *cilantro* is substituted in popular Mexican Spanish.
Interestingly, fresh coriander leaves are now available in many supermarkets in
the southwestern United States, where they are labelled "Mexican cilantro."

In the other category of euphemisms, an unpleasant idea is avoided by very
oblique reference. Thus, originally "toilet" referred to personal grooming, and
even today a woman may go to the "powder room," even when her face needs no
powdering. Likewise, a person may go to the "bathroom" who doesn't need a
bath or to the "restroom" when he isn't the least bit tired.

In American English, the three areas in which euphemisms seem to have
flourished most abundantly are the excretory functions, sexual organs and activities, and death. A fourth area might be business, where corporations do not
report "profits" but rather "earnings." But there are probably more ways to say a
person has died without using the verb "die" than almost anything else. Thus, a
person has "passed on," "passed away," "gone to his reward," "gone to the big
roundup in the sky," "been gathered to the bosom of the Lord," etc. The reader
can no doubt think of many others. One class in sociolinguistics at California

State University, Fullerton, succeeded in collecting more than a thousand such euphemisms for dying. Euphemisms are, of course, reflective of some very basic cultural attitudes and, therefore, of considerable sociolinguistic interest.

According to Haas (1964a:489–491), the Creek Indians in Oklahoma avoided the use of certain words of their own language when white people were around. These words were those bearing some phonetic similarity to the "four-letter" words of English. They avoided these words even though it was unlikely that a white person not knowing Creek would catch these words in the stream of Creek speech. The avoidance originated with the increase of bilingualism among the Creeks and as they came to assimilate the white man's taboos. Thai students studying in the United States also attempt to avoid certain Thai words resembling English obscene words, such as *phrig* "chili pepper." Among the Nootka, the English word *such* bears so close a resemblance to Nootka /sač/ "vagina umens" that Anglo teachers cannot get their students to utter the English word under any circumstances.

The case of the use of taboo words in public protest in the United States in the 1960s was, in effect, an attack on linguistic restrictions, which symbolized the attack on the social system itself. As Labov (1971a:63) indicates, "The strength of the norms which are being challenged here is hard to overestimate. The reactions of the Kent State grand jury to the language of the students provides some evidence. It must be remembered that the violation of a norm does not destroy the norm; in fact, this behavior would lose its significance if the social sanction did not exist." It was allegedly the shouting of obscenities at the National Guard soldiers that triggered the massacre of the Kent State students in May of 1970. Some taboos are connected with the belief in the magical nature of language, that somehow words have power in themselves. Thus, in some societies a person's name is kept secret, lest one gain power over the person by being able to utter his name. People also will change their names as a result of religious conversion, ethnic assimilation, or ascension to a throne or to the Papacy. Similarly, many women now feel that by giving up their maiden name upon marrying, they are giving up some of their power. This notion was common even in the women's movement of half a century ago (Jespersen 1925:175). Cities or countries will take new names and thereby hope to acquire new identities, as when Petrograd became Leningrad or the Gold Coast became Ghana.

Another category of taboo words is that of racial and religious epithets, hurled at people to insult and degrade them. Again, like other taboo words, they are in fact uttered and live on in the language. In fact, taboo words are very much alive and recently have become the subject of a specialized publication, *Maledicta; the International Journal of Verbal Aggression* (Volume 1, Number 1, Summer 1977), published by Reinhold Aman in Waukesha, Wisconsin, with contributions by linguists, anthropologists, psychologists, folklorists, etc.

Discussion questions

1. Are there any groups to which you belong that use special languages or special forms of the language? Describe their language usage.

2. What is the relationship between the socialization and language acquisition processes?
3. Describe the major stages through which a child goes in learning his first language.
4. There is much more to child language acquisition than the child's merely imitating what he hears adults saying. Explain.
5. Explain the difference between linguistic competence and communicative competence.
6. Describe some routines which children learn other than the *hi, bye-bye* or *trick or treat* routines and which you have observed. Do adults learn linguistic routines also? Explain.
7. Explain the Sapir-Whorf hypothesis. How strongly is it supported by empirical evidence?
8. Are you and your friends and acquaintances using more taboo words than formerly? Why do you feel this is happening? What age or sex differences do you observe in this regard?

5

Microsociolinguistics

By microsociolinguistics is meant the study of the relations between linguistic and social structures at the level of face-to-face interaction. At this level we are observing the linguistic and nonlinguistic behavior of individuals, rather than of categories, groups, or aggregates of people, as in macrosociolinguistics. The two levels of analysis are, of course, intimately related, and a prime task of the sociolinguist is to establish connections between the two.

According to Ervin-Tripp (1971b:16), microsociolinguistics includes "studies of the components of face-to-face interaction as they bear on, or are affected by, the formal structure of speech. These components may include the personnel, the situation, the function of the interaction, the topic, and the message and the channel." Unlike studies in "communication," microsociolinguistics is concerned with relating characteristics of the language or language variety to characteristics of the communicators or the communication situation. As sociolinguistic rules have been characterized in the literature, they are microsociolinguistic. It seems anomalous to speak of macrosociolinguistic rules. These are not part of the native speaker's competence, but rather are perhaps only large-scale empirical generalizations or "laws."

There are a number of viewpoints in the field converging on the notion that social and linguistic phenomena are of the same order. If this is the case, and much research appears to be based upon this assumption, then the same linguistic data can be used to analyze both linguistic form and social categories. Thus, rather than trying to correlate linguistic form with social information collected elsewhere, we can consider the linguistic forms actually chosen as simply a realization of the social meanings and categories.

There is a particularly intimate relationship between the study of social interaction and the study of language in use. The study of social interaction in sociology has been dominated by a school of thought known as symbolic interactionism. This particular theoretical perspective emphasizes the notion that, when people interact with each other, they are reacting to the meaning (to them) of others' behavior, rather than to what they are actually doing—that is, all behavior is interpreted symbolically. People react more to symbols than to acts or things.

Man lives in a world of symbols; he interprets his physical and social world in terms of symbols. Many, perhaps most of the symbols with which people have surrounded themselves are linguistic symbols or at least have direct linguistic representation. The study of people's reaction to such symbols is particularly instructive. Witness the phenomenon of violence as a reaction to the hurling of a racial epithet; the avoidance of words referring to death; or the fact that the mere uttering of one of the most frequently used words in the English language, *fuck*, has gotten people arrested or shot. Formerly books were confiscated by postal and custom officials if they contained the word; it does not even appear in most contemporary English dictionaries.

One obvious area where the study of language and the study of social interaction overlap is the analysis of conversation, perhaps the most pervasive and ubiquitous of all human activities. In conversational analysis, we are interested not only in what people are saying and how they are saying it but also what they are doing at the same time they are talking to each other. Looking at conversation from a sociological point of view, we are interested in the group memberships of the participants, their role relationships, the social categories to which they belong, etc., for all of these potentially affect the nature of the interaction which takes place, as well as the content and form of what is said (see section 5.5). Mead (1934) asserted that the self is acquired through the process of social interaction, as individuals' subjective experiences are objectified by mutual acceptance of symbols. Mind is basically a social phenomenon, and language provides increased control over the organization of the social environment. Language and mind are interdependent, and both arise out of the process of social interaction.

Although language has its origins in the face-to-face situation, it can be readily detached from it and communicate meanings other than those connected with the here and now. We can speak about all sorts of things that are not present at all in the face-to-face situation, including things we have never experienced and never will. People speak as they think, and speaker and hearer hear what each says at virtually the same instant. The two are constantly reinforcing each other's subjectivity, thereby creating a world perceived as objective by both. In the course of a conversation, one's meanings become more "real" to the speaker (Berger and Luckmann 1967:32–40).

Essential to any sociolinguistic study is consideration of the social organization of speakers, whether in a speech community or as part of an interaction network. Whether and how social interaction takes place is determined to a considerable degree by the communality of linguistic codes possessed by any potential actors. Each person interacts with other persons, who, in turn, interact with other persons. The way in which interaction is structured and the social networks thus formed are highly dependent on the availability to and adequate use of speech varieties by the actors and vice versa. We can begin by looking at who speaks to whom, when, for what purpose, and with what results. Small networks feed into large networks, which can usually be identified with social categories, and thus the micro- and the macrolevels are linked.

In complex societies almost every person is not only a member of several networks but also commands a *repertoire* of different languages, dialects, varieties, or styles which he is able to use at will depending on the situation (see Chapter 6). He can also switch from one to another in the course of a given situation. Fishman (1972c:47–48) has stressed the necessity of obtaining reliable descriptions of existing patterns of social organization in language use and behavior toward language before we can attempt to explain why or how this pattern either changes or remains stable. The researcher attempts to establish the systematic nature of code choice and code change in a given community.

5.1 Microfunctions of language

There is not an infinite or indefinite number of ways people use language for their own ends. There is really a rather limited number of basic things we do with language. As Searle (1976:22–23) has indicated, "We tell people how things are, we try to get them to do things, we commit ourselves to doing things, we express our feelings and attitudes, and we bring about changes through our utterances. Often, we do more than one of these at once in the same utterance."

Robinson and Rackstraw (1972:11–12) cite some others: "To ask for or give knowledge or beliefs about the physical and social world external to oneself and report on 'private' states (referential function) often by making statements or posing questions; to control other people's behavior, often by issuing commands; to relieve tensions by exclaiming; to order one's own nonverbal behavior; to attract or retain attention; to joke or recite or create poetry; to conform to social norms; to identify one's status; to derive the role relationships between speaker and listener; to teach someone else the language."

Whereas in sociology, functionalist theory is not concerned with individual motivation for certain actions, sociolinguistic theory takes into account both the intent of the speaker and the consequences for speaker, hearer, or others, as well as for the sociocultural structure. Furthermore, linguists are especially concerned with the means employed—in other words, what do people hope or expect to accomplish with language, what actually is accomplished, and how is it done? Consider the following:

1. Would you mind handing me the ledger, Abigail?

Abigail's boss hopes to get the ledger, and let us assume for the sake of argument that she (that is Abigail's boss) does in fact get it, so that is what is accomplished. The means employed is that of a question but of a particular form, a polite type of question, and one whose intention is clear: the speaker is uttering a request. Abigail's boss could just as well have said:

2. Gimme the goddamned ledger, Abby!

Here the intent is no less clear, although this utterance is better characterized as a command rather than as a request and its function may not be quite the same. That is, the boss may get the ledger, but in (2.), Abigail might get quite upset if this is not the boss's usual way of addressing her. This personal function might be either manifest or latent, depending on the speaker's intentions.

This particular example has been chosen, at least in part, to emphasize the point that most instances of language use are for the purpose of inducing changes in the hearers, either motor or intellectual/emotional, rather than merely to "communicate" ideas from one person to another.

The utterances of very young children are functionally simple, as each utterance normally serves just one function. Halliday (1973:353) notes that language develops in response to the child's personal and social needs and suggests what some of these needs might be:

1. Instrumental—language is used to satisfy some material need.
2. Regulatory—language is used to regulate the behavior of others.
3. Interactional—language is used to maintain and transform social relationships.
4. Personal—language is used to express individual identity and personality.
5. Heuristic—language is used to investigate speaker's environment.
6. Imaginative—language is used in fantasy and play.
7. Representational—language is used to express propositions.

Although Halliday explains child language in terms of seven specific functions, he explains adult language in terms of three more general functions: (1) the *ideational,* or the expression of content, that is, the speaker's experience of the "real" world; (2) the *interpersonal,* aimed at the establishment and maintenance of social relations, such as social roles; and (3) the *textual* function whereby language provides links with itself and with the situation in which it is used (Halliday 1970:143). Any adult utterance normally fulfills more than one function, e.g. *Like I said, I'm kicking you out, you bum!,* where all three functions can be identified. Another scholar, Leech (1974) has come up with a somewhat different list of functions:

1. Informational—conveying information
2. Expressive—expressing the speaker's or writer's feelings or attitudes
3. Directive—directing or influencing the behavior or attitudes of others
4. Aesthetic—creating an artistic effect
5. Phatic—maintaining social bonds

Consider, for example, the following sentences, illustrative of each of these functions.

1. The dog chewed up the book. (informational)
2. Well, for goodness sake, look at that! (expressive)
3. Bring me a beer, will ya? (directive)
4. Quoth the raven, never more! (aesthetic)
5. Good morning, Mr. Wong. (phatic)

Again, more than one of these functions can be carried out by a single utterance, in fact the multifunctional utterance is undoubtedly the rule rather than the exception. It must also be noted that these classifications are all impressionistic and intuitive, certainly neither scientific nor exhaustive. Undoubtedly the phatic and directive functions are those of greatest interest to the sociologist, whereas the social psychologist ought to be particularly interested in the expressive function. It should be further noted that any of these functions can be carried out by paralinguistic or kinesic means, as well as by the verbal act.

Some ethnographers of communication (see section 5.3) have been active observers in classrooms, studying interaction between teachers and pupils. Many different types of analysis have been carried out, some of them recently developed. One scheme sometimes used is an older one of Bales (1950), which can be used to analyze any type of interaction within small groups in terms of the functions of language, that is, what the speakers are doing with language. These functions are classified as follows:

1. Shows solidarity, raises other's status, gives help, reward
2. Shows tension release, jokes, laughs, shows satisfaction
3. Agrees, shows passive acceptance, understands, concurs, complies
4. Gives suggestion, direction, implying autonomy for other
5. Gives opinion, evaluation, analysis, expresses feeling, wish
6. Gives orientation, information, repeats, clarifies, confirms
7. Asks for orientation, information, repetition, confirmation
8. Asks for opinion, evaluation, analysis, expression of feeling
9. Asks for suggestion, direction, possible ways of action
10. Disagrees, shows passive rejection, formality, withholds help
11. Shows tension, asks for help, withdraws out of field
12. Shows antagonism, deflates other's status, defends or asserts self

Categories 1 through 3 represent the positive social-emotional area, while 10 through 12 represent the negative social-emotional area. The remaining categories represent the neutral task area. Bales bases his classification on the notion that interaction in a group accomplishes two main objectives: (1) it gets a job done (task area) and (2) it maintains social relationships among the members of the group (social-emotional area).

Not all the microfunctions of speech are manifest, that is, intended and/or obvious; they may be unintended and/or hidden. For example, speech gives information about the speaker whether or not he realizes or desires it. We can often easily determine various social categories to which a person might belong, by his speech alone: regional, ethnic, or national origin; social class; educational level; and in some instances, occupation or religion.

People also like to play with language. They may enjoy the sound of their own voices, with or without an audience, and may talk at great length with cats, dogs, or other pets, as well as to supernatural entities or forces from whom no immediate response is forthcoming. People may further engage in various kinds of language play, such as verbal dueling, nonsense rhymes, children's verses, and disguised languages, as well as glossolalia ("speaking in tongues"), which is sound-making rather than language.

Verbal dueling, such as that of Turkish teenagers, Eskimo songs, West Indian Calypso, or United States black ghetto youth, serve a number of functions, such as providing a verbal substitute for physical assault, thus avoiding physical violence. The duelers, usually youths, are able to test norms and limits and, hence, their own position of dominance in the group. In this word play, youths are being prepared for the adult world, where competition will be carried on on a different basis (Farb 1974:125) (see section 9.2).

The rationalistic view of man fostered by contemporary linguistics has tended perhaps to overemphasize man's logical nature. That man's use of language can be also nonlogical has been pointed out by Firth, who claims that scholars have deceived people by "persistently defining language as 'the expression of thought,' 'a medium for transmitting ideas to another individual,' 'a code of signs of symbols standing for concepts, ideas, and feelings,' a means of 'manifesting outwardly the inward workings of the mind.' Metternich was much nearer the mark when he pointed out to the professors that one of the commonest uses of language was for the concealment of thought and that, generally speaking, the very last thing a man of affairs wanted to do, assuming such a thing to be possible, was to manifest the inward workings of his mind" (Firth 1970:99).

To quote Firth further (1970:100–101), "Common speech is not the instrument of pure reason. It is as full of feelings, of the 'animal' senses as the common social life in the routine service of which we learn it. As Pareto said, 'Ordinary language, at best, reflects the facts of the outer world very much as a bad photograph that is a complete botch. It is serviceable in everyday life just because it is a manifestation of feelings.' "

5.2 Microsociolinguistic analysis

It has been only in recent years that serious attention has been paid to techniques of studying linguistic behavior in face-to-face interaction with a view to controlling for the social variables involved. Anthropologists have developed techniques of participant observation and worked on the classification and analysis of various types of speech events in different cultural contexts. Sociologists have been active in two areas particularly: ethnomethodology and the analysis of conversation. Sociolinguists use the concept of domain to categorize the regularities that obtain between varieties of language and socially recognized functions and situations. Such domains are not established a priori but are constructs emanating from detailed sociolinguistic analysis. Nevertheless, most are readily identifiable by the native speaker who is familiar with the fact that, because of the role relationships in which he finds himself, he is expected to use one variety, say, at home and another one in dealing with governmental officials, at church, at school, in the marketplace, etc. Domains are normally used to describe patterned linguistic variations at the level of the community, rather than at the level of the small group or nation state. The construct of domain provides a link between the micro- and macrosociolinguistic levels of analysis. Attitudes toward varieties may reflect attitudes toward the domains in which they are used.

A role relationship defines the mutual rights and obligations which people expect of each other, as, for example, between parent and child, teacher and student, friend and friend, or merchant and customer. An important recognition of the nature of the role relationship is revealed in the way people talk to each other, including such matters as proper use of respectful or deferential forms, informal slang, humor, etc. Not only is a certain way of speaking expected, but speaking in that fashion helps to validate the claimed statuses. The content and form of language reflects the extent to which the claimed rights are being honored. Speech, for example, will mark whether the interaction is a personal (informal and fluid) or a transactional one (where mutual rights and obligations of participants are stressed).

Culturally defined roles have characteristic linguistic repertoires, whereas class and other statuses are ordinarily marked by distinct styles of speaking. In the course of his social biography, the speaker is socialized to one or more repertoires and styles, although in the specific situation their use is influenced by the reciprocal definitions of the situation by the participants and any institutional constraints.

Linguistic interaction can also be viewed as a process of decision making, in which speakers select from a range of possible expressions. Choice is not a matter of complete individual freedom on the part of the speaker but is subject to grammatical and social constraints in the interest of intelligibility and accepta- bility of sentences, respectively. Both are matters of social convention. Speech styles often tip off the listener to what he is about to hear. When we are away from our usual surroundings, we may mislabel our speech by using an inappropriate style. Thus, style is a label one puts on one's speech. Analysts, such as Gumperz (1967), emphasize the notion that the nature of social relationships and the social categorization of the environment are the major social determinants of speech. Other factors, such as institutional setting and educational and other statuses, are significant only to the extent that they influence speakers' percep- tion of their social relationships.

An important alternative approach to microsociolinguistic analysis is that of the ethnomethodologists, who question the basic assumption of a stable system of symbols and meanings which are shared by the members of a society. They emphasize, rather, that the social construction of reality is an ongoing process of interpretation. They have adopted as their fundamental postulate the dictum of William Thomas: "If men define a situation as real, it is real in its consequences." Unfortunately, they manifest no concern for or attempt to link up with macro- sociological concerns.

The ethnomethodologists are phenomenological sociologists who are con- cerned primarily with what linguistic categories mean to the members of society in everyday life and their implications for members' actions. They reject the notion of innate language ability and postulate language as a developed skill which is internalized. They view meaning not as determined by abstract struc- tures but rather as an accomplishment of members as they engage in social interaction (Coulter 1973). The meaning of words according to this perspective is determined by the context in which they are used. It is not possible to delineate the meaning of words in some more general way. For the ethnomethodologists, words are essentially indexical expressions. They study how conversationalists make sense out of the utterances they hear.

Ethnomethodologists are interested in the socially situated use of language through a concern with the commonsense understandings that enable participants to enter into and sustain social interaction. They make meticulous analyses of recorded conversations to understand deep situational meanings. Some, such as Sacks, emphasize the objectivity of their findings, while others, like Cicourel, are more concerned with getting at the deeper meanings. For them, language is not something used in interaction; language *is* interaction. The language of researchers and subjects both generates the interaction between them and is product of that interaction (Deutscher 1975:176).

Ethnomethodological studies are concerned above all with practical reasoning. Their analyses of the internal organization of conversation clearly emphasize the speaker-hearer as practical analyst and practical reasoner. They look particularly at how the speaker-hearer produces and recognizes features of the talk which have consequences for the interaction. At the standard pace of conversation, speakers and hearers experience the most mundane features of talk and interaction in order to orient themselves to the delicate and rather complex features of the unfolding interaction (Turner 1974:11).

Whether social phenomena determine individual psychic states or vice versa, or, at least, which is prior in analysis has been a cogent issue in sociology ever since Durkheim opted for the primacy of social facts. In doing microsociolinguistic analysis, we observe that, in a conversation, speakers make certain choices, exercise certain options, while, at the macro level, we observe the social patterning of linguistic behavior. While some scholars are of the opinion that relatively stable patterns are generated from the individual choices, others treat individual choices as derived from stable sociolinguistic patterns.

A formulation of a sociolinguistic rule is basically a generalization of observed regularities. The most current formulation deals with such rules in terms of what have come to be called *alternation*, which concerns choice among alternative ways of speaking, and *co-occurrence*, which concerns interdependence within alternatives (Ervin-Tripp 1972:213). Thus, the speaker chooses a language or style; then within the code he chooses certain linguistic variables (phonological, lexical, or syntactical) which will necessarily co-occur with each other (cf. section 6.3). The speaker sizes up the situation in which he finds himself, decides on the norms which apply to the situation at hand, and chooses from available alternatives, depending on his knowledge and intentions.

In referring to intent, we must consider both the referential and the social information which the speaker wishes to convey. Gumperz (1972c:220) has pointed out that "The communication of social information presupposes the existence of regular relationships between language usage and social structure." We cannot ascertain a speaker's social intent unless we are familiar with the norms for the use of various linguistic alternatives which that particular speaker observes, depending on the social settings in which he finds himself and the subgroups to which he belongs. When we can formalize these relationships, we are able to classify the various linguistic forms into distinct dialects, styles, and registers.

There are a number of different linguistic devices available for the conveying of social information, such as choice of lexical, phonological, and syntactic variants; sequencing and alternation of utterances among speakers; choice of message form—that is, whether to convey a message by conversation, sermon, lecture or some other form; and code switching. Like grammatical rules, code selection rules operate below the level of consciousness and may be independent of the speaker's own intentions. In any case, interpretation of both referential and social information must take into consideration the total context of what has been said before and what is said afterwards. Social relationships appear to act as intervening variables between linguistic structures and their realization in speech.

5.3 Ethnography of communication

Ethnographers are anthropologists who write detailed accounts of how a given people, generally non-Western, goes about its culturally standardized daily and seasonal activities. One of the most pervasive activities of man is, of course, communication. Ethnographers have been quick to grasp this point, although it has been only in recent years that specific attention has been paid to the ethnography of communication. Basically, they treat such concepts as role, status, social identities, and social relationships as communicative symbols which are signalled in the act of speaking. In order to interpret a message in a particular context, one must have knowledge of the social values associated with the activities, social categories, and social relationships implied in the message. For example, while some societies place a great deal of value on verbal abilities, others admire silence. Thus, the Paliyans of southern India speak very little and generally not at all after age forty. Talkative people are regarded as abnormal and offensive (Farb 1974:143).

The ethnographer of communication focuses on how people actually talk, that is, what happens in a conversation, a speech, a telling of a joke, or any other speech event. This approach has overlapped with that of social psychologists studying social interaction in small groups and with the work of the ethnomethodologists. The ethnographers of communication have stressed the notion of communicative competence, the speaker's knowledge of sociolinguistic rules: when to use a particular variety or style, when to be silent, and the use of linguistic forms appropriate to the situation. They are not interested in an abstract, idealized speaker-hearer in a completely homogeneous linguistic community, as is Chomsky, but rather in actual speakers in socially and linguistically heterogeneous communities. They are concerned not only with what they know, but with what they actually say.

This approach involves the systematic description of communicative behavior as culturally standardized, viewed in the sociocultural context within which it occurs. All such patterns of behavior and their interpretation are taken to be problematic and to be established by empirical means. We investigate the communicative activities within the context of a given community or social network. Languages and their varieties are simply part of the resources upon which the members draw. Not only may the same linguistic means be made to serve various ends, but the same communicative ends may be served by different linguistic means. To untangle the interrelations, we have to examine the community's cultural values and beliefs, social institutions, roles, history, and ecology.

What elsewhere in this book is called "speech event" is referred to by Hymes as a "communication event," even though the latter is really a broader act, including the use of gesture as well as the transmission of language through writing or mechanical means. The starting point, at least, of the ethnography of communication is the description of specific communicative acts in specific cultures in terms of a predetermined frame of reference with which to guide the analysis. The frame of reference which Hymes (1974b:10) has devised for the ethnographic analysis of a communicative event is as follows:

(1) the various kinds of *participants* in communicative events—senders and receivers, addressers and addressees, interpreters and spokesmen, and the like; (2) the various available *channels*, and their modes of use, speaking, writing, printing, drumming, blowing whistles, singing, face and body motion as visually perceived, smelling, tasting, and tactile sensation; (3) the various *codes* shared by various participants, linguistic, paralinguistic, kinesic, musical, interpretive, interaction; and other; (4) the *settings* (including other communication) in which communication is permitted, enjoined, encouraged, abridged; (5) the *forms of messages,* and their *genres* ranging verbally from single-morpheme sentences to the patterns and diacritics of sonnets, sermons, salesmen's pitches, and any other organized routines and styles; (6) *the attitudes and contents* that a message may convey and be about; (7) the *events* themselves, their characters as wholes—all these must be identified in an adequate way."

This and similar frames of reference have been used to analyze ceremonies, sermons, verbal dueling, conversations, code switching, etc. in various societies. Bauman and Sherzer (1974) point out that the available scholarly literature considers, for the most part, the ways that languages and their uses are the same, rather than recognizing that there are differences in the purposes to which speech is put and the way it is organized for these purposes. Speech communities are inherently heterogeneous. There are different speech varieties available to its members, norms for speaking which vary from one segment of the community to another. Definition of speech community is fairly easy when one is dealing with the kinds of units which anthropologists study, such as villages, tribes, small preindustrial towns, etc., but the ethnographers of communication have been somewhat evasive concerning the identification of speech community in the large, modern, complex, industrialized societies.

As pointed out elsewhere, a speech community is an aggregate of people sharing at least one linguistic variety, as well as a body of sociolinguistic rules concerning the use of the varieties in their repertoire. People can share sociolinguistic, that is, speaking, rules without necessarily sharing a particular linguistic variety. When speaking rules are being shared among contiguous languages, we may speak of this as a *speech area.* For example, Czechoslovakia, Hungary, Austria, and southern Germany form such a speech area since they share norms as to greetings, acceptable topics, and what is said next in conversation, even though most speakers do not know the other langauges (Hymes 1972d:54–55).

5.4 Discourse analysis

Inasmuch as grammar deals with the system by which sound is related to meaning, grammarians have, for the most part, confined their analysis to single sentences. Yet, it is obvious that the meaning of many sentences is not clear without considering the sentences which precede or follow in the same conversation. For example, linguists studying reported speech (Zwicky 1971) generally confine their discussion to individual sentences and reports of sentences. But to do so is to ignore the nature of discourse. For example, as Sherzer (1973:273) has indicated, "If John asks Harry *Are you going to the movies?*, and Harry replies, *Yes*, then John can later report to Mary that *Harry said that he was going to the movies* in spite of the fact that all Harry said was *yes*. Any adequate account of reported speech must describe this and other aspects of the discourse properties of reporting."

It follows that if analysis of language is to be realistic, one must observe actual speech and not merely concoct sentences out of one's own intuitional resources. The social context, as well as the linguistic context, of each sentence must be considered. In discourse analysis, the first step is to distinguish what is said from what is done. We attempt to relate sentence types, such as statements, questions, and imperatives, by means of discourse rules to the set of actions done with words. There is no simple one-to-one relationship because, for example, requests for information can be made with statements, or they can be made by means of questions or imperatives. Some other types of actions are very complex in the relationship of words to actions—for example, refusals, challenges, retreats, insults, promises, or threats. The discourse analyst tries to show that one sentence follows another in a coherent manner.

Discourse rules include rules of interpretation (with their inverse rules of production) and sequencing rules, which connect actions. Other elements of discourse are based on shared and unshared knowledge and notions of role, rights, duties, and obligations associated with social rules (for example, cf. discussion on directives in section 5.6, also the collections edited by Freedle 1977 and 1979).

Lakoff (1972:907) notes that in order to be able to predict how rules are going to apply, one has to be able to identify the assumptions about the social context of an utterance, as well as any other implicit assumptions made by speakers. She observes that the following sentences are in descending order of politeness, although under other more ordinary circumstances, *must* imposes an obligation, *should* merely gives advice that may be disregarded, and *may* allows someone to do something he already wanted to do. The fact that the sentences are spoken by a hostess at a party is reflected in the inverse order to politeness expressed by choice of modals:

(1) You must have some of this cake.
(2) You should have some of this cake.
(3) You may have some of this cake.

Such distinctions are sometimes made in other languages by different honorifics, as in Japanese.

Although silence is the absence of speech, it often can communicate some-thing. For example, as Key (1975b:116–117) notes, "It can convey respect, as in the presence of a great person or an elder or at a funeral or coronation; comfort, to a distressed loved one who wants to be quiet; companionship, when watching a sunset; support, when a toddler is learning to tie a shoe; rejection, when a black employee wants to join the office chatter; reprimand, as to a child, or a peer, when words would be too embarrassing; consent as an answer to a challenging state-ment; and no consent, as an unspoken answer."

In some American Indian groups, an acceptable social visit may consist of going to a friend's house, sitting silently for half an hour, and then leaving without saying anything. In such a cultural setting, speech is not necessary if a person has nothing to say. A teacher may discover that a particular boy cannot and will not speak to a girl in the class because they bear a certain kinship relation to each other in the Navaho community (Hymes 1961:60–61).

Work impinging upon discourse analysis has been carried out primarily by the generative semanticists on the one hand, and on the other by sociologists doing fine-grained analysis of conversation. The generative semanticists, focusing on the analysis of the sentence, recognize aspects of discourse but force them into the structure of sentences, as if discourse had no structure of its own. On the other hand, those studying language from the perspective of the ethnography of communication and social interactionism have been developing rigorous ways of analyzing discourse in terms of the dimensions of speech usage and the nature of discourse rules. They have studied how, in coherent discourse, utterances follow each other in a rational, rule-governed manner, as well as the selection of speakers and the identification of persons.

One particularly active field of research the past few years has been the analysis of children's discourse (see, for example, Ervin-Tripp and Mitchell-Kernan, eds. 1977). A number of scholars have been analyzing children's turn-taking, sequencing, etc. They are beginning to realize the wide range of interactional strategies which children use, which reveal their assumptions about the nature of the participants and the most appropriate and effective way to use language in interactions with them (Boggs and Lein 1978). Studies have focused on both child-child and child-adult conversations. It appears that the child learns conversational strategies at the same time that he is learning grammar. In any case, it appears on close examination that children are very skilled interactants indeed.

5.5 Speech events

One cannot study speech in totality or in abstraction only; one must focus on some clearly definable and delimited segments for analysis if such analysis is ever to be validated, and replicated, if necessary. One such unit of analysis which has been proposed is the speech event. This unit has a beginning and an end, follows a socially recognized patterned sequence, and is generally an entity recognized as such by the people, with a socially accepted designation, for example, a con-versation, joke, sermon, interview, prayer, or political speech. Some societies or communities have their own rather unique speech events, and many of these have been studied by the ethnographers of communication. For example, in the United States the activities known as *jiving, shucking, playing the dozens,* etc. in the black community have been among the most frequently studied (see section 9.2).

The investigator studying speech events in a particular community cannot just simply make a detailed list of them and describe each. He must determine the categories which are meaningful to the members of the speech community and the functions they fulfill for them.

Special rules of speaking mark off certain speech events from everyday verbal behavior. These rules involve not only choice of word and topics but also such factors as selection of syntactic and phonological alternates, intonation, speech rhythm, and discourse structure, as well as role and setting constraints. They are often bounded by certain opening and closing routines. For example, if we hear "Dearly beloved, we are gathered here today . . ." we know a wedding is about to be performed, or if we hear "Did you hear the one about the . . . ," we anticipate that a joke is about to be told. Every child knows that "Once upon a time" announces a fairy tale and that "They lived happily ever after" closes it.

In some types of speech events, co-occurrence restrictions apply much more rigidly than they do in others. For example, public ceremonies or religious rituals prescribe modes of speaking in very narrow terms, whereas in intimate conversation a wide range of alternate sequences is ordinarily permissible. All types of discourse, however, show some form of co-occurrence restrictions. One would be surprised to hear a sentence like *I ain't never gonna analyze no empirical data no more* unless someone were trying to be funny. In this case, the humor derives from the fact that we expect "ain't" to co-occur with informal speech forms and "empirical data" in more formal discourse. Co-occurrence rules in multilingual repertoires tend to be more rigid than in monolingual ones (Gumperz 1971:157).

A major topic concerns the way in which people interpret, that is, make sense out of what is going on in a conversation. There is a particular relationship between what is being said and what is being done, as well as, of course, the social and linguistic context of the conversation. Speakers make assumptions concerning what is going on in the conversation, who says what, what has been said before, and by whom, and whether people are lying, joking, telling the truth, etc. If someone says to us *Drop dead!,* the first interpretative task is to figure out whether the statement is to be taken literally or not, seriously or not, by evaluating the circumstances. For example, if one were a seriously ill, cardiac patient, it wouldn't be very funny.

The analyst needs to look at such things as how conversations are begun and ended, as well as the factors determining a person's right to speak at a specific point in the conversation. He looks at the linguistic means used by speakers to make excuses, convince, cajole, mock, flatter, and so on. There are understandings of how topics may be introduced, avoided, or changed. Lulls and silences have their particular significances.

*Throughout this book an asterisk indicates an unacceptable sentence.

A conversation begins with an initial utterance by one of the speakers. The latter has a wide choice of expressions to use for this opening utterance which will serve not only to initiate the conversation but also to convey some of his assumptions about this speech and social community and his place in it, as well as the way in which he has conceptualized the social nature of the relationship with the other speaker and the situation in which the conversation takes place. Farb (1974:108–109) claims that all conversations are opened in one of six ways:

1. A request for information, services, or goods
2. A request for a social response
3. An offer of information
4. An emotional expression of anger, pain, joy, which is often a strategy to solicit a comment by a listener
5. Stereotyped statements, such as greetings, apologies, and thanks
6. A substitute statement to avoid a conversation about a subject the speaker anticipates the listener will broach

Two utterances are required for either opening or closing a conversation. The second utterance signifies agreement with what the speaker of the first utterance is trying to do, that is, open or close. For example, in American English, "O.K.," "I gotta go," and "well" frequently signal the desire to end a conversation and may be considered "pre-closings."

It seems patent that all conversation has two basic features, namely, in a given conversation, no more than one person speaks at a time, and in the course of the conversation, the speakers take turns speaking. We may postulate a turn-taking machinery to explain the co-occurrence of these features. This machinery orders speaker turns sequentially in conversation. For example, there are procedures for organizing selection of the next speaker and for determining when and under what conditions transition to a next speaker may or should occur. These procedures operate utterance by utterance rather than being predetermined completely in advance by extraconversational factors. Schegloff (1972b:35) claims that the validity of the rule that one party speaks at a time is proven by the fact that, where there are four or more persons and more than one person is talking, we can say not that the rule has been violated, but rather that there is more than one conversation going on. But before a conversation is started, there must be a way of determining who is going to speak first. In telephone conversations, for example, the person who answers the telephone speaks first, saying something like "Hello" or "Grubb Construction Co.," whereupon the caller says something like "This is Joe Gomez. May I speak to Mr. Ma, please." The answerer then says, "This is he," or "I'll get him." Only if someone violates the rules of telephone conversation by discourtesy or by saying something "strange" do we realize that such conversations are patterned, following quite definite rules.

In the midst of rewriting this section of the book, my home telephone rang, I picked up the receiver, and the following exchange ensued ("A"=answer, "C"=caller):

A: Hello?
C: Hi!
A: Hello!! (somewhat more emphatically)
C: (hangs up)

The caller had obviously reached a wrong number. Once she had ascertained this fact, she terminated the call without enquiry, explanation, or apology. This appears to be not at all unusual in telephone conversations in the United States. There are cultural differences in this regard. Thus, in France, for example, the sequence for the caller at the beginning of a telephone conversation is as follows (Godard 1977):

(1) Check number
(2) Name oneself at the first opportunity
(3) Excuse oneself (optional in case of intimacy)

The French conceive of the telephone as an intrusion, for which apologies are required. In the first place, the caller verifies the number, so that misdialings are caught immediately. It is up to the caller to identify himself first. This is contrary to common practice in the United States. Godard, who is from France, once answered the phone, to the caller's surprise at encountering a nonnative speaker:

A: Hello?
C: Oh! Who are you?
A: Who are you?

It is true that, in the United States, children are often instructed to say something like the following when they call: "This is Johnny Jones. May I speak to Jerry, please?" or in answering the phone, to say something like "Cohen residence," but these norms, if indeed they are norms, appear to be rarely observed. It would appear that more generally speaking, the American caller considers the answerer more a conduit of communication than a person, whereas the reverse is the case in France. Cf. another call received by Godard in her home in Philadelphia:

A: Hello?
C: Is Jane at your house? Can I speak to her, please?

In France the sequence would be in such a case:

A: Allo?
C: Checks number.
A: Oui.
C: Identifies himself.
A: Greetings. Identifies himself.
C: After greetings and a few words, asks for intended audience.

Rather than regarding the call as an intrusion, in the United States people will ordinarily interrupt another conversation or any other (or almost any other) activity and answer the telephone. The ring of the telephone has a definite imperative quality. In the United States, a positive value appears to be attached to the act of telephoning itself, and the caller seems to have more rights than the answerer (Godard 1977).

Duncan (1972:283) has described three basic signals for the turn-taking mechanism in conversation, namely (1) turn-yielding signals by the speaker, such as intonation, drawl, body motion, pitch, loudness, completion of a sentence or the use of stereotyped expressions, such as "but uh," "or something," or "you know"; (2) attempt-suppressing signals by the speaker, such as movement of the speaker's hands; (3) back-channel signals by the hearer, such as "mm-hmm" or nods of the head, indicating that he will not take his turn at speaking. Speakers use and respond to these signals in a relatively structured manner.

It often happens that the turn-taking mechanism does not work perfectly, and one speaker interrupts another, or his speech overlaps with another's. Such overlaps and interruptions apparently do not occur in a random fashion but are influenced by interlocutors' roles. For example, in one study of eleven cross-sex and twenty same-sex segments of two-party conversations, West and Zimmerman (1974) showed that overlaps were distributed symmetrically in same-sex conversations, but, where the speakers were of opposite sex, males initiated all of the overlaps. There was no difference between the rate at which men interrupted men and women interrupted women, but in the cross-sex conversational segments, 96 percent of the interruptions were initiated by males. The same authors have demonstrated that parent-child interactions are very similar to male-female interchanges in the exercise of interpersonal power. Parents and males interrupt children and females far more than the converse. They conclude, "With respect to conversational interchanges, it is generally the case that the child's right to speak is problematic and that many of the proprieties and courtesies routinely accorded by adults of equal status are usually ignored in the case of children." This and similar studies certainly weaken the popular stereotype of women as talking more. Conversational analysis is obviously a source of sociological data on power relationships. For example, instances have been noted, particularly in the non-Western world, where a tribal chief or other dignitary will speak through an interpreter to an addressee from another ethnic group, but who understands and speaks the language perfectly well. This practice helps to maintain social distance by preventing direct conversation between the two individuals in question. A similar phenomenon in some modern societies is the custom, still utilized by some women, of not addressing a waiter or waitress in a restaurant directly but, rather, speaking through her escort.

One important theme running through the work of some analysts is the use, by speakers and hearers, of knowledge of the social world in encoding and decoding speech. One interesting and significant problem is formulating place, that is, the means chosen to indicate the physical location by the speaker of some person or object he is mentioning. Some choice must be made, as there are a number of different ways to indicate the "same" place. In a given conversation, however, not all possible formulations would be considered equally correct. Account must be taken of the location of the object, as well as of those taking part in the conversation (Schegloff 1972a). Thus, for example, if someone should ask me where my Xerox copy of Schegloff's article is, I could say, right there, in the third drawer, in the file cabinet, upstairs, in my study, in my files, at home, in California, or back in the States.

In analyzing questions and answers in the context of a conversation, Sacks has identified a rule to the effect that the speaker asking the question has the right to speak if he receives an answer and has a right to ask another question, thus providing for another answer and a further question, and so on. Court transcripts are clear examples of such a cycle. Telephone calls are structured in such a way that the person who calls selects the first topic for discussion. In face-to-face social contacts, the speaker uttering the first greeting has the right to talk again when such a greeting is returned and has the right to select the topic (Turner 1970:209–210). In many cases, however, only a simple exchange of greetings may take place.

Schegloff and Sacks (1973:235) reject the notion that their findings relate to some general features of conversational rules in American English, for they do not believe that an ethnic or national language is a relevant putative boundary for their materials and findings. Their approach is to look for standardized invariant rules of discourse, for example, in the sequencing of conversations. To the extent that these rules are culture-specific, however, different rules imply different subcultures and vice versa. The consequences for social interaction in such a case can be significant. As Labov (1971a:64–65) points out, speakers of a given dialect may be able to interpret the grammatical rules of another dialect but may not be able satisfactorily to interpret rules of discourse relating to the interpretation of the social significance of actions, such as in the ways of indicating politeness, anger, sincerity, or trust. We interpret sentences rapidly and unreflectingly in terms of social relationships that are not overtly expressed. We are able to do this because of our knowledge of the social system and our familiarity with our interlocutor's social categories and the cultural associations they carry for him. When we are unaware of these social categories and cultural associations, we may very well misunderstand what is being said.

One of the most extensively studied microsociolinguistic phenomena is that of code switching, in which a person in the middle of a conversation, or even in the middle of a sentence, changes from one language, dialect, or style to another. Such switching may take place because the speaker may be able more easily to convey his meaning in the other language, dialect, or style, or the switch itself may convey social meaning.

In order to analyze code switching, we must take into account not only what is said, but the social situation in which the conversation takes place, particularly the role relationships and group memberships of the interlocutors, as well as their attitudes toward the various languages, dialects, and styles, and the speakers who habitually use them. Speakers know when to shift from one variety to another. A shift in situation may necessitate a shift in language variety, and conversely, code shifting may indicate a change in the nature of the immediate social relationship of the interlocutors, as well as a change of topic or motivation for speech.

These are all cases of *situational switching*. On the other hand, there is *metaphorical switching* where there has been no change in situation or topic, but where a person may switch to another language or style to convey humor, warmth, irony, ethnic solidarity, etc.

Scotton and Ury (1977) suggest that a speaker code switches either to redefine the interaction as appropriate to a different social arena or to avoid, by means of repeated code switching, defining the interaction in terms of any specific social arena. Each social arena (e.g. identity arena, power arena, transactional arena) has its own norms concerning the type of behavior expected. It is a strategy by which the skillful speaker uses his knowledge of how language choices are interpreted in his community to structure the interaction so as to maximize outcomes favorable to himself. Thus, in Kenya, for example, a speaker might switch from the local language to Swahili to indicate his perception of the interaction as a transactional, e.g. commercial one, or switch to English as symbolic of power, especially if his interlocutor is weak in English.

Metaphorical switching is possible only because there are previously agreed-upon norms governing the use of certain varieties or styles in particular situations. It is in violation of the norm that the switching has its impact. On the other hand, situational switching is called for by the norms—as the situation changes, so does the variety or style which is required. The norms allocate a particular variety or style to particular kinds of topics, places, persons, and purposes. For example, many speakers in the United States shift back and forth between pronunciations like *doing* and *doin'*, depending on the status relationship between speaker and hearer, and the topic and setting of the conversation. Such shifting is sometimes beyond the conscious awareness of both speakers and listeners.

In several studies of Chicano code switching, whenever Chicano identity was an underlying theme, Spanish was used by the speaker (for examples of Chicano code switching, see section 9.3). In another study, in a small Norwegian village, Blom and Gumperz (1972) showed that, of the two varieties of Norwegian spoken in the village, the local one was used in issues related to community identification, while the national standard was used in topics more national in scope. It was pointed out that code switching did not occur in friendly gatherings of people who composed a network of local relationships, regardless of topic. In a situation with both local and nonlocal relationships, however, code switching would be based on topical variation. Speakers conveyed social information by switching from the local dialect to the standard langauge.

5.6 Speech acts

Much smaller units of analysis than the speech event are the speech acts out of which the speech events are composed, that is, such entities as statements, commands, questions, promises, threats, etc. Speech acts have been studied from different perspectives by both philosophers and linguists, and the sociological relevance of their work is becoming increasingly apparent. Most utterances investigated by students of speech acts can be classified as both "serious" and "literal," as those terms are used by Searle (1969). He contrasts "serious" with play acting, teaching a language, reciting a poem, practicing pronunciation, etc., and he contrasts "literal" with metaphorical, sarcastic, etc.

It is clear that a large percentage of speech acts in ordinary conversation are not serious in nature, for example, the widespread "kidding" which takes place in face-to-face groups or the culturally stylized "sounding" in the black vernacular culture. Obviously, knowledge of the social situation and of the rules of discourse is imperative for deciding (on the part of either speakers or analyst) whether a given utterance is to be taken seriously and/or literally. Thus, not only linguistic competence but also communicative and social competence is involved.

Whereas the ethnographers of communication (Ervin-Tripp, Gumperz, Hymes, etc.) analyze speech acts as units of linguistic structure, generative semanticists, such as Ross, Lakoff, and McCawley, support an approach known as the performative analysis. The latter assumes that the structure of speech acts, such as declaring, questioning and commanding, are coded in the form of abstract underlying sentences which contain a verb like *assert, say,* etc., as well as the pronouns *you* and *I.* For example, all declarative sentences would have as part of their abstract underlying structure something like "I assert to you that. . . ." Thus, in a sentence like "Frankly, this just won't do," *frankly* modifies the deleted underlying performative verb (Sherzer 1973:271).

In speaking, a person is characteristically performing at least three different kinds of speech acts, which Searle (1969:23–24) calls *utterance acts* (uttering words, morphemes, sentences, etc.), *propositional acts* (referring and predicating), and *illocutionary acts* (stating, questioning, commanding, promising, etc.). Although one can perform an utterance act without performing a propositional or illocutionary act, one cannot normally perform an illocutionary act without performing propositional and utterance acts. The same propositional acts can be common to different illocutionary acts, and conversely the same illocutionary act may involve different propositional acts.

Searle (1972:137) argues that illocutionary acts, such as asking questions or making statements, are rule-governed and that therefore it is possible to state a set of necessary and sufficient conditions for the performance of that particular type of illocutionary act. Then, it should be possible to derive the set of semantic rules which marks that particular type of illocutionary act. One often states directly what one is doing by saying, for example, *I promise you that . . .* or *I hereby appoint you. . . .* The sentence is said to be felicitous if the illocutionary act succeeds. A bet, for example, cannot succeed unless both parties agree. Likewise, if a command is to be heard as a valid command, then, where A is the speaker and B the hearer, B must believe that A believes that:

1. X needs to be done
2. B has the ability to do X
3. B has an obligation to do X
4. A has the right to tell B to do X (Wootton 1975)

The social distribution of rights and privileges becomes an explicit and formal part of the knowledge required to identify valid commands. Interlocutors' knowledge about the rights and obligations of various participants in speech settings is of crucial importance, although such knowledge is for them only part of that involved in making and evaluating speech acts. Sociologists ought to be able to make some strong contributions to this point in the light of their long-standing interest in social norms and the distribution of social statuses. Norms and their applicability on particular occasions, however, are to some extent indeterminate and negotiable.

A *performative sentence* is specifically an utterance which itself describes the speech act which it performs. It is syntactically marked by having a first person subject (I or we), with the verb in the simple present tense (*ask, bequeath, declare*). The only possible indirect object is *you*. The sentence cannot be negative, and it is possible to insert the adverb *hereby*. The following sentence manifests all these characteristics.

I hereby promise you my loyalty.

The following sentences demonstrate the fact that not all verbs referring to speech events can function as performative verbs:

*I hereby remark that the room is dingy.
*I hereby persuade you to vote for Schlupp.
*I hereby denigrate your profession.

For every nonperformative sentence, it is possible to find one or more performative equivalents. Thus, a sentence like *I order you to go!* is explicitly performative, while *Go!* is implicitly performative.

The illocutionary force of an utterance is not ordinarily marked by a performative formula. There are a number of more subtle means of indicating what the speaker is trying to accomplish by speaking, such as word order, intonation, special morphemes, or deletion, depending on the language. Normally, simple sentences have one and only one illocutionary force (Saddock 1975:10–11).

Austin (1962:13) has noted that performatives have a different legal standing than other types of utterances. According to the law of evidence, a report of what someone said is not ordinarily admitted as evidence, that is, it is regarded as hearsay unless what the person said was performative in nature, for example, a promise. The reason for this is that the report is regarded not so much as a report of something that was said but rather a report of something that was done—an action.

A number of different types of performative acts have been studied in detail, for example, *directives*, which Ervin-Tripp (1976:29) has shown can be expressed in a variety of syntactic forms. They occur systematically according to familiarity, rank, territorial location, difficulty of task, whether or not a duty is normally expected, and whether or not noncompliance is likely. She has identified six types of directives, ordered approximately according to the relative power of speaker and addressee.

Need statements	I need a match.
Imperatives	Gimme a match.
Imbedded imperatives	Could you give me a match.
Permission directives	May I have a match.
Question directives	Gotta match?
Hints	The matches are all gone.

Need statements and imperatives are ordinarily used with subordinates or familiar equals, while at the other extreme, question directives and hints are used when there is a possibility of noncompliance. Imbedded imperatives and per-mission directives are used with unfamiliar interlocutors or possibly in speaking with superiors.

When we consider the consequences or effects which illocutionary acts have on the actions or thoughts of the hearers, we may speak of *perlocutionary acts.* As Searle notes, "For example, by arguing I may *persuade* or *convince* someone, by warning him I may *scare* or *alarm* him, by making a request I may *get him to do something*, by informing him I may *convince him* (*enlighten, edify, inspire him, get him to realize*). The italicized expressions above denote perlocutionary acts" (Searle 1969:25). Perlocutionary effects may be intentional or unintentional, suggesting a connection with the concept of manifest and latent functions.

Discussion questions

1. What are the most important purposes people accomplish with language? In this connection, how does form relate to function?
2. What is a *domain*? What are the principal domains in which you as an individual use language? How do these relate to your various social roles?
3. What are some of the topics dealt with in the analysis of discourse?
4. Observe some conversations during the next day or so and check how many started in each of the ways described by Farb.
5. Does the discussion of telephone conversations in this country agree with your experience? What do you say, and what do people at the other end say ordinarily at the beginning of such conversations?
6. Observe some conversations involving sex, age and status differences among speakers, and summarize what you observed with regard to the frequency of interruption of one speaker by another.
7. What is code switching? Discuss your observations of others' code switching and your estimate of why they are doing it.
8. State the necessary and sufficient conditions for the performance of some illocutionary act like a threat, order, declaration, question, etc.

6

Language varieties and their significance

Large-scale societies are heterogeneous both socioculturally and linguistically. On the one hand, there are different social classes, ethnic groups, religious denominations, occupations, etc.; on the other hand, different languages, dialects, and styles are used. The relationship between these two types of heterogeneity is one of the central concerns of the sociology of language.

Grammar books purport to describe the normal and general usage of a particular language, but frequently what they are describing is a specialized variety, and they fail to mention different styles of usage in the language. As Crystal (1971:61) indicates, "What we normally refer to as '*the* English (or French) language' is in reality not a single, homogeneous entity, about which we can speak absolutely; it is rather a conglomeration of regional and social dialects, personal and group styles, all of which are different from each other in various degrees."

Opinions vary as to whether ethnographical description must precede the description of language varieties within a society or vice versa. Some analysts group speakers solely on the basis of linguistic differences and then describe some of the social characteristics of the linguistically defined groups. Other analysts base their description of linguistic differences on the basis of previously determined socioeconomic groups. While the division of groups on a linguistic basis is a more reliable indication of sociolinguistic differences than the use of some objective socioeconomic index, when we describe linguistic differences in terms of predetermined groups, we are able to take advantage of what we already know from the objective indices of social class, for example. The most desirable course of action would be to attempt to take full advantage of the insights to be derived from both perspectives (Wolfram and Fasold 1974:16).

It must not be assumed that there is necessarily a one-to-one correspondence between group membership and speech variety. People may be multilingual or multidialectal, or speak "better" or "worse" than the majority of the social group to which they belong. A person may even pattern his speech after that of a group to which he does not even belong, that is a reference group.

81

Sociolinguists seek to establish relationships between the use of particular language varieties and other social phenomena. They also wish to look at a particular community or society as a unit and examine how its structure is related to the language varieties utilized by its members. Thus, for example, one is interested in the number of speakers of each language variety and in their characteristics. Data are often collected in this regard in censuses and surveys of populations.

Language questions involved in censuses include questions about mother tongue, languages used in the home, and all languages spoken. Definitions and criteria have varied widely among countries, and even in the same country, from one census to the next. For example, Spanish-speaking people in the United States have been variously recorded as being of "Spanish origin," having a "Spanish mother tongue," or as "living in a household where at least one person speaks Spanish." Thus, it is difficult to ascertain the linguistic composition of the population or to study changes over time with reference to language maintenance or shift (Lieberson 1966).

We can describe human communities in terms of their linguistic repertoires. Each repertoire is conceived of as consisting of a series of functionally related codes, such as genetically distinct languages, dialects, and superposed varieties of the same languages or different styles, depending on the community's history. Many scholars now use the term *variety* as a nonjudgmental and nonemotional technical term in order to avoid using such judgmental and emotion-laden concepts such as language, dialect, standard, etc. We need precisely such a term because what is or is not a language and how it is to be classified may represent major emotional, political and ideological issues.

Ferguson (1971:30) defines *variety* as follows: "Any body of human speech patterns which is sufficiently homogeneous to be analyzed by available techniques of synchronic description and which has a sufficiently large repertory of elements and their arrangements or processes with broad enough semantic scope to function in all normal contexts of communication." A language would then consist of one or more varieties which might share a single superposed variety, such as a literary standard language. All these would have substantial similarity in phonology, grammar, and lexicon and would normally be either mutually intelligible or else be connected by a series of mutually intelligible varieties.

A regional variety is a variety thought to be characteristic of some particular geographical region. Such a variety is, of course, never completely homogeneous, being characterized by considerable internal variability (as are all language varieties) and differentiated from other similar regional varieties more in quantitative than qualitative terms. If, as a result of migration, persons speaking a particular regional variety come to be concentrated in another geographical area but are separate socially from other speakers by endogamy and maintenance of their own subculture, we may consider their speech now some sort of social variety. For example, southern whites and blacks have brought their speech patterns to northern United States cities. Some, particularly among the poor, will then be recognized as speakers of "Hillbilly English" or "Black English," social rather than regional varieties.

If the speakers of a social variety maintain (or are forced to maintain) the boundaries of their group so as virtually to regard themselves as a separate society of people, their speech may come to be regarded as an ethnic or religious variety, or even as a separate language, depending on the degree of social and linguistic separation between these speakers and other groups in the same society. In any case, their own variety will be used for intragroup communication and a different variety for intergroup communication.

An important question relates to accounting for the origin and persistence of a multitude of language varieties in human communities. Each language variety can be considered as fulfilling some particular function or functions in the community. If a function is no longer needed, the language variety which fulfills that function may become obsolete; or, if a language variety dies out, its functions may be shifted to another variety. Cause-and-effect relationships, however, are difficult to establish in such cases. Fishman (1972c:51) indicates that a speech community ordinarily maintains a functional differentiation of the linguistic varieties in its repertoire. Different varieties will be used for different purposes and in different settings. It is difficult to maintain two or more varieties with the same function. In such a case, one variety must either displace the other or a new functional differentiation be developed.

All varieties of all languages are equal in the sense that all may expand or contract as functions change, and all can be influenced and penetrated by the influence of other varieties. The extent to which these events occur is determined by the norms of the speech community and the extent to which its speakers observe these norms. These norms can change as the community changes in self-concept or objective circumstances or in its relations with other communities.

Language varieties survive because of their functional differentiation, and their status derives largely from the functions they serve. Such varieties have certain symbolic values, frequently by social consensus because they represent certain ethnic or class antecedents or certain interests in the society.

As contrasted with modern societies, traditional societies show extreme internal linguistic diversity. In such societies, it sometimes happens that political administration, religious affairs, literary activity, and ordinary conversation are carried on in different languages. A classical or foreign language may be used in governmental and religious institutions, with the local populations generally speaking a variety of unwritten languages, e.g. Latin and local vernaculars in medieval Europe. The low rate of literacy tends to favor concentration of power in a small elite. Internal linguistic diversity comes to symbolize the extremes of social and political stratification. As societies modernize, there is a reduction of the gap between the literary and administrative languages, on the one hand, and the popular varieties, on the other. Language standardization tends to correlate with increasing literacy as standard languages become more accessible to all.

Nida (1975:143) distinguishes three types of languages: (1) *international,* for example, English, French, or Spanish, which is used in countries of various nationalities and accepted as vehicles of communication in international affairs; (2) *national* languages, e.g. Polish, Dutch, and Greek, which are used as vehicles of communication within a given country; and (3) *ethnic or regional* languages (or dialects), e.g. Welsh, Kikongo, Zulu, and Cree, which serve as vehicles of communication for more restricted groups within a given country. Some societies use only one language, some two or three, or more. In a society with a typical three-language structure, a world language is used for the communication of specialized information but some national language for elementary education and local government administration, the in-group language being utilized on a much more circumscribed basis. For example, in Kenya, the three languages are English, Swahili, and a local language.

Two-language structures are common throughout the world, as, for example, in many Latin American countries where Spanish and an indigenous language or languages are used. On the other hand, native speakers of one of the world languages typically live in a one-language situation. The United States, France or Germany, for example, are basically one-language societies, although they have large linguistic minorities.

Linguistic diversity and variation serve to communicate social information about the speaker, as well as to provide specialized codes for communication within groups of technical or other specialists. If the variation is one of style rather than of language or dialect, social mobility is encouraged, and the society is more open. Standardized languages in modern nations help to foster this kind of openness. On the other hand, oppression of the poor or of minorities may help maintain a high degree of linguistic diversity, and groups will regard their own variety as a mark of social identity.

Groups share linguistic characteristics because their members communicate with each other more than with nonmembers. This is true of ethnic and national groups, social classes, and geographical groups. Slang, professional jargon, and criminal argot all serve as boundary-maintenance mechanisms, as do all secret or semisecret languages—in fact, all language varieties. As Leach has noted, ". . . for a man to speak one language rather than another is a ritual act; it is a statement about one's personal status; to speak the same language as one's neighbors expresses solidarity with these neighbors; to speak a different language from one's neighbors expresses social distance or even hostility" (Leach 1954:49, quoted by Sibayan 1974:221–222).

A language imposed from above over a number of regional or social varieties is known as a superposed variety of a language. Some varieties like vernaculars are acquired by interaction in face-to-face groups, while the superposed variety is acquired by symbolic integration into some more abstract entity like nation, region, or social class, usually by formal education. The first type of variety is preserved by communication gaps between the speakers of different varieties. The second type is acquired and maintained even without face-to-face interaction. Thus, one might acquire, for example, a colloquial dialect at home and a standard language at school. In modern, open societies, e.g. the United States or West Germany, the speech community is more likely to utilize several varieties of the same language, but in more traditional, closed societies, e.g. Peru or Afghanistan, the speech community is likely to use varieties of several different languages. The more roles are compartmentalized and made difficult of access through personal achievement, the more linguistic compartmentalization we are likely to find as well (Fishman 1972b:27).

The matter of determining to which language a particular variety belongs is largely determined on sociocultural and political, rather than on primarily linguistic, grounds. Thus, regional dialects form a continuum such that, for example, Germanic dialects merge imperceptibly into each other, as do also the Slavic dialects. But because a political boundary intervenes, the people on one side of the border consider that they are speaking a dialect of German, for example, and on the other side a dialect of Dutch, despite the fact that they may be closer to each other—in fact, mutually more intelligible with each other—than each is with its own standard language. Yet, the latter serves as a reference point and is likely to influence the dialect in its own direction.

In dealing with language varieties, how do we define "different" or "same"? How do we know whether we are dealing with one variety or several? Are A and B varieties of the same language, or are they different languages? For example, is what we call "Chinese" a single language split into a number of different dialects, or does it "really" consist of a number of different languages? Which criteria are the most relevant in this connection—the narrowly linguistic ones or the more broadly considered, sociocultural ones? To what extent do political and ideological considerations and different cultural perspectives influence the answer to this question? Chinese linguists and their colleagues in the other communist countries argue that to say there are several languages is, in effect, to say that there are several nations; and since China is clearly a single nation, Chinese must be considered a single language, despite the great differences among the largely nonmutually intelligible dialects. The grammar is fundamentally the same, and the phonology has correspondence rules. Furthermore, although there is no unified spoken language, the Chinese have had a unified written language for thousands of years (De Francis 1972:462–463). On the other hand, it is equally obvious that Swedish, Danish and Norwegian, although largely mutually intelligible, are separate languages, rather than varieties of a single "Scandinavian" language.

William A. Stewart has devised a scheme for classifying language types on the basis of the presence or absence of four attributes:

1. *Standardization*—acceptance of a formal set of codified norms
2. *Autonomy*—uniqueness and independence of the language
3. *Historicity*—normal development over time in association with some national or ethnic tradition
4. *Vitality*—use of the language by an unisolated community of native speakers (Stewart 1968:534–537).

Type	Standardization	Autonomy	Historicity	Vitality
		Attributes		
1. Standard	+	+	+	+
2. Classical	+	+	+	−
3. Artificial	+	+	−	−
4. Vernacular	−	+	+	+
5. Dialect	−	−	+	+
6. Creole	−	−	−	+
7. Pidgin	−	−	−	−

As examples of each of the seven types, we could cite the following:

1. Standard: Standard English, standard French, German
2. Classical: Latin, Ancient Greek, Sanskrit
3. Artificial: Esperanto, Interlingua, Novial
4. Vernacular: Colloquial American English, colloquial Mexican Spanish
5. Dialect: Sicilian, Plattdeutsch, Canadian French
6. Creole: Gullah, Haitian Creole, Chavacano
7. Pidgin: Pidgin English, Chinook Jargon, Sabir

Fishman (1972b:21) has pointed out that the four criteria used in Stewart's classification (standardization, autonomy, historicity and vitality) are not objective characteristics but rather highly evaluational characteristics; and as these evaluations change, so does the perceived type. Again, the sociologist of language does not so much classify varieties as he reports classifications of varieties which societies or subgroups have made. Thus, in the United States, for example, the typical native English speaker will learn a vernacular (that is, the ordinary spoken language of the home) and the more formal standard language at school. He might also learn a classical language at school, such as ancient Hebrew or Latin. He may also speak a dialect: regional (e.g. New York City), social class (e.g. lower class), or ethnic (e.g. Black English or Chicano English). In these cases it would be difficult to state how dialect differed from vernacular. Both are home-learned and home-used colloquial spoken languages. Few Americans are avid Esperantists, but Esperanto can be learned and used in classes and clubs throughout the country and is used as a medium of communication in international conferences. Unless an American has been to the Sea Islands of Georgia or to Jamaica, he is unlikely to have encountered a creole, although many Hawaiians speak a variety of English sometimes referred to as a pidgin, sometimes a creole.

Stewart's typology is not necessarily an exhaustive one. For example, a type not mentioned by Stewart is the *koine* which perhaps might be considered as a form of the vernacular, although a *koine* may also become standardized. A *koine* is a simplified form of a language characterized by the incorporation of features from several regional varieties of a single language, but which is never detached from the language it issues from. The most famous of the *koines* is the common Greek spoken about 300 years before the Christian era all over the eastern Mediterranean. In a *koine*, interdialect differences have been reduced (levelled). For example "*koine*-ized colloquial Arabic," attempts to level the wide differences among the Arabic dialects by suppressing localisms in favor of features which are more common and better known (Blanc 1960:82–85).

Bell (1976) adds three other language types to Stewart's scheme. One he calls *Xized Y*, that is, a language heavily influenced by another language but utilized for normal purposes in a particular community as either a first or second language, e.g. Indian English (the language spoken by many Indians and Anglo-Indians in India and heavily influenced by the languages of that country). Another type is *interlanguage*, the variety used by the foreign language learner who has incompletely learned the language—English, for example. The third type is *foreigner talk,* a simplified form of the language used to communicate with foreigners with a minimal, if any, knowledge of the language. Bell points out that we can illustrate all of the types with examples of English varieties. The remaining types with examples are as follows:

Standard: Standard English
Classical: King James Bible English
Vernacular: Black English (see section 9.2)
Dialect: Cockney
Creole: Krio (West Africa)
Pidgin: Neomelanesian (New Guinea)

(Concerning standard languages, see section 6.1; dialects 6.2; pidgins and creoles 6.4).

6.1 Standardization

The concept of standard language is one of the most universal and theoretically critical concepts of the field. There are questions of how standard languages arise historically and under what social circumstances they change or give way to other language varieties. We are particularly interested in the actual processes by which the language variety recognized as standard gains and maintains its standard character, that is, the processes of standardization.

The concept of standard language was first explicitly developed by linguists of the so-called Prague School, who characterized it as a codified form of language, accepted by and serving as a model for a larger speech community (Garvin 1969:237). A standard language thus conceived must be flexible enough in its codification to allow for modification in response to culture change. Another property of a standard language is "intellectualization," involving a systematization of the grammar and explicitness of statement in the lexicon, in the interest of more definitive and accurate expression. Thus, printed prescriptive grammars and dictionaries are made available and obligatory.

It has been suggested that a number of different functions are fulfilled by the standard language. One of these can be called the *unifying function,* for it unites individual speakers and groups within a larger community, and another the *separatist function,* which opposes the standard language to other languages or varieties as a separate entity, thus serving as a symbol of national, ethnic, or class integrity and identity. Another function is the *prestige function,* for a standard language confers a special prestige upon those who have mastered it; and finally, a *frame-of-reference* function, in that the codified norm provides a basis for evaluating "correctness" (Garvin and Mathiot 1978). Dittmar (1976:8), however, defines the standard language as "that speech variety of a language community which is legitimized as the obligatory norm for social intercourse on the strength of the interests of dominant forces in that society."

The standard-nonstandard dichotomy is in a number of respects parallel to the well-known folk-urban dichotomy or continuum. For one thing, folk speech as a variety of language has not been affected by language planning. Folk speech, nonstandard language, or the vernacular, however these are conceptualized, are certainly unplanned developments arising from the "natural" processes of language and society. Standard languages, on the other hand, arise out of a process of fairly self-conscious social and linguistic planning. In addition to the deliberate planning, we are compelled to observe the social forces at work. Among the latter, the process of urbanization stands out as particularly significant, and a standard language may be considered a major correlate of an urban culture. The degree of language standardization is often a measure of the urbanization of its speakers (Garvin and Mathiot 1968:365–366).

The concept of standard language is sometimes confused with two other similar concepts, namely *official* language and *national* language. An *official* language has been officially recognized by some governmental authority. A *national* language can refer either to a language serving an entire nation state or to a language functioning as a national symbol. Thus, for example, although there are many speakers of standard German in the United States, in no place does it serve as a national or official language. On the other hand, for millions of Spanish-speaking persons in the United States, Spanish constitutes a national language, as in some Chicano communities in the Southwest, Puerto Rican communities in the Northeast, and Cuban colonies in Florida. In some of these localities, it has reached official status as well. On the other hand, it is clear that, at the national level, English is the national language of the United States, even though this fact lacks a constitutional basis. Many other countries, however, state in their written constitutions what the official language or languages are to be.

It is also necessary not to confuse the notion of standard language with the notion of written language, although there is considerable overlap in meaning. While written and standard language are characterized in terms of linguistic variables, official language and national language are matters of political decision or ethnic reality. The standard and the written language require the active cooperation of the speech community; an official or national language requires only passive acceptance.

The first printed grammars and dictionaries of the modern European languages coincided with the rise of their countries to wealth and power in the fifteenth and sixteenth centuries. The first printed grammar of any modern language was Nebrija's *Gramática de la Lengua Castellana* of 1492. Part of the same movement was the first academy devoted to winnowing out the "impurities" of a language, the Accademia della Crusca, founded in 1582 to promote the Tuscan dialect of Florence as standard Italian. It was, in turn, the model for Cardinal Richelieu's Académie Française, founded in 1635 as part of his policy of political centralization. He asked its members "to labor with all the care and diligence possible to give exact rules to our language and to render it capable of treating the arts and sciences" (Robertson 1910:13). Similar academies were soon founded in Spain (1713), Sweden (1739), and Hungary (1830). Their chief products were dictionaries. The English, however, resisted the idea of an Academy and instead accepted the dictionary of a private citizen, Samuel Johnson (1755). The United States declared its own linguistic independence by following the dictates of another private citizen, Noah Webster, whose dictionary has been the model for all that followed. Although in all European countries the Ministries of Education exercise control over the spelling and grammar of their written languages, uniformity has been secured in the United States by voluntary means (Haugen 1966b:57–58).

What usually happens in the standardization process is that one particular variety of language becomes accepted throughout the area where it is spoken as the "best" form of the language, along with the increasing uniformity of the norm itself and its explicit codification. There are basically two steps in the process: first, a model is created for imitation, and second, this model is promoted over rival models. The question, then, is to ascertain how a particular model comes to be selected and developed as a candidate for standardization and, secondly, the means by which its promotion is carried out, as well as the social factors influencing successful or unsuccessful promotion.

Europe is the first area in which the standardization process took place or, at least, has been seen in the full light of history. It understandably first developed where we find the earliest highly urbanized societies. The cases of Latin, Arabic, and Chinese are not pertinent here, for these were classical, rather than standard, languages, and Greek at its most widespread is best regarded as a *koiné*. Looking at the historical record, there are a number of generalizations we can make about the emergence of standard languages in Europe. The basis for each was educated middle-class speech in an important urban center, e.g. London for English, and Paris for French, as it was displacing some earlier language as the normal written language, e.g. Norman French in the case of English, and Latin in the case of French. Sometimes a single author or small group of authors served as models for the written standard, e.g. Dante for Italian, or Martin Luther for German. In each case, the emerging standard served as a symbol of either religious or national identity. This is true of both the earlier standards, such as English, French, or German, as well as the newer standards emerging during the last two centuries, such as Magyar, Albanian, or Macedonian (Ferguson 1968a:32).

Standardization may emerge in stages, starting with the origin of regional standard languages. If a particular region then acquired political, economic, or cultural dominance over the other regions, it would acquire linguistic dominance as well, e.g. the ascendancy of Castile and, hence, of Castilian over the rest of Spain in the fifteenth century. This was followed by the social downgrading of the various regional standards now looked down upon as "mere dialects." In the next stage, the standard language developed a literature, with a resulting split between a more formal or literary variety, now taught in special institutions such as schools, and the less formal, everyday, colloquial variety. Finally, the literary language may become the exclusive norm, such that illiterates are effectively blocked from command also of the spoken standard, where one is recognized (Hall 1960:195–197).

These processes of linguistic modernization lasted from about the eleventh to the nineteenth century in Europe. Similar processes can be identified in the contemporary modernizing countries of the Third World. A feature common to both is the positive role played by developing nationalism (see section 10.1). In Europe, nationalism consciously promoted the standardization of the major vernacular languages. The new standard languages shattered the dominance of the classical and other older languages and, thus, also the linguistic unity of the European elite. On the other hand, this was a small price to pay for developing links of communication between the elite and the masses within each nation.

Although a standard language develops out of regional dialects, it is modified by speakers at places like the royal court and universities, by prominent writers, and by the public school system. The upper classes normally are those which adapt to these changes such that a gap develops between their speech and the rest of the population, and their speech becomes a model for the latter.

Although in most cases, the standard language is the language of a prestige group, in others a particular variety may become standardized by default, that is, a dialect *not* spoken by socially stigmatized groups may become the standard. Wolfram (1971:98) believes that this may be the most operative definition of Standard American English. Not all languages have standard varieties, although some languages have more than one standard (e.g. Norwegian or Serbo-Croatian), and a variety can become standardized or destandardized as attitudes and functional needs change.

It should be pointed out that the standard language has both special social status and special linguistic characteristics. In addition, special attitudes are usually reserved for the standard language. A characterization of standardization in terms of psychological reaction by a hearer has been provided by Wolfram and Fasold (1974:20–21): "If his reaction to the *form* (not the content) of the utterance is neutral and he can devote full attention to the meaning, then the form is standard for him. If his attention is diverted from the meaning of the utterance because it sounds 'snooty,' then the utterance is superstandard. If his attention is diverted from the message because the utterance sounds like poor English, then the form is substandard." Thus, for example, Fasold reacts emotionally to "Is it not?" as superstandard, "Isn't it?" as standard, and "Ain't it?" as substandard. The standard referred to in this connection is the informal, spoken standard of educated persons.

To ask such questions as "Where is English best spoken?", "In what part of France do they speak the most correct French?", or "Where is the purest German found?" is to imply a belief in the existence of some standard or superdialect, the superiority of which cannot be questioned. Sometimes we are told in matters of correctness in writing to follow the best authors. But the classic authors use obsolete language, and it is not clear how one goes about identifying the "best" contemporary authors. Furthermore, the decision is then simply transferred to something outside the purely linguistic domain.

In 1890, Jespersen proposed to define, as the best Danish, the speech of those by whose pronunciation one cannot tell what part of Denmark they come from (Jespersen 1925:46). In the United States, standard English is often referred to as *network English,* for the language used in network radio and television broadcasting cannot ordinarily be identified with any particular part of the country and, hence, escapes the possible stigma of a regional dialect. Ethnic accents are similarly scrupulously eschewed. The differences between standard and non-standard, on the one hand, and between "high" and "low" languages in a diglossic situation (see section 7.3), on the other hand, are parallel but not identical. In each case, the first mentioned is the most prestigious, is spoken by the most prestigious class, and supported by the most powerful institutions in the society.

Two kinds of criticisms have been levelled at the concept of standard language. One is that the concept is too narrowly defined, that a standard language should include a number of varieties all to be considered standard. For example, in the United States, this would mean that a number of regional and ethnic dialects would all be considered standard, such as Black English, Southern English, New England English, etc. Such a criticism emphasizes the point that the variety of English used on network television ought not be considered the only form of standard American English.

The second line of criticism is that the notion, or at least the term *standard* is normative and ought to be replaced by a more neutral, descriptive one. One possibility is replacing the standard-nonstandard distinction by a distinction between *academic* and *popular*. By *academic* would be meant that variety taught in and used as a medium of instruction in academic institutions from kindergarten (or even from Head Start or other preschool programs) through graduate school, and by *popular* the language spoken by the people, naturally and in an unself-conscious manner, when they are not being constrained by institutions or persons to observe some artificial norms. This variety is often referred to as "vernacular." Thus, every normal person in every society has command of at least one popular language variety, while command of the academic variety will ordinarily require special study and effort. Such a language variety will exist only in those societies which maintain the institutions necessary for the creation, propagation, and regulation of an academic language. The degree of closeness of relationship between academic and popular varieties will vary socioeconomically, regionally, and ethnically, as well as from one society to another. In some situations, the two will not be closely related at all. In the case of closely related varieties, the differences may be lexical, morphological, syntactic, or phonological; the differences also may have different degrees of significance for different speakers, depending on their social position and their self-evaluated linguistic position.

6.2 Dialects

Ferguson (1971) defines dialect as follows: "A dialect is any set of one or more varieties of a language which share at least one feature or combination of features setting them apart from other varieties of the language and which may appropriately be treated as a unit on linguistic or non-linguistic grounds." He describes the extent and nature of dialect differentiation in terms of two major variables: density of communication and interspeaker attitudes. The more frequently people speak to each other, generally the more their speech tends to become identical. A close social unit will then express its group solidarity by its own unique speech. Less prestigious speakers normally will attempt to emulate the more prestigious ones.

The term *dialect* can be utilized only in connection with the term *language,* as the former is always a subdivision of the latter, although a given language may exist in only a single dialect. But it must be recalled, as discussed above, that whether a given variety is a separate language or a dialect of another language is ordinarily determined by sociopolitical considerations. (Max Weinreich once defined a language as "a dialect with an army and a navy.") Before we can accept such terms, we must know the entire language classification to which the terms belong. It is not the task of the sociologist of language to set up such classifications but rather to describe and analyze the behavior of speech community members toward such varieties, as they argue over their status and policies toward them.

The term *dialect* is sometimes used in a number of different senses other than the one utilized here. For example, differences in pronunciation, without grammatical or lexical differences, are best referred to as *accents* rather than as dialects. Most regional variation in American English is perhaps best understood in this fashion. Because the term has not attained a precise and widely accepted definition, some scholars have either given up the concept or chosen the neutral term *lect* which would include any variety of speech, even that of an individual (idiolect), or else refer simply to language *varieties.*

One popular usage is utilized in the popular entertainment field, where an actor, particularly a comedian may mimic or parody foreign-accented speech or tell so-called "dialect" jokes. Some such actors are ingenious and often convincing and/or amusing, but this use of the term "dialect" has little to do with the linguist's use of the term.

Another usage is to refer to a distinction between "written languages" and "spoken dialects," particularly in the Third World countries, with the frequently made remark that a particular country or society does not really possess a language, only unwritten dialects. This attitude is not confined to uninformed outsiders. It is frequently shared even by some educated members of the societies themselves because of a tendency to equate "real" languages only with written languages. Colonialized peoples in some cases have been taught to denigrate their own languages (as well as their cultural forms), although some of the now liberated peoples have reacted against this attitude and are beginning to take a strong pride in their native vernaculars.

Traditional studies in dialectology have emphasized geographical dialects. An interest in the speech of the provincial folk was a direct outgrowth of early nineteenth century European Romanticism, with its glorification of the "folk," in whom the national culture and values were presumably to be found in their purest and most laudable form. This was in origin primarily a European phenomenon, as the French, for example, were discovering their local *patois,* and the Germans were researching their provincial *Volksprachen*. It must be pointed out that the dialectal differences found in Europe are much greater than what are to be found in more or less linguistically homogeneous countries, such as the United States. Thus, while all geographical varieties of American English are mutually intelligible, all German dialects are not, nor are French dialects, Italian dialects, etc. In such cases, the very fact of their mutual nonintelligibility raises the question of whether we are really dealing with separate dialects or separate languages. In areas covered by closely related languages or closely related dialects, linguistic features ordinarily have a continuous distribution, that is, speech varieties may merge almost imperceptibly into each other. Thus, in parts of pre-Columbian America, a linguistically very heterogeneous area (for example, in California), Indians in one village would note differences between their own speech and that of a neighboring village, but these would be unimportant. Two villages away, the speech might seem "strange," while three villages away they might have difficulty understanding the language and find the language of four villages away completely incomprehensible. This is admittedly an extreme case but points out the nature of continuous distribution. In a country like Italy, the dialects of neighboring provinces may be very similar, whereas the differences two provinces away would be marked. For example, a Sicilian and a Piedmontese from northern Italy would be completely unable to understand one another unless, of course, they shared some other common speech variety, for example, standard Italian—itself originally based on the dialect of Florence. Some other dialect continua include the chain of German, Dutch, and Flemish dialects running from Switzerland to the North Sea, the chain of Romance dialects found in Italy, France, and Spain along the Mediterranean, and the entire Slavic area. Ferguson notes that "Within a dialect continuum mutual intelligibility is proportional to geographical distance and not directly related to political and standard language boundaries. Rural populations on both sides of such a boundary usually have no difficulty in understanding each other, while they might be unable to comprehend geographically distant varieties spoken in their own language area" (Ferguson 1971:35). In such cases, a standard language has been *superposed* over the local speech. The superposed variety serves as a special style to be used on formal occasions or to communicate with outsiders. The local population is thus bidialectical or bilectal.

The matter of continuous distribution has been emphasized by the study of linguistic geography, which has plotted the spatial distribution of linguistic features (words, phonemes, etc.) on maps or "linguistic atlases." Scholars were especially interested in using geographical evidence to arrive at historical conclusions as to how differences had arisen and spread. One deficiency of this approach was that it was basically unidimensional, that is, it looked at distribution on a geographical plane and ignored the vertical socioeconomic dimension. It emphasized the spread of linguistic features as a result of prestige imitation, that is, a feature was copied because it was utilized in some area (for example, a capital city) believed to have prestige. Nevertheless, it failed to note the flow of prestige up and down the class ladder. In other words, the function of social dialects was not clearly understood.

In recent years, the study of social dialects has been one of the most vigorously pursued areas in all of sociolinguistics, particularly in the United States. Recent studies there have shown that social dialects are not differentiated from each other by discrete sets of features but by variations in the frequency with which certain features occur. In other words, the differences are matters of degree and not kind. Social dialects are distinguished from each other not by one dialect using a certain pronunciation or a certain word or syntactic construction not used in other dialects but rather by using such features more frequently or less frequently. Thus, in American English, for example, both middle- and working-class speakers may regularize the third person present of the auxiliary do (He don't work), but such a form is found with much greater frequency among working-class speakers. (Concerning social and ethnic dialects, see sections 8.4, 9.2, and 9.3).

What keeps both regional and social varieties apart is both social barriers and social distance. Geographical barriers or distance in themselves may create the social distance or barriers, but the absence of geographical barriers may not necessarily mean the absence of social barriers. A dialect continuum can be either social or geographical, there being a chain of dialects connected by similarity but with those dialects at the ends of the chain being very different from each other. In India, there are caste dialects, which are somewhat more discrete entities than social class dialects. Social dialects may be based on social class, ethnicity, or religion. For example, in Baghdad and in other cities in lower Iraq, the Muslims, Christians, and Jews each speak quite different dialects of Arabic, each with its own phonology, morphology, and with its own syntactic and lexical peculiarities. The Jewish and Christian dialects are spoken for the most part at home and with coreligionists, while the Muslim dialect is used in public and other intercommunal situations, at least by those Jews and Christians who control the Muslim dialect. For example, take the word for bread which in the Muslim dialect is /xubuz/, in the Jewish /xebz/, and in the Christian /xebez/.

The Muslim dialect appears to have been heavily influenced by the speech of the Bedouins who have immigrated to the cities in recent centuries, whereas the Jews and Christians, because of social isolation, have conservatively retained the older urban dialect. The Jewish and Christian dialects resemble each other more than either resembles the Muslim dialect (Blanc 1964).

In the Serbo-Croatian of Bosnia Turkisms (words of Arabic, Persian or Turkish origin adopted during the Ottoman period) are more commonly used by Muslims than by Christians, both in the countryside and in the city of Sarajevo. Lockwood (1975:53) indicates that "When a Moslem enters a gathering of both Moslems and Christians, he will invariably say 'merhaba i dobar dan'—good day (Moslem expression from Arabic) and good day (Christian expression from Serbo-Croatian)—thus automatically categorizing his listeners into ingroup and outgroup. In similar circumstances, a Christian will use only 'dobar dan.' " Some of Lockwood's informants said that Moslems, Serbs (mostly Orthodox), and Croats (mostly Catholics) each used different terms for certain items, but he found it difficult to verify these contentions. The important thing was that the inhabitants believed that such differences exist.

6.3 Styles and Registers

That language varies by geographical area, ethnicity, and social class is perhaps more obvious than the fact that language also varies according to situation. Furthermore, the two kinds of variations are interrelated in various interesting ways. There are a number of dimensions along which language can vary. Perhaps the most frequently encountered is the formal-informal dimension. How formally one person will speak to another will depend not only on the situation (for example, a job interview, as contrasted with friends chatting at a neighborhood bar), but also on the relative statuses of the interlocutors (for example, speaking with a high political or religious dignitary as contrasted with one's haberdasher). Rules for the use of such styles are so much a part of the competence of the individual speaker that he is likely to be shocked, or at least surprised, to hear them violated: *How're ya doin', your Holiness?* In fact, when a person wishes to de-emphasize the formality of a situation or to reduce status differences, one of the most effective means, and undoubtedly the commonest employed, is to change one's language to a much less formal style. This is, of course, also an effective way of insulting people if that is desired. Style switching is undoubtedly closely connected with the structure and dynamics of personal interaction.

Studying the speech community, we observe the various ways of speaking and the conditions under which each is used. The point of departure is perhaps what it is the speaker wishes to convey by way of referential and social meaning. Style is important precisely because *how* something is said is part of what is said. Choice of language variety or of one word rather than another to express the same thought conveys primarily social information. As Giglioli (1972:16) notes, "Sociolinguistic choices may inform the hearer about the speaker's social and regional origin as well as the nature of the social situation at hand, about shifts in the topic of the conversation and so forth. However, social meaning transmitted through style switching or other sociolinguistic devices is effective only when the participants share common cultural norms and common background knowledge about the particular situation in which they are engaged." Thus, for example, a bilingual Spanish-English speaker talking to another bilingual will convey much information about ethnic identity or situation by choosing one language rather than the other, or by switching back and forth between the two languages.

The speaker is forced to choose between languages and styles and to choose specific words within the language and style. While these choices may be of different orders of magnitude or along different dimensions in a linguistic sense, basically the same social correlates are involved. Although linguistically different, switching from one language to another or switching from one style to another within the same language may carry the same meaning or at least fall within the same category of social meaning. All normal individuals command several styles of speaking within their language, so that they are able to express intimacy or social distance, or to indicate respect, insolence, seriousness, or humor. They may do this by switching languages, varieties, or styles. Religious seriousness is often emphasized by using a language not generally understood by the faithful, such as Latin, Arabic, or Sanskrit in some communities. (Hymes 1972d:58–59). The same conditions that determine the choice of pronouns or inflectional endings in one community may determine choice of language in another community.

We know we are dealing with a single speech variety or style when we notice that consistency is observed with reference to the co-occurrence of certain forms. For example, stylistically we can expect *right on* and *far out* to occur in the same discourse but not with *exquisite*; likewise, *ain't* may occur with *fishin* but not with *fishing*; nor would we expect *weltanschauung* with *freaked out*. But it is the very existence of normal co-occurence that allows departures from it to convey social meaning (Ervin-Tripp 1972:215).

A number of attempts have been made to classify styles of speaking or to identify the dimensions along which styles can be ranged or classified. One of the most famous such classifications is that of Joos (1962) with reference to spoken English. Joos identified five styles corresponding to different stages of the individual's socialization. The *intimate* and *informal* styles are used with close friends or family and with casual acquaintances. The *consultative* style is ordinarily used in semi-formal situations such as between strangers, between teacher and student, or employer and employee. The *formal style* is used for formal speaking or for writing. The first two styles may be considered private and the last two primarily as public styles. Within each geographical variety, there will be social class dialects; and within each class dialect, we expect to find various private and public styles.

The consultative style is the most neutral or unmarked of the styles. In using this style, the speaker supplies background information which he assumes the hearer needs to have in order to understand him. This style is for dealing with people who speak the same language but may possess a different personal stock of information. But it is not easy, says Joos, to go on treating the listener as a stranger. Therefore, the speaker tries to form a social group with him by the use of casual style. The two defining features of casual style, ellipsis and slang, mean that the addressee is treated as an insider who will understand what not everybody else might be able to.

Intimate style is characterized by extraction and jargon. Good intimate style goes a step further and fuses two personalities, according to Joos, whereas good casual style integrates two disparate personalities. Good consultative style produces cooperation without the necessity of integration of the individual personalities. The purpose of good formal style is to inform the addressee on an individual basis. It demands advance planning and is characterized by detachment and cohesion.

A fifth *frozen style* is used in print and declamation in situations where the addressee is not allowed to cross-question the author. This style is for those who are to remain strangers. Thus, style in part defines the social relationships of the speakers.

In consultative style, one might say "I believe that I can find one" but in casual style "I believe I can find one" or "Believe I can find one." Casual style has markers like "Come on!" On the other hand, formal style often has *may* or *might:* "May I help you" or "We may not see one another for some time." Intimate style relies heavily on shared context: "Ready?" whereas frozen style provides a very extensive context, expecting very little in the form of shared knowledge from the hearer or reader: "This work in its present initial form should be regarded as a progress report, designed primarily for other researchers in the field." There is perhaps an even more frozen style in English, as in many other languages, which is ritualized, that is, so that what a person is about to say is completely predictable or almost so: "Our Father, which art . . ."

Joos' classification is attractive in a number of respects but is based on anecdotal evidence and is difficult to apply on a rigorous basis. Furthermore, Joos characterizes the differences between various styles as qualitative, rather than quantitative, a difference that does not hold up when we look closely at actual speech behavior.

Two major dimensions along which styles are classified in the research literature are formality and degree of attention paid to one's speech. These two dimensions are not mutually exclusive, of course. The most intensive investigations into speech styles in actual use have been conducted by Labov, who insists that there are no single-style speakers. While some speakers show a much wider range of style shifting than others, every speaker studied by Labov and his colleagues showed a shift of some linguistic variables as the social context and topic changed. Labov ranges styles along a single dimension, measured by the amount of attention paid to speech, normally by means of audio-monitoring of one's own speech. The style in which minimum attention is given to the monitoring of speech and the least amount of hypercorrection (as in casual conversation) he calls the vernacular style. The most formal style would be used in reading aloud. He notes that the same linguistic variable can be used to signal either social or stylistic stratification, for example, the use of *ain't,* connoting nonstandardness and/or informality. People ordinarily identify careful speech with the patterns used by the next higher status group (Labov 1971b). Of course, they may misunderstand some of the usages of the group they are trying to emulate.

By the time the average child comes to school, he will have had three or four years of language training which has enabled him to master one or more informal speech styles and perhaps also to develop receptive competence in one or two others, perhaps from television. In school, of course, he is expected to learn a new formal style. He will soon learn also the relationships of social status to language style.

By register is meant a variety of language considered appropriate for a particular type of situation. Thus, different kinds of register are expected in, say, a church sermon, a diplomatic encounter, a family dinner, a sports broadcast, or a pair of lovers billing and cooing. The type of language appropriate to one of these situations might be insulting, amusing, ludicrous, or confusing if used under different circumstances. Ordinarily, the varieties in question will be styles, but under certain conditions different languages or dialects will be used.

An ethnographic approach requires that registers be considered from the viewpoint of the speakers, not that of the scientific observer, for how the interlocutors define the situation will determine (or at least affect) the particular style of speech utilized in that situation. The other factors affecting language usage are, of course, the topic and the intentions of the speaker. The native speaker possesses, as part of his communicative competence, knowledge of the rules of co-occurrence. As Halliday notes (1968:150): "The choice of items from the wrong register and the mixing of items from different registers are among the most frequent mistakes made by non-native speakers of a language. . . . Linguistic humor often depends on the inappropriate choice and the mixing of the registers."

As in the case of different dialects or different styles, so too the differences among the different registers are not so much differences in kind as differences in degree, in differing frequencies of the occurrence of particular forms. In some countries (for example, the United States), choice of register seems to be tied in with choice of style, whereas in Great Britain, it is choice of dialect that is associated with choice of register. One cannot give a radio commentary on cricket in cockney or sing popular songs in the Queen's English. On the other hand, in much of the Third World, there is often a tendency for the register to determine not the choice of dialect, but the choice of language, so that it becomes necessary to learn a second language in order to be equipped with a full range of registers.

When social institutions reach a certain degree of specialization, a significant range of their functions can be performed only by socially defined experts. They have specialized knowledge which they express in specialized language or styles, which may, in turn, influence the standard language. Luckmann (1975:39) notes that institutional styles of language arise primarily from the goal-oriented requirements of an institution with a complex division of labor. Styles associated with social strata, on the other hand, are based on a common life style and group solidarity, as well as concern for the maintenance of mobility barriers and transmission of family status. The linguistic variables serve as elaborate markers of identification that cannot be easily faked. Group solidarity may be reinforced by either class styles or occupational argots.

When we find groups which are socially different from each other, we expect to find linguistic differences as well, such as the different occupations to be found in a society, many of which are differentiated from each other by education, socioeconomic status, values, dress, etc. In some cases, occupational language peculiarities consist of terms necessarsy for their special activities but of little interest to outsiders. At times, a special effort is made to replace ordinary terms with special ones, particularly to avoid being understood by outsiders, even when addressed. Thus, lawyers or doctors may address their clients in such a way as to be understood in an unclear fashion, if at all. This emphasizes the expertise of the professional and maintains social distance between the professional and nonprofessional. Sometimes the lack of understanding is unintentional, as in the case of a social worker who doesn't realize that her middle-class speech is not entirely understood by her lower-class client.

Some occupations beyond the pale of respectability, for example, the work of thieves, pimps, prostitutes, and gamblers, have developed special vocabularies for ordinary words to the point that these argots, jargons, or cants may be regarded almost as separate languages. (Some semirespectable occupations, like that of sociologist, have also been credited with such forms of language.) Such secret languages may be useful in avoiding detection by the police and other authorities. Similar varieties have also been developed by youth gangs, whether delinquent or nondelinquent, most notably by some Chicano groups known variously as *pachucos, tirilones,* etc., who speak *caló* (see section 9.3).

Maurer (1955:4) defines argot as "specialized language used by organized professional groups operating outside the law; these groups normally constitute criminal subcultures, and the language is usually secret or semisecret." Argot is used only by professionals for the discussion of their business. Normally they speak it only in the presence of accepted underworld persons; hence, it is not used primarily for purposes of secrecy. They especially avoid its use in the presence of victims or potential victims. Some persons may speak an argot with wit and originality. Others may speak several argots fluently if they have had experience in more than one racket. Some criminals, on the other hand, shun argot completely. Terms from argot frequently find their way into the general language. There is, for example, an outflow of gambling argot from a professional center to semiprofessionals, legitimate gamblers, all players, and to the public at large (Maurer 1950:118–119).

Some subcultures, without an economically specialized institutional basis, like those of the underworld have adopted argot-like speech patterns. Such linguistic styles are typically unstable, for example, languages of the jazz world, of drug addicts, or of youth cultures existing on the borderline of professional crime. Such youth languages borrow from criminal argots, jazz language, and black slang, and are used for a wider range of functions than those of professional argots (Luckmann 1975:38–39). Languages of concealment may use either phonological transformations, such as Pig Latin, or else use a word that rhymes with the one they would conceal. They also invent new words or borrow words from languages with which others are not familiar. To a limited extent, certain argots and children's languages fall into this category.

Slang arises not from ignorance of the standard language but rather from the desire of a group such as a gang or occupational group to have speech forms that will distinguish it from outsiders. Some slang words like argot may enter general speech and, in some cases, survive there and even become incorporated into the standard language. Most slang, however, is ephemeral, changing as outsiders begin to catch on. It is difficult to give examples of current slang for the words may be obsolete even by the time this book is published.

In the view of Jespersen (1925:150), "Slang is an outcome of mankind's love of play, 'Spieltrieb': it is the playful production of something new, where, properly speaking, nothing new was required. In the light of pure reason the old word is good enough; it is only our feelings that cannot stand it any longer. Slang is a linguistic luxury; it is a sport and like any other sport, something that belongs essentially to the young. It is (or was, at any rate) a greater favourite with young men than with young women. One may describe it briefly as the fight against what is outworn and drab." Persons, however, learning the slang as part of a second language may fail to distinguish between standard and slang forms and use the latter inappropriately. That is, foreigners may fail to acquire the necessary socio-linguistic rules for the use of the various speech styles.

6.4 Lingua francas

The term _lingua franca_ refers to any language used to communicate across linguistic barriers. UNESCO (1953:40) has defined lingua franca as "A language which is used habitually by people whose mother tongues are different in order to facilitate communication between them." According to Samarin (1968), there are four special types of lingua francas, namely _trade-language_, a language used by some people as a second language in commercial situations over a large territory outside its native base (for example, Hausa in West Africa); _contact language_, a lingua franca whose use is not necessarily habitual, e.g. Latin or Greek in the ancient Near East; _international language_ which is used actually or virtually internationally (English perhaps comes closest to this); and _auxiliary language_ which generally refers to an artificially constructed lingua franca, such as Esperanto.

Lingua francas can be either natural, pidginized, or planned. The most important natural lingua francas in the history of Western Civilization have been the Greek _koine_, Latin, and French. The koine owed its spread to the military conquests of Alexander the Great but outlasted the empire and helped to spread Christianity. There would probably have been no audience for the new religion had not the koine been previously available as a contact language (Samarin 1968:661–663). Koines are always mutually intelligible with at least some forms of the standard language. Aramaic, and later Arabic, became lingua francas of the Near East, and Hindi became a lingua franca following the Muslim conquests of India in the 12th century.

While lingua francas are characterized in terms of function, pidgins can be characterized not only in terms of their limited functions but also in terms of their origin, structure and social context. A _pidgin_ is a contact vernacular which originated out of the contact of two unrelated languages, usually one European and one non-European and developed adjacent to a marine expanse, often by seamen. Probably some two or three million persons daily use some form of pidgin for communication purposes (De Camp 1971:21–22). It is not normally the native language of any of its speakers. There are also a number of pidgins in widespread use which are based upon indigenous languages, such as Kituba in Zaire or Police Motu in Papua, which are typically used by young male workers who leave their rural homes to work in the cities.

A _pidgin_ is ordinarily a simplified version of one of the languages, usually European, modified in the direction of the other. Usually grammatical distinctions are ignored which are unrelated to important semantic distinctions. The language thus developed, at least in its initial stages, is used for communication in a very limited number of situations, such as buying and selling goods or communication between foreman and worker. It is used to transmit referential rather than social meaning and lacks stylistic variation. The vocabulary thus is also very limited, and the pidgin becomes very easy for both parties to the transaction to learn and use. The social status of the pidgin leads to a decreased functional load which, in turn, leads to its simplified structure (Smith 1972:47).

Despite their contact origins some pidgins are not spoken by those who control the related standard language but rather by natives in subordinate positions who do not share a common language. For example, Chinese pidgin English is not spoken between speakers of English and Chinese but rather among Chinese who speak mutually unintelligible dialects, as Tok Pisin is used between members of different New Guinea tribes.

To give the reader an idea of the nature of a pidgin, a text of the Lord's Prayer in Pidgin English (New Guinea), as printed in the 1963 edition of the Four Gospels, is presented along with an interlinear literal translation (cited by Capell 1969):

Papa   bilong   mipela,   yu i stap long   heven.   Nem   bilong
Father   of   us,   you live in   heaven.   Name   belong

yu i mas   i stap holi.   Kingdom   bilong   yu i kam.   Laik bilong   yu
you must be   holy. Kingdom   of   you come. Will of   you

ol i   bihainim   long heven,   olsem   ol i   mas   bihainim   long
they follow   in   heaven,   the-same   they must follow-it   on

graun tu.   Kaikai   bilong   mipela   inap   long de nau,   yu
earth too. Food   of   us   sufficient   for   any more,

gipim   mipela.   Na   yu   lusim   sin bilong   mipela,   olsem   mipela
give-it us.   And you loose-it sin of   us,   as   we

tu   i lusim.   Pinis   rong   bilong ol   ol i   mekim   long mipela.
too loose-it. Finish wrong of   them they do it   to   us.

Na   yu   no bringim   mipela long samting   bilong traiim   mipela.
And you not bring   us   to   anything   to   try   us.

Tasol   tekewe   mipela   long   samting   nogut.
That's all (=but)   take away   us   from   anything   bad.

In West Germany, there are hundreds of thousands of temporary workers (euphemistically called *Gastarbeiter,* or "guest workers") from Greece, Yugoslavia, Spain, and Turkey who have developed a German pidgin for communicating with their German employers and neighbors. It apparently is sufficient for the needs of the factories where most of the *Gastarbeiter* are employed, but they are effectively isolated from the rest of German society. Their children are handicapped in attending German schools, although some bilingual programs have been established.

There are many other instances of pidgins or near-pidgins. For example, Weil (1977) identifies a variety of Hebrew she calls "sub-Hebrew" spoken by immigrants to Israel from India (the Bene Israel), which is characterized by a reduced diversity of syntactic construction, reduced attention to gender, tense and number, a reduced number of lexical alternatives, and increased emphasis on nonverbal language. Thus, they may say /kolnoa?/ ("cinema") to mean "Would you like to come to the cinema with me?" or /yerakot/ ("vegetables") to refer to different specific kinds of vegetables. Or a speaker may go to a grocery store, and if he doesn't know the name in Hebrew of the item he wants, he may simply say /ze/ ("this"), pointing to the desired item. The purpose of sub-Hebrew is to facilitate communication with other speech communities, as the Bene Israel generally speak Marathi and/or English.

When a pidgin becomes a medium of communication among non-Western speakers who speak mutually unintelligible languages (for example, persons from different tribes in New Guinea), it often happens that such persons marry each other and thus may utilize the pidgin as the language of the home. Their children will then speak the pidgin as their first language. If this occurs on a fairly large scale and there is a group of people who speak the pidgin as their first or only language, its functions will become expanded. Its vocabulary and new grammatical devices will be developed to convey all the semantic nuances necessary for the full life of a community. This latter development is called *creolization* and results in a *creole*. In fact, Pidgin English has become this in Melanesia, where it is now generally called Neo-Melanesian or Tok Pisin. Newspapers and books are published in Tok Pisin, and the business of the New Guinea legislature and other governmental bodies is conducted in this creole.

Hall (1972) has pointed out that pidgins and creoles have in some cases been standardized by the production of written grammars and dictionaries under the auspices of colonial regimes and missionary organizations. Newspapers, government communiques, Bible translations, etc., are then issued in standardized written form (cf. the Pidgin English text above). In such cases the problems of standardization involve the same types of considerations as the standardization of other languages, such as, for example, standardized orthography.

While contact cultures maintain their own integrity in the case of pidgins, creoles represent the outcome of acculturation. Although most of the vocabulary of a creole is shared with its "parent," the phonology and syntax are ordinarily so different that the two are mutually unintelligible. Smith contrasts pidginization and creolization by noting that the former involves simplification of form, restriction in function, and admixture of vocabulary to a base language, whereas the latter involves elaboration of form, expansion of function, and stabilization and incorporation of the lexicon into the referential framework of the new system (Smith 1973a:290–291). He further believes that any child's language is originally pidginized, but that as it develops, it undergoes a process analogous to creolization and eventually decreolization. On the other hand, pidgins are developed by adults, whereas creoles are developed by children.

A significant question concerns the conditions under which a pidgin does or does not become creolized. Generally, a creole will not emerge if the sociolinguistic situation which produced the pidgin in the first place remains unchanged. The pidgin must become the first, native language of its speakers at the same time that they are denied the opportunity of acquiring the corresponding standard language. This will occur as a result of largely unbridgeable social and racial gaps between elite and masses, or colonizers and colonized.

Once a creole has been established, there are several stages it can reach (Bell 1976:160–161):

1. Virtual stability in relationship to other languages
2. Change taking place in the form of
   (i) Extinction of the creole by the standard superposed language (e.g. Gullah by English in Georgia or Negerhollands by Dutch in the Netherlands West Indies).
   (ii) Evolution of the creole to a standard language (e.g. Bahasa Indonesia, Afrikaans, Maltese, or the Romance languages after the fall of the Roman Empire).
   (iii) Merging of the creole with the superordinate language to form a postcreole continuum, e.g. Jamaican Creole with standard English.

The low social status of pidgins and creoles (popularly regarded as corruptions of the standard rather than "real" languages) derives from the low social and ethnic status of its non-white speakers, as contrasted with the largely European speakers of the corresponding standard language. When opportunities for upward mobility for creole speakers become available, the situation may change fundamentally. If the creole is based on the standard language in use in the same community, and further when acculturation takes place between creole and standard speakers, a postcreole continuum is likely to emerge, replacing the original diglossia (see section 7.3) of pidgin and early creole. In other words, the creole is changing in the direction of the standard language but not at the same rate for all speakers. This *decreolization* process has been most closely observed in the case of English-based creoles in the Caribbean, for example, in Guyana.

Bickerton (1975:24) uses the term *basilect* to refer to that variety of Guyanese Creole most distinct from English, *acrolect* to refer to educated Guyanese English (a variety that differs from other standard varieties of the language only in a few phonological details and a handful of lexical items), and *mesolect* to refer to all intermediate varieties. At times he refers to upper mesolect, mid-mesolect, and lower mesolect. All of these are sections on a continuum, not discrete varieties, and each blends into the next.

Creoles are characterized by much internal variation and style switching and mixture, but the following set of possible realizations of the sentence *I told him* is a useful approximation to the correlation of linguistic form with social stratification in Guyanese:

1. /ai tɔ uld hIm/   6. /ai tɛl i/
2. /ai to:ld hIm/   7. /a tɛl i/
3. /ai to:l Im/   8. /mi tɛl i/
4. /ai tɛl Im/   9. /mi tɛl am/
5. /a tɛl Im/

According to Allsopp (1958, cited by Bickerton 1975) varieties 1–3 were characteristic of middle-class usage; 4–7 of the lower-middle and urban working classes; 8 of the bulk of the rural working class; 9 of old and illiterate (and predominantly Indian) rural laborers. The scale is from nearest to English to farthest from English.

A speech community can reach postcreole status if two conditions are met. First, the dominant official language and the creole must have the same vocabulary base. Otherwise, the creole either remains as a separate language (for example, Spanish-based Papiamento separate from Dutch in Curaçao) or becomes extinct. In addition, the society must provide for sufficient upward social mobility for the standard language to exert real influence on creole speakers; otherwise, the creole and the standard will not form a continuum but will remain sharply separated, as in the case of French-based creoles, e.g. in Haiti. Influence of the standard does not operate uniformly on all speakers, of course, for if it did, the creole would merge with the standard rather than form a continuum with it.

Creoles are spoken today by more than six million persons around the Caribbean and in West Africa. The largest group is that of the French-based creole speakers, who comprise perhaps four and a half million speakers in French Guiana, Louisiana (in the United States), and the Lesser Antilles; all are mutually intelligible. English-based creole speakers include a million and a half speakers in Jamaica, plus speakers in other parts of the Caribbean, Camerouns, Liberia, Hawaii, and Pitcairn Island. In the United States, an English-based creole called Gullah was once spoken widely in Georgia, South Carolina, and the nearby Sea Islands. It is still spoken to some extent on the islands but is almost extinct on the mainland.

Spanish and Portuguese-based creoles are widely used in Asia and in three islands off the West African coast. In the Caribbean, Papiamento is spoken by about 200,000 people in the Dutch colonies of Aruba, Bonaire, and Curaçao (De Camp 1971:17–18).

At one time, it was thought that pidgins originated when European language speakers used a simplified form of their language, a sort of baby talk, to speak to slaves or customers which was quickly picked up and modified in the direction of the local language in Africa, South America, the Caribbean, or the Pacific area, as the case may be. It seems rather more likely that pidgins derived from nonnative speakers' theorizing differently about the language of their colonial masters. Furthermore, all the early accounts report that the white planters were learning the creole from the slaves. Even more importantly, it became necessary to explain the fact that all dialects of Creole French, for example, including those in the Indian Ocean, are mutually intelligible. As De Camp (1971:19) indicates, the typological similarities shared by the Portuguese, French, English, and Spanish creoles are too great for coincidence. These creoles, furthermore, share much common vocabulary, including syntactic function words.

The most widely accepted hypothesis among creolists as to the origins of the European-language based pidgins and creoles is that they originated in a single proto-pidgin, probably based on the famous Sabir of the Mediterranean area in the Middle Ages, which gave rise first to Portuguese Pidgin in the fifteenth century, then to the various other pidgins through the process of relexification. This is a wholesale shift of vocabulary, with the structure remaining basically the same.

The relexification hypothesis is supported by the fact that some of the words in English creoles are derived from Portuguese, such as *pickaninny* from *pequenino*, or *savvy* from *sabe*, and many from West African languages, such as *njam*, "to eat." In addition, there are grammatical similarities among the different creoles which suggest a West African rather than a European origin, such as aspect and tense being indicated by preposed particles. Furthermore, Saramakkan, a creole spoken in Surinam, appears to be about halfway through the relexification process from Portuguese to English. The process stopped when the slave ancestors of present-day Saramakkan speakers escaped into the jungle (Trudgill 1974b:179–180).

Alleyne (1971:182) argues against the monogenetic theory of pidgins and creoles, and supports an explanation based on their similarities with West Africa languages, as well as on the similar social conditions throughout the Caribbean, principally the fact that the creoles became crystallized within the group of field slaves.

The various studies of pidginization and creolization are particularly important for the light they may shed on the question of the origins of some of the distinctive features of black speech in the United States. The slave traders generally dealt with the African dealers along the coast through interpreters, usually of mixed ancestry, who had learned French, English, Dutch, or Portuguese in the ports well enough to be able to work as interpreters and nothing more. About that time and under these conditions, Europeans rarely learned any African language. Thus, probably the slaves brought to the Americas from West Africa spoke, in addition to their own languages, originally a Portuguese-based, later an English-based pidgin. Because of diverse tribal origins and the policy of the slavers to separate slaves speaking the same language, the blacks came eventually to use the pidgin exclusively among themselves in the New World, with the result that it became creolized. The social isolation of the blacks, especially of the field slaves, from white society helped perpetuate this language, although the isolation was never complete. The house slaves spoke a language very close to that of their masters, so that a diglossic situation developed. With the constant impact of the standard language on the creole, decreolization affected all black speech, but to a lesser degree in the case of Gullah, which seems to have survived the decreolization process. Gullah still manifests thousands of words from two dozen different African languages, as well as some syntactic and phonological influence from West African languages. Elsewhere the process has gone so far that what is known as Black English is different only in minor details from other varieties of English. Some of the features of these varieties supposedly constitute evidence for its creole origins.

The similarities of seventeenth and eighteenth century black speech to present-day English-based creoles in the West Indies and West Africa form the basis of the hypothesis. Evidence is largely from literary and comparative work and is fragmentary and inconclusive, but it fits the facts better than the allegation that Black English is either merely a variant of Southern White English or a "corrupted" or "incorrect" form. It is, furthermore, in accordance with the frequently noted observation that oppressed, submerged people tend to be culturally very creative. Thus, we have evidence, indirect as it is, that Blacks in the past created their own language, an intellectual achievement of no mean proportions.

A special form of language planning involves the artificial creation of new languages for international communication to avoid giving any existing language an unfair advantage. Such an international auxiliary language is intended to supplement, not supplant, existing languages. There would seem to be a greater need for such a language, as the world has in some senses become less international. For example, at the Congress of Vienna at the end of the Napoleonic Wars, French was the sole official language; at Versailles at the end of World War I, French and English were the official languages; while currently at the United Nations, five languages are officially used, namely English, French, Spanish, Russian, and Chinese. As a result of this, each year hundreds of translators are busy translating millions of pages from the original language of the document to the other four languages. Such a situation derives, of course, not from linguistic practicality but from political considerations.

Descartes was the first person to construct an artificial language. Since then, there have been at least a thousand other attempts. Linguists have criticized these attempts, saying that existing constructed interlanguages and projects are all more or less deficient since we really do not know which is the most efficient structure of a language. Such critics assume we must first build a theory of language planning and then interlinguistics. On the other hand, McQuown (1964) believes that the major difficulty in adoption of an international auxiliary language is not the problem of deficiencies in the proposed languages themselves but, rather, political and social issues. Mainly, the world is not ready. Imperialist powers are also not about to willingly give up the prerogatives that have come from the world-wide use of their languages. When the time is ripe, any constructed language will do, as long as it can develop large technical vocabularies, internationally agreed upon. The only existing international language which comes close to these criteria is Esperanto. Although large technical vocabularies are not available, it has had wide practical use. There are even native speakers of Esperanto, who are called *denaska* ("from birth") Esperantists who have been brought up by Esperantist parents and have used Esperanto as the normal family language from their earliest childhood (Elgin 1972:78). But for the most part, speakers of Esperanto are native speakers of some other language and use Esperanto only by intention and with conscious effort. There are not enough native speakers of Esperanto to serve as a standard for usage, although presumably such a standard could be developed.

Zamenhof explained his motivation for devising an international language in a letter in 1895:

> "This place where I was born and spent my childhood gave the direction to all my future endeavors. In Bialystok the population consisted of four diverse elements: Russians, Poles, Germans and Jews; each spoke a different language, and was hostile to the other elements. In this town, more than anywhere else, an impressionable nature feels the heavy burden of linguistic

differences and is convinced, at every step, that the diversity of language is the only, or at least the main cause, that separates the human family and divides it into conflicting groups. I was brought up an idealist; I was taught that all men were brothers, and meanwhile, in the street, in the square, everything at every step made me feel that men did not exist, only Russians, Poles, Germans, Jews, and so on. This was always a great torment to my infant mind, although many people may smile at such an 'anguish for the world' in a child. Since at that time it seemed to me that the grown-ups were omnipotent, I kept telling myself that when I was grown up, I would certainly destroy this evil" (quoted by Boulton 1960:6–7).

As late as 1910, he naively noted that "What makes humanity unhappy is not the existence of the groups, but their interference—so far unavoidable—with one another. Every time I wish to deal with a member of another group, either I have to force on him my language and customs, or he has to force his on me. When this regrettable necessity of *forcing* disappears, inter-racial hatreds will disappear" (quoted by Boulton 1960:156).

Although Zamenhof's views were unrealistic and simplistic in nature, the language he created has indeed promoted international understanding and become a social force in its own right. Thus, the Nazis opposed Esperanto because it had been created by a Jew and was internationalist and humanitarian in orientation, with a new culture of its own. In *Mein Kampf*, Hitler had said that the Jews would try to establish a universal language in order to rule the rest of the world. In Nazi Germany, the teaching and use of Esperanto were prohibited, Esperanto organizations were liquidated, and some Esperanto speakers were actually sent to concentration camps and eventually murdered for no other reason. Almost the entire Zamenhof family perished. During the Spanish Civil War, local fascists executed the whole local Esperanto group in Córdoba. The teaching of Esperanto was prohibited in Fascist Portugal in 1948. Until after Stalin, Soviet Esperantists were classified as bourgeois, international, and cosmopolitan "anti-Soviet elements" and, during the great purge, deported from the Baltic republics to distant regions of the Soviet Union. In postwar Eastern Europe, Esperanto activities were suspended in East Germany (until 1961) and in Hungary, Poland, and Czechoslovakia (until 1969).

At present, however, the Esperanto movement is flourishing in Poland, Hungary, Bulgaria, and especially Yugoslavia, and is permitted in Czechoslavakia, Romania, and even in the Soviet Union. The 1959 World Esperanto Congress was in Warsaw and the 1978 Congress in Varna, Bulgaria.

In their study of repression of the Esperanto movement, Sadler and Lins (1972:215) conclude: "Curious indeed that a language 'lacking scientific or cultural foundation' and having 'neither a lexical basis nor a grammar of its own' variously described as an 'expression of cosmopolitanism,' the 'reactionary ideology of the imperialist bourgeoisie,' as an 'international anarchist language,' as 'a bridge to the rule of the international' and as 'Jewish poison' should have proved so effective a medium of communication across frontiers as to necessitate massive intervention by the security forces of numerous totalitarian regimes. And, should outlive them all one by one."

It should be noted that people are often attracted to the Esperanto movement for ideological rather than practical reasons but leave for the same reason; they conclude that an international language is not attainable. As Broadrib (1970:4) notes, "It is a striking fact that although within the past 25 years well over a million persons have formally studied Esperanto in school classes and in clubs, the actual number of Esperantists known to be active seems not to have risen at all. The number of active Esperantists—taking this to mean actual speakers of the language who are members of Esperanto groups or regularly purchase literature and take part in the movement—is in the neighborhood of 50,000, a figure which has remained fairly constant for nearly fifty years now."

Discussion questions

1. What is a language variety? What are the principal language varieties in use in your community?
2. What is a standard language? Do you feel that this is a valid concept? Is there one or many standards in this country?
3. Watch the evening network news on several different TV channels. Can you observe any regional features in the announcers' speech?
4. How does the sociolinguistic concept of "dialect" differ from the popular one?
5. Describe the different styles of speech you use and the situations in which you use them.
6. Discuss the ephemeral nature of slang. What expressions are on the way in and what expressions are on the way out in "your dialect"?
7. Do you know any speakers from the West Indies, Haiti, Hawaii, the South Pacific, West Africa, etc., where creoles are spoken? Ask them about the language varieties in use in their home communities.
8. Interview a foreign student about his difficulties with English when he first came to this country.
9. Under what kinds of social circumstances do pidgins and creoles arise? What social forces promote decreolization? Discuss the evolution of Black English in this framework.
10. What are the purposes of artificially constructed international languages? What has been the degree of their success in the past, and what appears to be the outlook for the future?

7

Multilingualism and the language community

7.1 Multilingualism

One of the most widespread and most interesting of all sociolinguistic phenomena is multilingualism. In many societies of the world, we find large numbers of people who speak more than one language. Generally, those who speak two languages are called bilingual, although there is no reason why the term multilingual cannot be applied to all persons speaking more than one language. It is a moot point whether there is a qualitative rather than a mere quantitative difference between the speakers of two languages and those who speak more than two.

It is rare to find an individual in any society who speaks more than one language with native-like fluency. Halliday (1968:140) calls such a speaker, who has completely mastered two languages and makes use of both in all situations, *ambilingual.* Most bilingual people restrict one of their languages to certain uses. One tends to predominate. Halliday furthermore considers any language learned by a child before school age as a native language, so it is possible to have more than one native language. An interesting fact is that native bilinguals, including ambilinguals, ordinarily cannot translate between their native languages, although they can learn to do so.

Since almost all bilingualism is asymmetrical, the question can be raised: How asymmetrical can a person's control of two languages be, such that we can still classify the person as bilingual? There is no unanimous agreement among scholars on this issue, although perhaps the most widely accepted definition of a bilingual is a person who can produce spontaneous meaningful utterances in two languages. Such a minimal definition may appear to be too generous in classifying persons as bilingual, but it is a sociolinguistically relevant one. Any case where there is a person producing spontaneous meaningful utterances in more than one language, there is potentially a sociologically interesting situation. It is not merely a linguistic phenomenon but generally involves interaction between different categories of people, that is, some sort of cross-cultural communication.

The compound-coordinate distinction is considered by many to be of significance. The distinction has been most clearly described by Macnamara (1967a:64): "Compound bilinguals are those who attribute identical meanings to corresponding words and expressions in their two languages. The fusion of meaning systems is said to result from their having learned both languages in the same context (e.g. a bilingual home), or one language through the medium of the other (the so-called indirect method). Coordinate bilinguals, on the other hand, are defined as those who derive different or partially different meanings from corresponding words and expressions in their two languages. The distinction in the coordinates' meaning system is said to arise because they acquired their languages in different contexts." This distinction is probably best understood as a continuum rather than a dichotomy.

One linguistic problem of the bilingual is keeping the two languages apart; most bilinguals do not succeed. To the extent that he does, and this is more likely to happen in the case of the coordinate bilingual, he is in a sense two separate speakers in one person. Inability to keep the two languages separate results in what is often referred to as *linguistic interference,* defined as "deviations from the norm of either language which occur in the speech of bilinguals as a result of their familiarity with more than one language" (Weinreich 1953:1). Specific kinds of interference are often referred to as "foreign accent," "language mixture," "unidiomatic expressions," "borrowings," etc. These phenomena may or may not be deliberate and may range from a slip of the tongue or a personal habit to a usage of the whole community.

The skills involved in bilingualism are production or encoding skills (speaking and writing) and reception or decoding skills (listening and reading). In each of these four skills, we can distinguish the phonological, lexical, syntactic, and semantic aspects. In other words, there is a total of sixteen dimensions along which skill can vary from complete fluency to minimal command. Thus, a person might have good syntactic control over the second language, but his phonology may be defective. He may speak one language very well but be illiterate in that language, or conversely be literate in a second language but virtually be unable to speak it. A person may also be perfectly able to understand a language but be unable to speak it. Macnamara (1967a) considers bilingual any person who "possesses at least one of the language skills even to a minimal degree in their second language." He would approach the description of bilingualism from the individual perspective in terms of how well the individual knows the languages he uses; what he uses his languages for; the extent to which he alternates between languages; when and how, as well as how well, he keeps the languages apart.

It sometimes happens that an individual, through extensive training in a second language, gains a proficiency in it which exceeds that of his mother tongue. In that case, perhaps it is more useful to speak of primary and secondary languages. Sometimes a secondary language is learned first. Among the Chontal Indians of Mexico, children are taught Spanish first and learn Chontal when, as adolescents, they enter the cultural life of the adult community (Waterhouse 1949). This is despite the fact that the nearest Spanish-speaking villages are two or three days away by horseback trails. Chontal seems to be a part of the adult culture, but the people are motivated to learn Spanish by the presence of the school. Parents want their children to do well in school and fear that knowledge of Chontal will impede the child's progress. Adults forbid the child to use Chontal and address him only in Spanish, although they prefer to use Chontal among themselves.

Some European scholars make a distinction between "local" and "cultural" (or "artificial") biligualism. Local refers to bilingualism that arises under natural circumstances in the family, in the playground, or during the first years at school. Cultural bilingualism characterizes the educated classes in many countries, although in some cases it is limited to reading knowledge in one language only.

As we consider bilingualism as a characteristic of societies, we look at the relative numbers and types of bilingual speakers. Most of the nations of the world are multiethnic and, hence, also multilingual. Bilingualism can result from migration, a wide gap between vernacular and standard versions of the same language, or from the revival and expansion of languages not spoken for centuries or used on a restricted basis, such as Hebrew in Israel or Swahili in Tanzania. In some of the new countries which have extreme ethnic diversity, former colonial languages have been adopted as national or auxiliary languages, so that, as a result, numerous new bilinguals have been created. Unfortunately, many large bilingual populations are being forced to function in their weaker language, a further burden on the decolonized nations. As Mackey (1967:19–20) puts it, "More and more people are tending to be bilingual through the necessity of becoming polysocial; that is, belonging to one group for one thing and to another for another."

Bilingualism inevitably results from the coming into contact of people with different cultures and different languages. Under such conditions, it is likely that more speakers from one of the speech groups become bilinguals than from the other. Socially based bilingualism is rarely symmetrical. There is actually no reason for a completely bilingual community, for a closed community in which everyone is fluent in two languages could get along just as well with one.

Given that a person is bilingual, on what basis does he decide to use one language rather than another in a given situation? Asked more broadly, in a particular community, what social forces impinging on the communication process are likely to encourage the use of one language rather than another in certain specific types of situations? Clearly, choices have to be made, as one cannot speak two languages simultaneously, though one can alternate languages in a single stream of discourse. The decision is not made by the individual alone, for there is sociocultural allocation of situations for the use of particular languages. In this connection, we make use of the concept of *domains* which refers to "the large institutional role-contexts within which habitual language use occurs in multilingual settings" (Greenfield and Fishman 1972:65). They can be considered social situations at the level of face-to-face interaction which involve language appropriate to certain places, role-relationships, and topics. In complex multilingual societies, the relevant domains would include family, friendship, religion, education, work, and government. For example, a bilingual Mexican American might use Spanish with family and friends, as well as at church, but use English at school, on the job, and in dealing with local government officials.

In some societies we find bilingualism without diglossia (see section 7.3). That is, there is a bilingual population, but no societal allocation of functions to the two languages. Such situations tend to be transitory in terms of the linguistic repertoire of the community. There has been, in these cases, massive dislocation of population associated with immigration and industrialization. The linguistic repertoire becomes less compartmentalized as the language of work and school come to be used in the home. A natural result is linguistic interference, such that the immigrants' speech may be ridiculed at the same time that their standard variety is given no official support (Fishman 1972b:104–105). Sedentary populations are much better able to resist the onslaught of foreign-inspired domination, as in the case of linguistic minorities in Europe.

Where linguistic minorities are large, their languages may be recognized as official languages, as in Canada, Finland, or Yugoslavia, or if the minorities are very small, a certain amount of local autonomy may be granted; or their linguistic rights may be unrecognized (see section 11.2). In these cases, members of the linguistic minority ordinarily are then forced to be bilingual. On the other hand, if they had their own nation state, they would not be forced to be bilingual. Minority groups sometimes use this as an argument for political independence. Therefore, national governments may seek to eliminate linguistic foci for political discontent by suppressing or at least discouraging the use of minority languages.

There is wide variation in patterns of language division in multilingual societies, for example, in the number and relative size of language groups, the degree of relatedness among languages and between standard languages and dialects, including the relevant literary traditions, the relation of language divisions to other societal divisions, and the degree of importance attributed to the language factor by each of the speech communities. There are several broad patterns: For example, in Indonesia, there is a number of closely related languages, one of which, Bahasa Indonesia, has the status of a lingua franca. In Morocco, there exists a number of languages, not closely related, of which only one, classical Arabic, has a long literary tradition. In much of tropical Africa, a country may have a number of unrelated languages, no one of which can claim a long literary tradition. In India, Pakistan, Sri Lanka, and Malaysia, there exists in each country a variety of languages, each with its own substantial literary tradition.

Where linguistic minorities enjoy substantial political power, they may be able to have the state provide bilingual education at public expense. Bilingual education programs vary widely in purpose, scope, method, and results (see sections 9.4 and 11.2). Thus, for example, bilingual education in Canada concerns primarily the acquisition by speakers of one of the official languages (English or French) of the other official language. In the United States, on the other hand, bilingualism is regarded not as the province of the elite but primarily of the poor, dispossessed, and disadvantaged Chicanos, Puerto Ricans, and American

Indians. Mackey's (1972a) study of the John F. Kennedy Schule in Berlin is a study of a program for elite students. A major finding is that students from fortunate home backgrounds in a favorable educational setting do not suffer from doing their school work in a foreign language. On the other hand, the results of the bilingual education of poverty-level Chicano children in the southwestern United States are somewhat inconclusive. What *is* clear is that many so-called bilingual programs are not geared to the maintenance of Spanish but rather to its use as a transition to English and monolingual education. Furthermore, many Chicano children do their schoolwork in their weaker language, whether English or Spanish, and the effects of this are not fully known. It should be noted that it is the younger, English-speaking, better educated, and more articulate Chicanos who have been the most forceful in demanding bilingual education programs. Their work has been made considerably easier by the Lau decision, which makes it mandatory for school districts to provide special education programs for children who do not speak English.

Two of the most widely discussed topics in bilingualism are choice of language and code switching. (Concerning the latter, see sections 5.5 and 9.3). An interesting example of language choice concerns Paraguayans, almost all of whom are bilingual in Spanish and Guaraní, the local Indian language. Among these people, Guaraní is the language of intimacy, indicating solidarity or identity with the person spoken to, whereas Spanish is more likely to be used with mere acquaintances. When Paraguayans are overseas, they tend to use Guaraní with their countrymen, even though they may have used more Spanish back in Paraguay. Formal relationships or topics are more likely to require Spanish. Guaraní dominates the rural areas, while the capital city Asunción is more bilingual. Jokes are told in Guaraní and anger expressed in the first language learned (Rubin 1968:523).

7.2 Second language learning

It is not entirely clear whether different processes are involved in first and second language learning (see section 4.3). The easily observed difference between the ease of childhood language learning and the difficulty of adult language learning is oft-cited evidence that there is indeed a difference, due possibly to some physiological or psychological ability lost by the adult. Since he has already acquired a linguistic system which, to him, embodies logic and good sense, the adult may be resistant to learning a new system of thinking. He has to process the new system through his old system, and the two may be far from congruent, hence the first is modified to fit the second. In other words, there occurs a tendency to transfer semantic, lexical, morphological, syntactic, or phonological features from one language to another (usually from the more familiar to the less familiar language).

The social contexts in which the two types of language learning take place are different from each other, as indicated above. The first language is learned in the everyday, ordinary setting of family living. The second language is typically learned in a more formal setting, characterized by secondary-group relations, frequently a school of some sort. Likewise, learning of the second language, whether in a formal or informal setting, more often than not involves contact and interaction with members of a different ethnic group.

It has been hypothesized that the nature of the relationship between the two ethnic groups (their relative numbers, power, etc.) and such factors as whether the learner is living in his own society or in one to which he has migrated will have an effect on the numbers of persons who, in fact, learn the second language, how well, and what attitudes they develop toward it. Especially significant in this regard seem to be the attitudes held toward the people whose language one is to learn. Presumably the more favorable the attitude, the more easily and fluently the second language will be learned.

The theory of second-language learning, developed by Lambert and his colleagues over the past decade and a half, maintains that the successful learner must be psychologically prepared to adopt various aspects of behavior of the other linguistic-cultural group. Ethnocentric attitudes impede learning. Lambert distinguishes between two different sets of motivation: *instrumental,* where the purposes of language study reflect utilitarian values, such as getting ahead in one's occupation; and *integrative,* where the student is interested in the other community in an openminded way. Perhaps he even wishes to be accepted as a member of that community, that is, the other group may become a membership group as well as a reference group, as his proficiency in the language increases. As Gardner and Lambert (1972:3) note, "Depending on how he makes his adjustment to the two cultures, he may experience feelings of chagrin or regret as he loses ties in one group, mixed with the fearful anticipation of entering a new and somewhat strange group. Thus, feelings of social uncertainty or dissatisfaction which often characterize the immigrant and the bilingual may also, we believe, affect the serious student of a second language." In a study of English-speaking students in Montreal, students with an integrative attitude were more successful in learning French than those who were instrumentally oriented. This orientation is probably developed within the family; that is, students with an integrative disposition had parents who were sympathetic to the French community and who themselves had integrative attitudes. On the other hand students may resent another group whose language they are compelled to learn through social or economic pressure.

Macnamara (1973:36–40) argues, on the other hand, that favorable attitudes are of only minor importance to success in language learning and that an integrative attitude is not necessarily more likely to lead to success than an instrumental one. He points out that conquered people have frequently learned the language of their conquerors, despite unfavorable attitudes toward them. Note, for example, the almost complete displacement of Irish by English. Macnamara further comments on the differences between first and second language learning, in that in the school the child sees language as a tool for communicating. The teacher, on the other hand, believes that language is to be respected and caressed for its own sake, with all due attention to the fine points of pronunciation and grammar, and pounces on all departures from perfection. Furthermore, school children are usually required to speak in full sentences in an unnatural manner. By way of contrast, when the child was learning his first language or dialect, the mother accepted everything the child said which was both true and mannerly, not bothering to correct his pronunciation or grammar until he was about five, by which time he had almost mastered his language.

Specialists in the field are convinced that second language learning is faster, more complete, and leads to greater retention if it takes place in informal, unplanned imitation and use in actual communication situations than if it is learned by formal study in a school or other special educational situations (Ferguson 1971:68).

Students who have learned a foreign language in school, even if they have learned it well, frequently find that they have difficulty in finding native speakers who are willing to speak the language with them when they travel abroad in search of practice. Their attempts to practice the language may be met with barely intelligible replies in English. The foreigner may have failed to learn how different language varieties are used in the country he is visiting. There may also be severe social barriers to interpersonal friendships, which means that the foreigner will not be able to practice the language or variety used within such intimate groups. Gumperz (1971:184–185) notes that, for example, "The Indian's persistent attempts to use English in interaction with Westerners serves as a boundary maintenance device marking the social differences. This can be overcome only after long periods of close contact." The best place to practice would be in the bazaar, characterized by impersonal transactions, or with monolingual villagers.

7.3 Polyglossia

A phenomenon related to bilingualism and often confused with it is the situation called *diglossia,* the use of two different languages or language varieties, a "high" formal, official one, and a "low" informal, colloquial one, in separate spheres of a given society or community. The original definition is that of Ferguson: "Diglossia is a relatively stable language situation in which, in addition to the primary dialects of the language (which may include a standard or regional standards), there is a very divergent, highly codified (often grammatically more complex) superposed variety, the vehicle of a large and respected body of written literature, either of an earlier period or another speech community, which is learned largely by formal education and is used for most written and formal spoken purposes, but is not used by any sector of the community for ordinary conversation." The defining languages are French/French Creole in Haiti, Katharevousa/Dhimotiki in Greece, German/Schwyzertütsch in Switzerland, and classical/colloquial Arabic in the Arab countries. Each of these situations has arisen out of different historical circumstances. The Arabic and Greek situations go back many centuries. Classical Arabic is fundamentally the language of the Koran, some thirteen centuries old, while Katharevousa is a largely artificial language which attempts to resuscitate various aspects of ancient

Greek, as well as "purify" the language of foreign words. Dhimotiki is ordinary, spoken Greek; Schwytzertütsch is the Swiss-German dialect of which its speakers are extremely proud. The Swiss situation developed as a result of isolation from the centers of German linguistic standardization. Haitian Creole arose from a creolization of a pidgin French, standard French subsequently being superposed.

The "high" formal variety (H) and the "low" colloquial one (L) have specialized functions, such that only H is appropriate in one situation and in another only L, with very slight overlapping between the two sets. Thus, H would be used in a sermon, personal letter, political speech, university lecture, or news broadcast, while L would be used in instructions to subordinates, conversation with family or friends, or in a radio or television soap opera. It is exceedingly important in these societies to use the right variety in the right situation. Speakers characteristically have a particular set of beliefs concerning H, namely that somehow it is more beautiful, more logical, and better able to express important thoughts and the like. These beliefs are widespread, even among those with little or no mastery of H.

Objectively considered, H is more standardized and, in most cases, grammatically more complex. Furthermore, according to Ferguson, "A striking feature of diglossia is the existence of many paired items, one H and one L referring to fairly common concepts frequently used in both H and L where the range of meaning is roughly the same, and the use of one or the other immediately stamps the utterance or written sequence as H or L." Thus, for example, in a Greek restaurant "wine" would appear on the menu as /inos/ (H), but the customer would ask the waiter for /krasi/, the Dhimotiki (L) word.

H is normally learned through formal education, and in the case of the classical administrative and liturgical languages—such as Latin, Sanskrit, and Arabic—the elaborate ritual and etiquette that surround their use could be learned only through many years of special training. Only a privileged few could afford the private tutors who were the only source of instruction. Thus, small elites tended to maintain guild-like control over their linguistic skills.

Diglossia differs from other situations involving functional differentiation, in that both varieties are used throughout the society, not just in certain social classes and ethnic groups. However, H is never used for ordinary conversation, and L may be standardized to varying degrees. As in other cases of functional differentiation, diglossia may also be the focus of ideological and political struggles. Thus, in Greece, for example, liberals have historically favored Dhimotiki (L) and conservatives Katharevousa (H), and changes in government have been reflected in changes in the official status of the two varieties. Thus, in the 1960s Dhimotiki was made the language of the schools by a liberal government, only to be replaced by Katharevousa with the military dictatorship in 1967 and reinstated in 1975 with the restoration of constitutional government. The problem had been, in any case, an artificial one because Katharevousa was artificially constructed from archaic forms and had never been a living language. There was never any benefit to be obtained by acquiring Katharevousa, as there is, for example, in acquiring standard German in Switzerland, as it was not used outside of Greece itself. Its imposition was long a form of class oppression (see especially Petrounias 1970, 1978).

Because H and L varieties are functionally separated, there is ordinarily no conflict between the behavior, attitudes, and values associated with one variety and those associated with the other. Each set is accepted as culturally legitimate. Values related to "L" are usually intimacy, solidarity, spontaneity, and informality, while the cluster related to "H" usually emphasizes status differences, ritual, and formality. The appropriate variety is used in the appropriate domain; L in domains such as family and friendship, while H is used in education, occupation, and religion. In ambiguous situations, interlocutors struggle to identify the domain, redefine the situation, and thus use the appropriate variety (Greenfield and Fishman 1972:65–66) (cf. discussion on code-switching in section 5.5).

It has been suggested that the concept of diglossia should be extended beyond the H-L dichotomous situations to characterize societies that utilize any kind of functionally differentiated language varieties, including separate languages, dialects, or registers. Thus, the term *polyglossia* may be more appropriate.

As a consequence of growing modernization and social complexity, the number of societies characterized by polyglossia or functionally differentiated varieties has greatly increased. Polyglossia and multilingualism may or may not occur or co-occur. Only the smallest and most isolated and least internally differentiated societies manifest neither, but such societies are rare. In some cases, masses and elite form a single society but two separate speech communities, in which case there is diglossia without bilingualism. Such societies are generally economically underdeveloped. As they begin to modernize and industrialize, they encounter very serious language problems. Bilingualism without diglossia stems mainly from the dislocation of populations, especially through immigration. The existence of separate languages without societally allocated functions tends to be a transitory phenomenon, that is, either functions are allocated, or linguistic assimilation is accomplished.

Although there are few nations that are really both bilingual and diglossic, major regions or social classes within a society may manifest both phenomena, for example, urban Paraguay (Spanish/Guaraní), Swiss-Germans (Standard German/Schwyzertütsch), pre-World War I Eastern European Jewish males (Yiddish/Polish, for example). Such situations involve role compartmentalizations, as well as functional allocation of linguistic varieties.

Fishman (1972b:91–106) has differentiated between stable bilingual societies with diglossia and unstable bilingual societies. In stable bilingual societies, languages tend to be reserved for different domains of life in the community, e.g. French and English in Canada; whereas in unstable bilingual societies without diglossia, the domain separation in language use disappears, and both languages come to be used alternatively, especially in the family and friendship domains. Take the case of Mexican Americans in the United States, where Spanish-English bilingualism along with code-mixing and code-switching, rather than Spanish alone, are now predominantly used in the home. On the other hand, with the spread of bilingual education, more and more Chicanos are encountering a bilingual situation in the school as well.

7.4 Speech communities

According to Fishman (1972b:22): "A speech community is one, all of whose members share at least a single speech variety and the norms for its appropriate use." The speech community ordinarily possesses a verbal repertoire more extensive than the verbal repertoire of any of its subgroups, while the subgroups have a wider verbal repertoire than any of their individual members. Of special concern from a sociolinguistic point of view is the totality of language varieties shared by members of a community, that is, its linguistic repertoire. We are interested in the presence or absence of polyglossia, the extent of multilingual-ism, multidialectism, etc. Different types of communities, nomadic, rural, tradi-tional urban, industrialized urban, etc. have different patterns in this regard. Each may form a speech community, which has its own rules for the conduct and interpretation of speech, and rules for the interpretation of at least one linguistic variety (Hymes 1972d:54). Interpretative rules enable the speaker-hearer to know what counts as a coherent sentence, request, statement requiring an answer, requisite or forbidden topics, marking of emphasis or irony, normal duration of silence, and normal level of voice, etc.

Gumperz (1968:466) has presented a description of the major types of speech communities. In the simplest, technologically least advanced communi-ties, such as those of hunters and gatherers, social interaction is limited to face-to-face communication, social stratification is minimal, and contacts with outsiders are relatively infrequent. There is some differentiation between casual, everyday speech and styles used in ritually defined situations, such as, for example, religious ceremonies or myth recital. Larger, more economically developed tribal communities may maintain some trade relations with other communities, and thus a measure of bilingualism develops, particularly in market towns. Pidgins will sometimes result from contact between an economically advanced society and a tribal group (see section 6.4). As economic development produces economic stratification, community bilingualism, speech stratification, or major stylistic variations may appear, as is true of most of the world today. Maximum internal linguistic diversity is characteristic of societies of an intermediate level of complexity, with peasant, herder, or tribal groups integrated in various degrees into the socially dominant groups, as for example in Indian caste society. In such societies, people may show language loyalty to varieties distinct from the vernacular, such as, for example, Latin in medieval Europe or Sanskrit and Persian in medieval India. On the other hand, in highly urbanized, industrialized societies, differences between standard and local dialects are minimized, which is a reflection of the fluidity of roles in a class as opposed to a caste system.

Social heterogeneity and linguistic heterogeneity are co-occuring phenom-ena. Societies which are more internally diversified and stratified tend to have more diversified linguistic repertoires (Fishman 1972b:55–56). Such internal diversity can be maintained in a stable fashion over very long periods of time and has been so particularly in traditional societies. Peoples have lived in close proximity to the same country or city without learning each other's languages to any significant extent, except for middlemen such as merchants or translators who may serve as links between divergent speech communities. In modern urban areas, particularly in Western countries where we also find social class, religious, and ethnic cleavages, the linguistic differences to be found are not between varieties so much (except for incursive immigrant groups) as quantitative variations in certain marginal lexical and phonological forms. Community boundaries may be emphasized by cultivating such variations, as in a situation reported by Labov, (1972g:1–42): Martha's Vineyard is an island off the coast of Massachusetts, which was formerly fairly well isolated from the mainland. In recent years, however, there has been a heavy influx of outsiders during the summer. Natives of the island have resented the economic domination and exploitation of their island by more powerful people from the mainland. Their ancestors had been landowners and ship captains, but there has been a steady downtrend in socioeconomic status. They have reverted to an older and less prestigious speech to identify with the older values. Those who most resent the intrusion of the mainlanders and who identify most closely with the local traditions have been exaggerating what was formerly a low-prestige, old fashioned pronunciation of certain vowels. Exaggeration of this pronunciation seems to serve the function of emphasizing group identity and solidarity and rejection of mainland lifestyles.

7.5 Language attitudes

What is customarily referred to as language attitudes actually encompasses a wide spectrum of attitudes, values, beliefs, and emotions regarding language. Though labelled as such by the sociologist or social psychologist, they are likely to be regarded as some sort of self-evident truth or "natural" feelings by the persons who hold them. The nonrationality, that is, the culturally and experientially conditioned nature of such attitudes, beliefs, emotions, and values is not ordinarily recognized. It is characteristic of such attitudes that they tend to be shared even by those who suffer most from them. That is, a speaker may regard as "incorrect" forms which he himself uses, or look down upon his own language or dialect as unworthy.

Cooper and Fishman (1974:6) consider language attitudes to include attitudes toward a language or toward a feature of a language, toward language use, or toward language as a group symbol. They do not consider that attitudes toward the speakers themselves are language attitudes, although they might be reflected by language attitudes. Research is aimed at discovering the nature, determinants, effects, and measurement of attitudes. Also important is the fact that attitude has served as a variable in many sociolinguistic studies.

Perhaps the most actively researched area of language attitudes has concerned judgments of certain languages or language varieties as better than others, which result in a higher evaluation of those who speak in that fashion. In every community we find attitudes and beliefs about the language of the community, as well as about other languages and language in general. These beliefs may or may not have a basis in objective reality or involve esthetic judgments not subject to empirical verification. Language attitudes are ordinarily conservative, for one must be convinced that changing his attitude toward a particular type of speech will not have repercussions he cannot handle. If change in linguistic behavior is proposed, the speaker must also be convinced that his change will not result in sanctions for violating the rules of the ideological system. This is at the root of much of the opposition to language and language attitude change (Smith 1973b:107–108).

Language attitudes seem to be extremely uniform throughout a speech community. Labov (1971b:248–249) says, "It seems plausible to define a speech community as a group of speakers who share a set of social attitudes toward language." Wolfram (1971:99–100) claims that speakers react to the social differences that the language differences imply. Such reactions are often based on stereotyped notions of linguistic and social differences which may or may not have any factual basis. Listeners are reacting to the supposed personality traits of the identified social categories, rather than the speech characteristics as such (Robinson 1972:95). (On the interrelationships among social evaluation, ethnic identity and language attitudes, see the excellent collections by Giles, ed. 1977 and Giles and St. Clair, eds. 1979.)

Some linguistic stereotypes have names, such as "Brooklynese" (Toity-toid Street), "Bostonian" (Pahk yaw cah in Hahvahd Yahd), "Southern drawl" (Y'all), etc. Some stereotyped features of United States working class speech are widely stigmatized but remarkably resistant and enduring like *dese* and *dose* for "these" and "those." There is a strong tendency for highly stigmatized forms to disappear, and in the last stages of disappearance to serve as a source of ritualized humor. Some people may consciously or unconsciously cultivate certain speech styles in order to be identified with and receive the same treatment as certain groups, or cultivate a style appropriate to a particular role.

Lambert, Tucker, and their associates at McGill University in Montreal have devised a technique for analyzing language attitudes known as the "matched guise" technique. The technique consists of having subjects listen to tape recorded excerpts which include bilingual or bidialectal speakers speaking in both of their languages or varieties. The subjects are asked to make judgments as to characteristics of the speakers without, however, realizing that the speakers recur in matched guises. Since the set of speakers for both languages or dialects is the same, any attitudinal differences found between the two sets of recorded excerpts must stem from attitudes toward the language variety and its speakers rather than the speakers actually heard. Thus, for example, lower class speakers are perceived as less intelligent or confident, although not less kind or good-natured (Fremder and Lambert 1973:244–245).

Several important findings have arisen from this work, such as the fact that subjective evaluations of social dialects or foreign languages are quite uniform throughout a speech community. These norms are acquired in early adolescence. Labov (1972g:310–311) has found a further important principle, namely that those speakers who use the highest degree of a stigmatized feature in their own natural speech show the greatest tendency to stigmatize others for their use of this form. It is important to recognize that very few speakers realize they are using these stigmatized forms. As Labov (1972d:533) notes, "They hear themselves as using the prestige forms which occur sporadically in their careful speech and in their reading of isolated word lists. Secondly, the subjective responses tapped by our tests are only the overt values—those which conform to the value systems of the dominant middle-class group. There are surely other values, at a deeper level of consciousness, which reinforce the vernacular speech forms. . . ." Labov (1971a:62) suggests what these values may be in a school situation: "There seems to be some permanent source of support for the nonstandard forms which leads many gifted speakers to prefer them. We are led to suspect the existence of covert values which do not normally appear in test situations. . . . The message that seems to be coming across to students can be paraphrased in this way: 'Don't talk like those big boys in the back of the room who beat up on kids and take their lunch money away; you should talk instead like the kids who sit up in the front of the room, get beat up, and have their lunch money taken away.' "

Some people have very strong attitudes about their language. For example, in general, Arabs believe that Arabic is the most perfect of all languages since God chose it as the medium through which to reveal the Koran. It is thought to be extremely rich in vocabulary as a result of its extensive "logical" derivation system, but Arabs may get defensive if you point out the chaotic nature of Arabic plurals, for example. Each believes his own dialect is closest to the classical (Ferguson 1968b). In eliciting responses to Ferguson's question "What Arabic is best?", Nader (1968:279) found that the answer depended partly on the informant's origin, for example, a person from Damascus visiting in Beirut would defend his dialect as the best, but in Damascus, he would say that the Bedouin dialect was best. No informant suggested that the dialect of some other town was best.

One hypothesis which has been suggested is that mutual intelligibility of closely related language varieties depends heavily on attitudes toward speakers of the other variety. Thus, for example, Russians and Serbs understand Slovaks better than the Czechs do, although the phonological and syntactic patterns of Czech and Slovak differ less than each does from Serbo-Croatian or Russian. It has been noted that as soon as members of a certain community in Nigeria recognized a related hinterland dialect, they refused to understand it. But some communities will make a great effort to understand despite great differences (Hymes 1973:65).

Acquisition of language attitudes is part of the process of linguistic socialization. Many preschool children have remarkably consistent notions on what is "correct" and "not correct" in language and can even make accurate judgments about the ethnicity of a speaker from speech alone. The prestige which various languages have in the schools is an interesting question. It seems rather certain that a language tends to have low prestige in areas where there are large numbers of native speakers of that language. Thus, Spanish has more prestige in Iowa than it does in Texas, and Navaho is much more highly regarded at the University of California, Los Angeles, than it is in Arizona. Some languages have had prestige because of certain supposed virtues they inculcated in the minds of those who studied them. Thus, Latin allegedly gave one a better grasp of English grammar, which was perceived as based on Latin, as well as providing a useful knowledge of the large English vocabulary based on Latin roots. French supposedly trained one in logic and supplied the student with instant culture. All languages, further- more, were deemed to give insight into a foreign culture which was quite impossible to get without a knowledge of its language. This last claim on the surface, at least, seems to have some validity. The claim has been made also that knowledge of another language gives one insight into a different way of thinking. What makes these claims less relevant, however, is that the languages most commonly studied in the United States have structures very similar to English and reflect cultures of the same general variety as American culture. A much stronger case could be made for Navaho, Japanese, Swahili, Chinese, Hebrew, Turkish, or even Russian, as mind-stretchers than for Spanish, French or German. Nevertheless, educators will urge and students will respond to the study of foreign languages for reasons quite alien to their supposed virtues. Thus, while throughout the world French is studied largely as a result of its prestige in earlier days and as a result of strenuous efforts by the French government to promote the teaching of French abroad, the great extent of English study abroad is a direct reflection of the enormous political, military, and economic power of the United States. No doubt as power relations change throughout the world, these will be reflected in the attitudes toward and the teaching of foreign languages.

Discussion questions

1. What is meant by bilingualism? How does it differ from diglossia? To what extent are these phenomena found in your community?
2. Are there any linguistic minorities in the city where you live? What language rights, if any, do they enjoy?
3. What foreign languages are taught at your university? Which are the most popular, and why?
4. Which foreign languages have the highest status in your university? Why do you feel this is so?
5. Would you describe the speech community to which you belong as homoge- neous or heterogeneous? Discuss why you think so.
6. Describe some of the commonly held language attitudes of the persons best known to you. How do you feel these attitudes originated?
7. Ask some of your friends or family members to describe the "worst" and the "best" speakers they know. What is the class and ethnic background of these speakers? Do these language attitudes appear to be a reflection of their attitudes toward the groups to which the speakers belong?

8

Language
and social inequalities

One of the most pervasive of all sociocultural universals is social stratification, that is, the unequal social distribution of prestige, power, wealth, and privilege. This involves also the ranking of persons and groups along various dimensions of stratification (education, income, occupation, etc.), as well as the identification of ranked categories, such as social classes, ethnic groups, castes, or estates. The social scientist is interested in how such social inequalities come into being, are maintained, changed, and how they affect and are affected by other social variables.

In other words, it is patent that in all societies there are persons who are more powerful than others, that is, who are able to command goods and services and deference from others with or without their consent. Likewise, some persons or families are wealthier than others, while still others have more prestige and respect than others. The wealthier and more prestigeful are also likely to be the more powerful, although these variables are by no means always perfectly correlated.

Linguistic inequality and social inequality are closely related. Christian (1972) has expressed the matter succinctly: "The ideal of linguistic democracy, in which the speech of every citizen is regarded with equal respect by all others, is perhaps the most unrealistic of all social ideals. Speech is one of the most effective instruments in existence for maintaining a given social order involving social relationships, including economic as well as prestige hierarchies."

Both language varieties and linguistic variables may be ranked. Socially diagnostic linguistic variables are those whose distribution differs on the basis of social rank. Stratification may be either *sharp* or it may be *gradient*, in which case there is a progressive increase in the frequency of occurrence of a variant in various social groups. Some variants may be socially *prestigious*, that is, they have been adopted by a high status group (e.g. "*To whom* would you like to speak") or they may be *stigmatized* variants, those features associated with low status groups (e.g. "Don't you have no more grapes left!").

Persons ranking higher on any of the dimensions of stratification, as compared with those ranking lower, not only generally speak differently (usually socially evaluated as "more correctly") but are also spoken of and addressed in a different fashion. The dimensions of stratification which appear to be the most sociolinguistically relevant are sex, age, socioeconomic status, and ethnicity. The role of language in supporting inequality based on these factors bears close examination. We do not speak to everyone in the same fashion; how we speak depends considerably on the identity of the person spoken to or about. An exceptional case, however, is that of Nootka, an American Indian language in which separate linguistic forms are used in speaking to or about children, fat people, dwarfed people, and hunchbacks (Sapir 1915). More usual are variations in men's and women's speech, and those based on socioeconomic differences.

8.1 Age

It is apparent to even the most casual observer that there are differences among the ways people of various age categories speak. In the popular mind, children's speech may be characterized as "childish" (in phonology, syntax, and lexicon as well), that of adolescents as "brash" or "vulgar," and that of the elderly as "old-fashioned." Such labels are, of course, only reflections of the attitudes of the labelers, although they may be related to real linguistic differences. Some of these differences are obvious and apparent, while others are much more subtle. The differences most easily noted by the layman are likely to be lexical in nature: the child uses "baby" words, for example, *bunny* rather than *rabbit* or *potty* rather than *toilet*; the adolescent attempts to use fresh slang, *that's cool* rather than *O.K.* (This observation will, no doubt, be long out of date by the time this reaches print.) The elderly tend to use words or expressions no longer in current use among the remainder of the population.

Persons in various age categories are referred to and addressed in different ways. Much as the kinship categories established in different societies are conventional as far as the degree of actual blood relationship is concerned, so recognized age categories are also somewhat arbitrary. We find cross-cultural differences, as well as historical changes, in this regard. For example, who is to be called a "child" or a "boy" or "girl" has varied widely from society to society and from one historical period to another. Such terminology is rarely accurate, and changes in terminology generally reflect changes in attitude, as well as age span covered. For example, witness the change in the last generation from "adolescent" to "teenager" to "young adult," not to speak of the coming and going of such semiderogatory terms as "bobby soxer" or "teeny bopper." Or witness the recent emergence of the term "senior citizen," which may be a euphemism.

Forms of address are indicative of social status, and those utilized with reference to age categories form no exception. In American society, perhaps in all societies, formality or politeness of address is typically correlated with the age of the addressee. Words are available to indicate objective age or to assign (for either flattering or derogatory purposes) a younger or older age. Thus, in Mexican

Spanish, for example, the term *joven* (young man or woman) is applied to an adolescent or young adult in perfectly neutral fashion (the "unmarked" usage), but to a child (who otherwise would be addressed as *niño*(a) or *muchacho*(a) in a flattering manner; whereas, used to address an adult (otherwise addressed as *señor, señora* or *señorita*), it could be interpreted either as deflating, derogatory, flattering, or jocular, depending on the circumstances. Such matters are primarily concerned with social identity and stratification.

One observation that goes back to the nineteenth century is that, even within the confines of one family, either noticeable or subtle evidence of ongoing linguistic change can be detected. Thus, for example, if in a particular speech community a certain vowel is, over time, being pronounced higher and higher, it may be possible, with the aid of the sound spectrograph to detect a rise in pronunciation from grandparents' to parents' or children's speech. In southern California, the pronunciation of *chair*, for example, has been changing over two generations to something almost homonymous with *cheer*; for many young people there, *Don* is homonymous with *dawn* and *hock* with *hawk*. Usually differences are more subtle than this; many age-graded differences in speech are below the level of consciousness of average speakers.

8.2 Sex

On the assumption that any social differences are bound to be reflected in linguistic ones, it comes as no surprise to note that language spoken by and about women is different from that spoken by and about men. The point has become even more interesting under the influence of the women's liberation movement. There are a number of subtle points connected with women's speech, where the differences apparently serve to maintain the generally inferior position which women occupy in virtually all societies.

There is considerable evidence that, although men speak more, females are superior speakers. Girls do better than boys in language skills in the early years of schooling. In the United States, some 75 to 85 percent of the children who have reading problems or who are in remedial classes are boys. The latter also stutter more than girls. On the other hand, in societies with high illiteracy rates, it is most often the women who are illiterate. In bilingual societies, it is most often the men who are bilingual (Key 1975a).

Differences between men's and women's speech may range from differences in pronunciation and grammar, which are scarcely noticed except by linguists, to obvious differences systematically taught to children. Since there are few barriers to communication between the sexes, differences between women's and men's speech must be accounted for on a different basis. Women's speech is frequently more conservative and evaluated as better than men's speech. This is contrary to usual stratification patterns, where the *more* powerful are believed to speak more correctly.

Actually, some studies show women to be linguistically innovative; others show them to be linguistically conservative. This apparent contradiction results from linguists failing to realize that women's role in language needs to be linked to the social position of women in the communities studied and to the related question of what women want to express about themselves in speech, as Gal (1978) has indicated. She has demonstrated that bilingual Hungarian-German speaking women in a town in Austria refuse to use Hungarian, which is symbolic of peasant status. They use German, the language of industrial life, and prefer the easier life of a worker's wife, refusing to marry peasants even though they themselves may be of peasant origin. The bilingual peasants are thus forced to marry monolingual German women from other villages, and their children become monolingual as well. Thus, the bilingual women's attitude toward peasant life is speeding the community's transition from bilingualism to monolingualism.

Anthropological linguists have uncovered a number of instances where, in a given tribe, men and women spoke different languages or different varieties of the same language. In Koasati, an American Indian language, men's and women's speech differ from each other in certain well-defined respects. For example, if the form used by women ends in a nasalized vowel, the men's form substitutes an s for the nasalization. At the time of Haas' study, only the middle-aged and elderly women used the women's forms. The younger women were already using the men's speech. Haas (1964b:229–230) notes that "Members of each sex are quite familiar with both types of speech and can use either as occasion demands. Thus, if a man is telling a tale, he will use women's forms when quoting a female character. . . . Moreover, parents were formerly accustomed to correct the speech of the children of either sex since each child was supposed to use forms appropriate to his or her sex." There are also linguistic sex differences of this type among a number of other American Indian communities and some peoples in northeast Asia.

Both scholars and laypersons have noticed that there are also differences between men's and women's speech in English. Not only this, they have noticed that the linguistic differences are reflections of the difference between the role of women in our society and that of men. What are some of these differences? In careful speech, women use fewer stigmatized forms, that is, socially defined "incorrect" forms than do men (Labov 1972a) and are more sensitive than men to the prestige pattern, particularly lower middle-class women. Labov claims that women are more sensitive than men to overt sociolinguistic values. Because language in this case is a reflection of social role, women are at a disadvantage by speaking "women's language"; but they put themselves in even more of a disadvantage if they try to speak "men's" language.

Women in Western societies at least appear to be more status-conscious and sensitive to the social significance of certain linguistic variables. On the other hand, because of the association of certain working-class values with masculinity, men may value working-class speech as a symbol of masculinity. The wider the difference in sex roles, the greater the difference between the sexes we find in their speech (Trudgill 1974b:93–95).

Robin Lakoff has claimed that language works in two ways to help maintain the social subordination of women, namely, the language of women and language about women. In the first place, she is referring to the fact that women's language differs lexically, syntactically, and phonologically from men's language, that is, they are statistically more likely to use certain forms than others. As an example, she cites the fact that women make finer discriminations of color than do men. Women have a much richer color vocabulary. In other words, while men make the important decisions of the society, women are allowed to make decisions of little importance to the world of work and power, like what color to call a certain garment. Then, women are not supposed to express themselves with forceful expletives, for example, *shit* rather than *oh, dear*. As Lakoff (1975:11) says, "Allowing men stronger means of expression than are open to women further reinforces men's position of strength in the real world; for surely we listen with more attention the more strongly and forcefully someone expresses opinions, and a speaker unable—for whatever reasons—to be forceful in stating his views is much less likely to be taken seriously." Likewise, words such as *adorable, charming, sweet, lovely,* and *divine* are generally considered to be "women's" words, as opposed to the more neutral use of *great, terrific, cool, neat,* and *groovy,* which can be used by either sex. Thus, it is that women are programmed in their language to express themselves in such a manner that their opinions will not be taken seriously by others. They help to perpetuate stereotypes and may even come to think of themselves as indecisive, incompetent, and silly persons.

Lakoff asserts that "tag" questions are more likely to be used by women than by men, for example, "The F.B.I. sure took a long time to catch Patty Hearst, didn't they?". She also says that women are more likely to answer a question with the rising inflection normally associated with a yes-no question. For example, if a husband asks his wife, and she answers:

Q. When do you want to go to the store?
A. Oh . . . about four-thirty?

In other words, in this answer, as in the sentence above with the "tag" questions, uncertainty, hesitancy and dependency are expressed. English-speaking women use more verb auxiliaries (*can, could, shall, would, may, might*) than do men, thus showing more indefiniteness, inconclusiveness, and uncertainty, whereas men's speech appears more definite and authoritative (Key 1975a:75–76).

Crosby and Nyquist (1977) refer to "female register" rather than "women's language." On the basis of three studies, one in an experimental situation, one at an information booth, and one in a police station, they noted that women, in fact, used the female register more than men do, except in the information booth, where perhaps because of the ritualized nature of the interaction, no significant differences were found. They argue that nonassertiveness is the central feature of the female register, with politeness less important. They attribute sex differences in the use of female register to sex differences in roles, rather than to the lower status of women, as Lakoff asserts. They further point out that sexism is harmful to men also because it limits their options of asking nonassertively and politely in situations where nonassertiveness and politeness are most functional.

Dubois and Crouch (1975) question Lakoff's generalizations about women's speech as based on introspection and unsystematic and uncontrolled observation, and present counter examples. Most telling is their study of an actual social situation in which 33 tag questions were used, *none* of them by the women present and only two statements with falling intonation.

Studying a corpus of 587 utterances produced in buying a train ticket in the Netherlands, Brouwer, Gerritsen, and De Haan (1979) could find few significant differences in the number of words used to deal with a set task, diminutives, civilities, or forms of language expressing insecurity (repetitions, hesitations, self-corrections, or requests for information). Another recent study by Edelsky (1979) also cast doubt on the assertion that more women than men use rising intonation when they answer questions to which only they have the answer. The 154 men and 165 women, approached by either a male or female interviewer and asked either where they were born or what their favorite color was, manifested no difference by sex in the use of straight rising intonation, except when women were approached by a female interviewer. Both studies suggest that intuitive studies present problems and that we need to pay more attention to people's *perception* of women's speech.

With reference to language *about* women, Lakoff claims that *lady* is a euphemism, a word to take the place of *broad* or related words, or to avoid the use of the word *woman* which has sexual connotations. Here again, the usage serves to rob women of their dignity and importance. The word *lady* implies politeness and nonimportance, so that a person referred to as a *lady sculptor,* for example, is not likely to be taken seriously while a *woman sculptor* might be, although there is no parallel expression *male sculptor* or *man sculptor.* As Lakoff (1975:23) points out, "We hear of *one-woman shows,* but not *one-lady shows.*"

She also has called our attention to the nonparallel usage of certain pairs of words, the meanings of which are commonly supposed to differ only in the sex of the person, such as *master/mistress, bachelor/spinster* and *widow/widower.* Consider the following sentences:

1. Roger grew tired of his wife and went out looking for a mistress.
2. *Ruby grew tired of her husband and went out looking for a master.
3. *Aisha is a mistress.
4. Hans Holbein is an old master.
5. *Suzy Slagel is an old mistress.
6. Where are all the eligible bachelors?
7. *Where are all the eligible spinsters?
8. Sarah is Samuel's widow.
9. *Alfonso is Laura's widower.

The fact that the asterisked sentences are generally unacceptable indicates that the pair meanings are not parallel at all.

Walum (1977) has pointed out that in practice women are defined in terms of their sexual desirability (to men); men are defined in terms of their sexual prowess (over women), for example, *dog, fox, broad,* and *chick* as contrasted with *dude* or *stud.* Likewise, *He's easy* and *She's easy* mean different things. And while a divorced woman is a *divorcée,* there is no commonly used term in English for a divorced man (except perhaps *swinging bachelor?*). She further notes some originally neutral words for women which have acquired obscene and/or debased connotations, while the corresponding words referring to males have retained their neutral character, for example, *lord/lady, baronet/dame, governor/ governess, master/mistress. Hussy* originally meant "housewife," whereas *broad* originally meant "a young woman" and had no derogatory connotations.

Not only do the words denoting females have certain derogatory connotations not shared by their male counterparts, but females are regarded as the possessions of males. One cannot just be a mistress, one must be somebody's mistress. Contrariwise, while a person might be somebody's widow, one cannot be someone's widower. There is a parallel instance in Spanish. For example, assume Marta Rosales marries Roberto Sánchez and subsequently becomes widowed. Her name while her husband is alive is Señora Marta Rosales de Sánchez, that is, "of Sánchez," but after his death she becomes Marta Rosales Viuda de Sánchez, that is, "widow of Sánchez," whereas neither marriage nor bereavement changes a man's name. (This usage is becoming obsolete.) Likewise in the United States a century or so ago, a widow would be called "Widow Smith," for example, rather than by her own name.

It is often asked whether the presence of grammatical gender in a language (for example, masculine and feminine in Spanish or French, or masculine, feminine, and neuter in Russian, German, or Latin), or the existence of different pronouns by sex (for example, *he* versus *she* or *his* versus *her*) necessarily indicates that the language, and hence the speakers, are more sexist in orientation than in cases where such distinctions are not made.

While gender is a common phenomenon among the world's languages, there are many languages which never had gender. It has been lost in some languages which once possessed it, for example, modern Persian. In other languages, such as English, the gender system has radically changed and lost almost all of its morphological and syntactic manifestations. According to Ibrahim (1973:24), no language which lost its gender system has *ever* reacquired it or anything like it at a later stage of its history.

In languages which have gender, the correspondence between natural and grammatical genders is almost perfect, that is, nearly all nouns that refer to male creatures belong to the class of masculine nouns, and nearly all nouns denoting female beings belong to the feminine class of nouns. Ibrahim (1975:3) claims that grammatical gender did not arise because of any social or psychological factors. The evidence from Semitic and Indo-European languages seems to indicate that gender was an accidental outcome of linguistic development. He rejects the notion that gender originated in primitive man's ascription of animistic sexual qualities to inanimate objects. It is rather a syntactic category related imperfectly to a semantic one, that is, sex. Of course, once gender becomes fixed as a grammatical category in a particular language, it can be used by its speakers for social and psychological purposes.

At times various spokespersons for the women's liberation movement have urged the abolition of "sexist" pronouns and advocated the use of a single set of pronouns for both sexes. Languages such as Chinese, Japanese, Persian, and

Turkish make no distinction in pronouns between the sexes; yet it can hardly be maintained that the societies in which these languages are spoken are necessarily any less sexist than, say, American or British society. The feminists do have a point, however. If doctors and lawyers are consistently referred to as "he" and elementary-school teachers and nurses as "she," there is no doubt that there is a fostering of sexist stereotypes of certain occupations as being either masculine or feminine.

Lakoff (1975) feels that language should be reformed only when it explicitly or implicitly demeans categories of people. Thus, for example, she does not consider pronominal neutralization in English (*he* used to refer to either gender) a serious problem. Consider the following, all of which could be uttered by a teacher without causing great surprise:

1. O.K., everybody hand in his paper now.
2. O.K., everybody hand in her paper now.
3. O.K., everybody hand in his or her paper now.
4. O.K., everybody hand in their paper now.
5. O.K., everybody hand in your paper now.

Number 1 disturbs many feminists, while 2 is proper only in a class consisting entirely of female students; 3 is awkward or clumsy for many speakers, while 4 would be indignantly denounced by Miss Fidditch as a barbarism; 5 is a nice way out of the sexist dilemma, but is it grammatical and/or logical? It is for me, but it is for others to judge whether or not it is preferable to the other forms.

Bodine (1975) interprets the current movement against sex-indefinite *he* as a counterreaction to the attempt by prescriptive grammarians over the past two and one-half centuries to displace singular *they* and *their* from the language. Such usage preceded the rise of English prescriptive grammar and has continued vigorously in the spoken language. In the written language, it was utilized by writers of such stature as John Ruskin, Walter Scott, and Jane Austen. Bodine claims that the effort to stamp out singular *they* was socially motivated. Both singular *they* and sex-indefinite *he* lack agreement with their antecedents by one feature, but gender has social significance, whereas number does not. She quotes sixteenth- and seventeenth-century grammarians who refer to the masculine as the "worthier" gender, an attitude which has not died. She cites a textbook published in 1967 to the effect that children should not use "he or she" which is "awkward" but instead follow the convention that "grammatically men are more important than women." Bodine points out that lack of agreement of number, as in the proscribed singular *they*, is no more "inaccurate" than the disagreement of gender, as in the accepted sex-indefinite *he*. *He or she* is no more "clumsy" than the *one or more* or *person or persons*, which are acceptable to the prescriptivists. (This author has no objection to either *he or she* or singular *they*. I am simply more comfortable with sex-indefinite *he* and have used it throughout this volume, as the careful reader will have observed.)

Somewhat different and perhaps more to the point is the changing of occupational titles to remove designation of sex as when *fireman* is changed to *firefighter* or *chairman* is changed to *chairperson*. Whether changing of nomenclature is likely to improve women's social position is a moot point; that it will improve their self-image is very likely, and the impact on children is likely to be momentous in terms of their aspirations for later life.

While the title *Mr.* is unmarked for marital status, *Miss* indicates a woman who has never married and *Mrs.* a woman who is, or was, married. Therefore, to eliminate this discrepancy in requirement to reveal marital status, many women have adopted *Ms.* in place of either *Miss* or *Mrs.* Lakoff (1975:42) is of the opinion that "Until society changes so that the distinction between married and unmarried women is as unimportant in terms of their social positions as that between married and unmarried men, the attempt in all probability cannot succeed. . . . The attempt to do away with *Miss* and *Mrs.* is doomed to failure if it is not accompanied by a change in society's attitude to what the titles describe."

8.3 Forms of address

Some languages make very elaborate distinctions, depending on the relative rank of the interlocutors. Some of these distinctions are lexical, as when very complimentary terms are applied to the superior person, his possessions and actions, and humble terms to those of the speaker of inferior rank. In other cases, special honorific verb forms are used in reference to the superior person. This honorific function may be carried out in different fashions; in one language lexically, in another morphologically, in still another syntactically. Since forms of address are dependent upon the relative status of the interlocutors, they must be considered in the context of the stratification system of the overall society. In English, for example, a person can potentially be addressed by name, title, kinship term, nickname, or some combination of these, for example: Alexander, Your Honor, Father, Uncle Alexander, Judge Cohen, Alex or Honey.

Precisely which forms will be used on a given occasion depends on that society's sociolinguistic rules, the situation, and the intentions of the speaker. In the simplest of societies, persons are generally addressed and referred to by either kinship term or name, though in some nonliterate societies the person's real name is never used, some substitute name being used in its place. In very complex, highly stratified societies, forms of address likewise may be highly stratified and elaborate, especially if statuses are primarily ascribed rather than achieved. Societies like the modern industrialized ones where most statuses are achieved have relatively simple address systems. On the other hand, in the Ottoman Turkish Empire a very elaborate system was used. Of the Turkish pronouns meaning "you," *sen* was used for children, intimate friends, servants, or pupils, while *siz*, or even politer forms, was used for equals. In addressing a superior, one used *efendim, zatiniz,* or *zati aliniz* (literally "my master," "your person," and "your exalted person," respectively). An even politer term was *hakipayiniz* ("the dust of your feet"), that is, out of humility the speaker addresses the dust of the other person's feet. Superiors were likewise generally addressed and referred to in the third person plural, for example, *zati aliler,* that is, "the excellencies," meaning either "you" or "he." Contrariwise, in polite Ottoman circles, a person never used *ben*, "I" but rather *bendeniz* or *kulunuz*, that is, "your slave" or "your servant" (Hagopian 1907).

In Persian today, in certain situations one uses different verbs in addressing superiors or equals. Thus, for example, in referring to what a person (intimate or inferior) has said, one would ordinarily say:

/če gofti?/ "what did you say," but to an equal or superior
/če farmudid?/, lit. "what did you command?" but conversely to indicate "I
    said . . ." one would use the humble expression
/arz kardam/ . . . lit., "I made the petition . . ."
Similarly special honorific verbs are used for "to be present," "to depart" and "to arrive," viz.
/tašrif daštan/ "to be present" lit. "to have honoring"
/tašrif bordan/ "to depart," lit. "to carry honoring"
/tašrif avardan/ "to arrive," lit. "to bring honoring" (Lambton 1953) These expressions can never refer to oneself.

In Japanese, choice of verb may indicate the status relationship which the speaker desires to express. For example, there are four verbs meaning "to give" as follows:

/sašiageru/: receiver of the action is greatly elevated
/ageru/: receiver of the action is somewhat elevated or equal to the giver
/yaru/: receiver of the action is equal to or somewhat lower than the giver
/kureru/: the action is sharply downgraded, and the meaning is usually
    derogatory (Goldstein and Tamura 1975:24)

The speaker (or a member of the speaker's group when talking to outsiders) may never be the receiver of an action using *sašiageru*. There are also strict rules as to what verb is used depending on the giver. In any case, from the specific verb form used, it is clear what the relative statuses of giver and receiver, speaker and hearer, are, assuming that the speaker is following correct polite usage. The speaker must take into consideration both status (age, sex, socioeconomic position) and group affiliation. In Korean, the form of the verb must indicate whether a person is talking to another person of the same, higher or lower status, and whether this is happening in a comparatively reverential, contemptuous, or indifferent manner (Schlauch 1955:271).

In English, if we wish to show respect, humility, or neutrality, we can use a series of devices, such as intonation, circumlocution, euphemism, idioms, gestures, etc. In English, a distinction was formerly made between an informal *thou* and a formal (originally plural) *you*. The former has dropped out of use except from Quaker speech (actually *thee*) and when addressing the deity. The distinction still survives in a number of European languages which, because they are more highly inflected than English, manifest it also in the form of the verb, for example, French *tu lis* versus *vous lisez*, "you read." The two forms, often referred to as T and V from the shape they take in French, are used similarly in a number of European languages. They are often referred to as the familiar and polite forms.

In many cases the polite form is also used to address more than one person; in fact, this was its former use. For example:

	Familiar	Polite
Spanish	tú	usted
French	tu	vous
German	du	Sie
Russian	ty	Vy
Italian	tu	Lei
Macedonian	ti	vie

For many centuries, these languages followed the rule of nonreciprocal T-V between persons of unequal power (the more powerful person using T and receiving V) and the rule of mutual V or T between persons of roughly equivalent power, with T signifying intimacy and the V formality. In other words, the system was two dimensional, the T-V distinction coming to signify solidarity (the "us" versus "them" distinction) as well as the power differential. Over the past hundred years or so, the solidarity dimension has gained ascendancy over the power dimension. So, for example, while in early nineteenth century Europe children were called T but called their parents V, we now find reciprocal T. And whereas a century or so ago employees called their employers V but received T, we are now more likely to find reciprocal V. What they seem to have now is a simple, one-dimensional system with reciprocal T for the solidarity and the reciprocal V for the nonsolidary relationship, although the right to initiate the reciprocal T belongs to the more powerful member of the dyad (Brown and Gilman 1960).

American society takes a somewhat different approach to matters of mode of address. Of course, we have specific honorific titles of honor like *Your Honor, sir, Mr. President*, etc., but the main distinction now made in mode of address is a choice between first name and title plus surname. Brown and Ford (1961) studied forms of address in American plays and collected data on actual usage and self-reported usage in American English. The principal option between first name (FN) and title plus last name (TLN, for example, Mrs. Calderón, Dr. Said, Rev. Fujimoto) is dependent on the relationship between speaker and addressee. There are three patterns, reciprocal use of FN, reciprocal use of TLN, and the nonreciprocal situation where one person uses FN, and the other uses TLN. Apparently the distance between the two mutual forms of address is only a very small increase in intimacy, sometimes just a short conversation.

The nonreciprocal pattern results from either age differences (children addressing adults or adults addressing other adults about 15 or more years their senior by TLN), or a difference in occupational or social status (person lower receiving FN, for example, physician and patient). Mutual TLN indicates considerable distance and formality, but the mutual FN indicates only a slightly greater degree of intimacy. The result is that one form, TLN expresses both distance and deference, while the other form, FN, expresses both intimacy and condescension. In the development of a personal relationship, there is usually a progression from mutual TLN to nonreciprocal TLN/FN, to mutual FN with the growth of intimacy. As in the European T-V situation, the higher status person ordinarily takes the initiative in the reduction of social distance. The virtual abandonment of nonreciprocal address in American English is an obvious parallel to the abandonment of the nonreciprocal pattern for second person pronouns in other European languages. If language reflects society, a reasonable conclusion is that these changes are reflective of a decrease in social inequality, at least at the level of personal interaction.

In cases of ambiguous status relationships, a person speaking English may avoid using any term of address at all, although this strategy involves very careful and skillful wording of sentences. This is not possible, of course, in languages like French, Spanish, Italian, Japanese, Persian, and others where one obligatorily must use a verb or verb form which indicates status relationships.

8.4 Social class

Social class is one of the most highly developed and explored concepts in the social sciences, yet there is widespread disagreement as to how to conceptualize it and how to study it. One has schemes all the way from the Marxist division of society into bourgeoisie and proletariat to W. Lloyd Warner's famous six-fold division into the lower-lower, upper-lower, lower-middle, upper-middle, lower-upper, and upper-upper classes. Then there are a number of socioeconomic scales devised by sociologists which emphasize primarily such factors as education, occupation, and income, and which divide a community into anywhere from two to ten *classes* or *status groups*. The rationale for these schemes is not always clear or empirically validated; yet results appear to be consistent enough with other variables, particularly linguistic ones, to be satisfactory in a sort of rough-and-ready way for the practical purposes of the sociolinguist.

It would appear that the more stratified the society, the greater is the linguistic differentiation. So, for example, in India there is a sharp division between social strata such that the great social distance separating the strata in the general consciousness is usually expressed in correspondingly conspicuous caste dialects. In one village studied by Gumperz (1971:14–15), among Hindi speakers differences between the speech of the touchable and untouchable castes were found to be much greater than those between Muslims and Hindus.

In modern, open societies with considerable movement up and down the socioeconomic ladder, lower-class speech characteristics will also be normally found in the working and lower-middle classes as well, though not as frequently, for example, in American English the so-called double negative, *he don't* for *he doesn't*, or *runnin'* for *running*. The codes referred to by Bernstein as *restricted* and *elaborated* (see below) are found at all social levels. Although the upper levels are better able to utilize elaborated codes in a wider range of situations, they also use restricted codes in situations like cocktail parties and religious services. Thus, the range of speech repertoire is wider at the upper socioeconomic levels, and variables characteristic of lower class speech also characterize informal usage at the higher levels.

The speech of the more advantaged classes normally shows less regional diversification than does the speech of the lower classes, who are less likely to communicate with each other over long distances. Thus, for example, one finds much more geographical variation within a single Arab country like Lebanon or Syria than one finds among the elite speakers of Jerusalem, Damascus, and Beirut, all of whom speak substantially the same dialect, and whose speech resembles each other more than it does the lower-class rural dialects in the same country of which these cities are the capital. Likewise, elite speech in cities throughout the United States manifests much less variation than do regional or social lower-class dialects.

Perhaps one central idea that emerges out of all the sociolinguistic studies relating social class to language usage is that there is a noticeable, and socially marked distinction between middle class and nonmiddle class (that is, "lower" or "working" class) speech in a number of societies, especially American society, which has been the most studied from this point of view. People are aware of the differences, especially those unsure of their status, or aspiring to a higher one. On the other hand, Ross (1962) claims that the English upper class is clearly marked off from the others solely by language. The differences, apparently the result of both home and public school socialization of the upper class, are lexical and phonological, rather than morphological or syntactic. Thus, for example, U (the upper class) pronounce *medicine* and *venison* as three syllables, but non-U as two; or in U speech *Berkeley* rhymes its first syllable with *bark* but non-U with *smirk*. And whereas non-U say *to take a bath*, U say *to have one's bath*. Non-U say *wealthy*, but U say *rich*. But Ross points out that the distinction between non-U *serviette* and U *table-napkin* is perhaps the best known of all the linguistic class-indicators of English. And whereas non-U may say *Pardon!*, in the three instances of failing to hear a speaker properly, bumping into someone, or after hiccuping or belching, the U speaker in these three instances respectively says *What?*, *Sorry!*, and nothing.

Now let us turn to middle-class/working class differences. Studies of Black speakers in Detroit, Michigan and of Norwich, England, for instance have shown that the use of -s for the third person singular present tense of verbs (e.g. *he doesn't*, rather than *he don't*) is correlated positively with social class. Its lack ranges from 0 for the Middle-Middle Class to 97 percent for the Lower-Working Class in Norwich and from 1 percent for the Upper-Middle Class to 71 percent for Lower-Working Class Blacks in Detroit. The biggest gap, corresponding to the social division between manual and nonmanual occupations, is between the Lower-Middle Class (2 percent) and Upper-Working Class (70 percent) in Norwich and between the Lower-Middle Class (10 percent) and the Upper-Working Class (57 percent) among Black speakers in Detroit. Thus, the dialect continuum shows a clear break between middle- and working-class speech indicative of a social barrier. It also shows a much wider gap in England than among Black speakers in Detroit (Trudgill 1974b).

A well-researched case concerns the pronunciation of the consonant r in New York City. Up until the time of the Second World War, the more prestigious pronunciation deleted ("dropped") this sound except before a vowel. But about that time the pattern reversed itself and the r-less pronunciation began to become the stigmatized form, perhaps as a reflection of emerging national norms. In the 1960s, Labov (1972f:51) studied the social stratification of r, that is, the degree to which speakers deleted an r except when followed by a vowel. He analyzed the pronunciation used in three department stores of varying levels of prestige (see section 1.3). He found that 62 percent of Saks' employees, 51 percent of Macy's, and 20 percent of Klein's used all or some r in deletable position, with an even sharper stratification for percentages of those not deleting at all.

From this and other studies, Labov (1972e:115) determined that in New York City in casual, everyday speech, only the upper-middle class showed a significant degree of r-pronunciation. But in more formal styles (e.g. reading aloud), the amount of r-pronunciation for other groups rose rapidly.

Labov has coined the term "linguistic insecurity" to indicate the degree of discrepancy between what a speaker believes are the "correct" forms and the forms which he believes he himself uses. His studies show that lower-middle class speakers have the greatest tendency toward linguistic insecurity, and therefore show a very wide range of stylistic variation, by their conscious striving for correctness. They incur in this process a high degree of hypercorrection (see section 8.5). They manifest strong negative attitudes toward their native speech patterns.

Basil Bernstein (1972a) has studied class-related speech differences in Great Britain among children which he characterizes in terms of language usage (sociolinguistic or speech codes) rather than in terms of dialects (linguistic codes). A particular linguistic code is capable of generating any number of speech codes. What he calls *restricted* and *elaborated* speech codes result from systems of social relationships. Both the Sapir-Whorf hypothesis (see section 4.5) and Bernstein's ideas are based on the premise that different linguistic forms produce different social experience. But Bernstein asserts that it is primarily social structure that determines linguistic behavior which, in turn, reproduces social structure. Sapir and Whorf emphasized differences between cultures, Bernstein between classes. Bernstein distinguishes between what he calls universalistic meanings, those in which principles and operations are made linguistically explicit, and particularistic meanings in which they are relatively implicit. For example, a sentence like *My father has been over at the poker club a lot* is relatively more explicit than *He's been there a lot*. Bernstein argues that elaborated codes orient their users to universalistic meanings, whereas restricted codes orient their users to particularistic meanings and in each case are realized differently and used in different types of situations. The class system limits access to the acquisition of elaborated codes. It is much more difficult for the working class to acquire them. Restricted codes are more tied into specific contexts, where interlocutors share a narrow base of experience and assumptions. Elaborated speech variants are less tied in to the context, and speech is edited to make it intelligible to those who do not necessarily share the same background and assumptions.

It is difficult to characterize linguistically the differences between elaborated codes and restricted codes because Bernstein has given so few examples, but the former appears to utilize a greater proportion of uncommon adverbs and

conjunctions, adjectives, passive verbs, subordinate clauses, and the pronoun "I."
The sentences are longer in elaborated speech and have a more varied vocabulary. The syntax is more complex. Delivery is slower and more edited. Restricted
speech uses expressions like *Don't you know* and *Isn't it so* which ask the hearer
to fill in background information. More is left implicit.

Restricted codes use a high proportion of pronouns, especially *you* and *they*
and tag-questions. Working-class children tend to use more pronouns as subjects
or objects of sentences, but this may be an economy of speech. In one of
Bernstein's projects, all of the children were asked to look at the same pictures, so
they and the researcher obviously all knew to what the pronouns referred. The
responses of the middle-class children thus might seem somewhat pedantic.

Elaborated speech is "autonomous," that is, minimally dependent on paralanguage or the hearer's background information. Autonomous speech carries the
full burden of communication. In folk communities with a minimal division of
labor, virtually everyone has shared the same experiences, hence restricted
speech suffices. But as societies have greater complexity and diversification, it
becomes more and more necessary to be explicit in speaking with persons with
whom one shares few common experiences. Hence, Kay (1977) postulates an
evolution of speech styles from less to more elaborated, as societies modernize
and become more complex. Restricted speech can still be used within homogeneous groups of whatever type, but elaborated codes become necessary for more
and more types of communicative tasks. Social evolution produces speech
communities in which situations calling for autonomous speech occur with
increasing frequency, that is, situations where one needs to communicate precise
information on an unfamiliar topic of an affectively neutral kind with someone
with whom he shares a minimum of common experience. Thus, formal education and academic language are merely particular instances of this general trend.

According to Bernstein, there are differences in the relative orientation of
social class groups toward the functions of language. He notes that certain
aspects of children's speech are closely linked to differences in the social,
cognitive, and affective functions of communication which supposedly originate
in the social class structure. Children's readiness and ability to profit from educational experiences and practices are strongly affected by such functions.

One of Bernstein's studies showed that middle-class mothers placed much
greater emphasis on the use of language itself than did working-class mothers.
The latter placed relatively greater emphasis on the use of language in the transmission of basic skills (Bernstein and Henderson 1972:126). When they explain
the meaning of words to children, middle-class mothers more frequently choose
abstract or context-independent definitions, while working-class mothers more
frequently choose concrete or context-dependent definitions.

Cook-Gumperz' research (1973:210) showed that the middle- and working-
class mothers used different patterns to present rules to their children, as parental
perceptions of control relations vary by class. She discovered that working-class
respondents tended to use more restricted code and positional strategies;
something like: *I'm your mother, and I'm telling you to do that!* Another finding
was that both lower-class and middle-class mothers employed a varied linguistic

and strategic repertoire, but the range of styles by middle-class mothers was greater.

Bernstein claims that elaborated codes are more likely to be utilized in families where the unique attributes of members are relatively more manifested in the processes of interaction and communication, rather than their positions in the family, that is, their statuses. The two types of family Bernstein refers to as person-centered and positional, respectively. Children from positional families are more likely to develop restricted codes only, so that they may encounter serious difficulties in the schools, where elaborated codes and universalistic meanings are stressed. The child's particularistic orders of meaning and social relationships clash with the school, and they find it difficult to acquire the language of control (Bernstein 1971:vi, 196).

A further point is stressed by Bernstein (1972:174–176): "So far as the child is concerned, in positional families he attains a strong sense of social identity at the cost of autonomy; in person-centered families the child attains a strong sense of autonomy, but his social identity may be weak. . . . Elaborated codes give access to alternative realities, yet they carry the potential of alienation of feeling from thought, of self from other, of private belief from role obligation."

Bernstein has claimed that since middle-class speakers frequently use *I* while working-class speakers more frequently use *we,* middle-class children have greater personal judgment, sense of identity, and maturity. But an opposite interpretation of the facts is possible, namely that the *I*-user manifests egocentricity and thus immaturity and self-interest, whereas the *we*-user manifests an emerging sense of solidarity and sympathy for others. One's values will obviously influence the choice of interpretation (Roeper 1975:342).

Some writers have attempted to identify one language as "restricted" and another as "elaborated" in multilingual diglossic situations. But as Whitely (1971:12–13) notes, any language can occur in both restricted and elaborated codes, although one language may act as a restricted code in one setting and as an elaborated code in another.

Edwards (1976) studied two groups of eleven-year-old school children in England, one working-class and one middle-class, and found that the working-class children did not use either a more restricted vocabulary or a simpler syntax. This study points up the weakness of studies of Bernstein and their statements of social class differences based on inadequate linguistic derivation from the concept of codes.

Van den Broek (1977) interviewed four middle-class and four working-class informants in the Flemish town of Maaseik in two different situations, one formal and one informal. Standard Dutch was spoken in the formal situation and the local dialect in the informal one. He used five measures of syntactic complexity to test Bernstein's theories. In the formal situation the middle-class subjects exhibited a greater degree of syntactic complexity than the working-class subjects. In the informal situation, however, there was no significant difference between the two groups, so that the middle-class subjects manifested less complexity but the working-class subjects significantly *more* complexity in the informal than in the formal situation. Apparently the working-class subjects were more relaxed, were not intimidated by the situation, and could express themselves more elaborately. This study and others add fuel to the argument that the "restricted codes" or "deficient speech" of the lower classes may be largely an artifact of the testing situation.

Attempts have been made to transport Bernstein's British-specific concepts transatlantically and to apply them to the United States class situation. These attempts must be rejected on a number of grounds. In the first place, the American class system is not the British class system. Secondly, although Bernstein has denied that the lower class is linguistically deprived, a number of American scholars believe that Bernstein's work allows them to make this assumption. Thirdly, there is much evidence that economically deprived people may be gifted verbally, given a nonoppressive communication situation. Furthermore, it is highly likely that not all middle-class verbal habits are functional, even in the academic environment. Middle-class high school and college students often needlessly complicate their syntax to the despair of their teachers. Jargon and empty elaboration abound in learned journals. The elaborated style is out of place in many situations, especially intimate ones, where one would like to be able to say, *You know what I mean.* This is what it means *to have some one to talk to* (Hymes 1973:76).

Dillard suggests (1972:38) that a better word for Bernstein's *code* would be *strategy of discourse* and notes further that Bernstein may have overlooked the fact that lower-class groups have their own types of elaborated code. Working-class children may actually use elaborated codes in different contexts than middle-class children and prefer not to use them in others. The two codes are more a matter of variability in use rather than representing differences, and stem as much from family structures as from social class.

Kochman (1972:236) for his part has suggested that Bernstein's codes can be characterized in terms of style, specifically those of Joos (section 6.3), as a continuum from restricted to elaborated, corresponding to an intimate-casual-consultative-formal-frozen continuum.

A Marxist critic, Dittmar (1975) argues that the study of language and class in Western societies promotes the very social stratification that it analyzes, since both the deficit and the difference theorists do research which supports the status quo. Arbitrary empirical measures are, in fact, chosen with the guidance of a particular set of values aimed at social crisis management. Other Marxist analysts have for some time attempted to explain why the working class has not developed the class consciousness necessary for revolting against the conditions which oppress them. One factor according to Mueller (1973) is that because, in general, the working classes do not have access to elaborated codes, they are not able adequately to articulate their concerns and utilize abstract thinking to analyze their conditions and to devise the necessary means for changing it. According to Mueller, this is a matter of what he calls "arrested communication" derived from a particular socialization pattern and which prevents members of the working class from transcending their social context. As a result, they continue to accept their subordinate position in society.

Considerable doubt is thrown on this conclusion by the fact that ethnic minorities among the proletariat may be bilingual or biloquial. Furthermore, in the United States, the Black Panther Party and the Black Muslims grew out of a nonmiddle-class background yet had no difficulty articulating their concerns and organizing themselves using an elaborated code (Lee 1977).

That black people are not linguistically deficient in any regard but only different is amply proved by the cultivation of the verbal arts in the black community (see section 9.2) and in many other ways. Yet some educational psychologists still persist in equating nonstandard dialect with linguistic and cognitive deficiencies which they feel can be remedied by rote drill in standard forms. The following quotation from Fasold (1975:202–203) illustrates this approach:

> A film showing the corrective program developed by a team of educational psychologists for children alleged to have these language deficiencies was screened for linguists at the 1973 Linguistic Institute in Ann Arbor, Michigan. It contained the following sequence:
> Earnest White teacher, leaning forward holding a coffee cup: 'This-is-not-a-spoon.'
> Little Black girl, softly: 'Dis not no 'poon.'
> White teacher, leaning farther forward, raising her voice: 'No, this-is-not-a-spoon.'
> Black child, softly: 'Dis not a 'poon.'
> White teacher, frustrated: 'This-is-not-a-spoon.'
> Child, exasperated: 'Well, dass a cup!'
> The reaction of the linguists, after they had finished applauding and cheering for the child, was a mixture of amusement, incredulity and anger.

This author was present at that screening and can vouch for the fact that we did indeed applaud and cheer our small heroine and wonder at the linguistic naïveté of those educational psychologists.

8.5 Social mobility and hypercorrection

Just as social structures are never static but are in a constant state of flux and change, so too the people who operate within these structures are frequently on the move from one position to another within those structures. Such movement can be on a daily basis as when, for example, a woman is a housewife during the day and a student at night, or a person who is a school teacher during the academic year may operate a camp during the summer months. A person may change jobs or occupations temporarily or permanently, move from one part of the country to another, or change his religion or ethnic affiliation. All of these have been referred to as instances of social mobility, and ordinarily involve differences in linguistic behavior. The term, however, is most frequently used in connection with movement to a higher status level, that is, upward social mobility.

In many countries, because people are having laws and other social arrangements made for them in languages which they do not understand, the bilingual who is familiar with the local and government languages may become a necessary and valuable go-between. Lawyers or civil servants or professional contact men may fill this role. Such persons gain access to power and mobility through the linguistic situation. In many Third World countries, the young man, for instance, who learns the language of government, feels he has joined an educated elite and has acquired middle-class status. From interpreting to his own people, he will want to move up to a white collar job in the capital (Le Page 1964:17–18).

The expansion of bilingual education in the United States has opened up many opportunities for bilinguals to be upwardly mobile. On the other hand, minorities and the poor who do not acquire some standard variety of English will find their opportunities for upward mobility blocked. The educational system serves the dual function of teaching occupational, intellectual, and social skills useful for mobility, as well as providing an opportunity for learning the approved middle-class speech variety.

When a person aspires to a higher status, he generally attempts to emulate the ways of the category of people into whom he wishes to move, that is, his *reference group*. But because he was not originally socialized into that group, his knowledge of their ways, including their linguistic ways, is likely to be far from perfect. For example, he is likely to comprehend certain of their linguistic rules in an incomplete way, so that he tends to overgeneralize some of them to cases to which they do not apply. This leads to the phenomenon known as *hypercorrection.* De Camp (1972:87) has defined it as "an incorrect analog with a form in a prestige dialect which the speaker has imperfectly mastered." We can, however, identify cases of hypercorrection only if we know the social status of the speaker's dialect relative to the accepted standard of the community.

Thus, for example, in English *I* is used for subject of a verb, and *me* for direct or indirect object and after a preposition. Consider the following sentences from the point of view of academic English:

1. Harry and I ate the bagels.
2. Sam gave the bagels to Harry and me.
3. The beagle bit Harry and me.
*4. Me and Harry ate the bagels.
*5. Harry and me ate the bagels.

Sentence 4 violates the rule that the first person pronoun must come after the *and*, and both 4 and 5 violate the rule which requires *I* to be the subject of the verb. Thus, how often have our teachers or parents corrected us and said, *No, Harry and I, Harry and I!* This lesson has been overlearned by some speakers, that is they believe that one always says *X and I*, as a unit whether in subject or object position, thereby giving rise to the following nonacademic sentences:

*6. Sam gave the bagels to Harry and I.
*7. The beagle bit Harry and I.

Some readers will undoubtedly retort at this point, that sentences 6 and 7 are *correct*, at least "in my dialect." True enough, and in American English one increasingly hears constructions of this type. But the point is that this is an innovation, one which originated in hypercorrection through linguistic insecurity. It is now entirely possible that this may become the norm for academic English, as one hears this more and more frequently. One even hears it in the mouths of prominent people, on television and even in print, supposedly the bastion of conservative language.

Some hypercorrection is phonological. Some southern dialects substitute the sound [iy] for word-final unstressed schwa [ə], for example, Sary rather than Sarah, or sody for soda. The author of this book was called Penaloosy by a southern sergeant in the U.S. Army. Some speakers, aware that this is a nonacademic variant strive to "correct" their speech but in the process may correct final iy syllables to schwa even where other dialects of American English have iy as well, so one hears the hypercorrect Missourah, for example. People aware of dropping their r's may attempt to replace them even where they never were. For example, one native speaker of an r-less dialect known to this author consistently says Warshington (D.C.) as well as Califohnia.

A particular linguistic variable may become so associated in the popular mind with a particular variety that it becomes, in effect, a stereotype. The person then who wishes to convey the impression that he is speaking that variety will use the variable, or even overuse it, that is, in places where the rules of the variety do not call for it: Whom may I say is calling? for Who . . . . Such hypercorrection is typical of persons with high levels of linguistic insecurity. For example, Labov has reported the extensive centralization of the diphthongs /ay/ and /aw/ (i.e. the first member of the diphthong sounding like schwa) on Martha's Vineyard by the natives of Portuguese and Indian descent, who felt insecure vis-à-vis the old Yankees in being "real" islanders.

Discussion questions

1. Describe age differences among speakers, illustrating with your own observations.
2. According to Lakoff, what are the two principal ways in which language is used to help keep women subordinated to men?
3. Observe carefully the speech of men and women (in both same-sex and cross-sex conversations) and report any peculiarities in the speech of one sex not noted in the other. Offer an interpretation of the observed differences.
4. Observe carefully what kinds of speakers (by age, sex, class, occupation) are most likely to use he (and him, his), he or she (and him/her, his/her), or they (and them, their) as a sex-indefinite pronoun. Do you find any differences along these dimensions?
5. Look for advertisements which offer courses or books on vocabulary enrichment, speech improvement, "better English," etc., and analyze the kinds of appeals made to the potential customer.
6. With what persons do you use first name? With which do you use title plus last name? How do your role relationships with one group differ from those you have with the other?

7. In what ways is the European T-V distinction similar to the English FN/TLN distinction?
8. If there are any former New Yorkers living in your area, observe the cases in which they "drop" their r's. Ask them how they feel about their speech now that they are in a new environment. Have they made any effort to change it? Why (or why not)? (In the absence of New Yorkers, you could interview displaced New Englanders or speakers of southern, r-less dialects.)
9. Discuss the concept of elaborated and restricted codes and the criticisms which have been leveled against it.
10. The poor are not linguistically deficient, only different. Discuss this statement.
11. Do you know people who say things like "Joseph is going with the teacher and I"? In what ways, if any, are they different from the people you hear using the standard "with the teacher and me"?

9

Ethnic
and linguistic minorities

An *ethnic group* is a population which claims a common ancestry for itself and is set apart from similar populations in the same society on the basis of one or more social characteristics, such as genetic inheritance, culture, language, religion, or tribal, regional, or national origin. Where they are numerically, politically, or economically weak, they are often referred to as *ethnic minorities*. Some of them may be referred to popularly (often incorrectly) as *races* or *nationalities*. Ethnic minorities, like other socially differentiated groups, usually have their own distinctive language or language varieties and, hence, are often *linguistic minorities as well*.

These situations have arisen as a result of different types of historical processes. In much of Europe and Asia, national boundaries have been drawn in such a way as to include members of the nationality of an adjoining country or populations left behind from earlier migrations and conquests. Thus, there are, for example, Germans in Belgium, Albanians in Italy, and Hungarians in Yugoslavia. Some populations have no state of their own and, hence, are a minority everywhere, such as Armenians, Kurds, or Rom (Gypsies). (On Romani sociolinguistics, see especially Hancock 1979.) All over the world, Europeans have conquered non-European peoples and established various forms of racist colonialism. Thus, in the United States and elsewhere in the New World, we have various Native American and Black populations, as well as the conquered Mexicans in the U.S. Southwest. Most of the Third World is now free of colonial domination, but colonies had been often set up without regard to tribal or other ethnic boundaries, so that virtually all Third World countries are multiethnic and have linguistic minorities; in fact, some have no linguistic majority. In many countries, particularly in Africa, tribal affiliation forms the basis of ethnicity. A final major form of ethnicity has emerged as people from the economically less advanced countries have emigrated to the more advanced ones, either on a temporary or a permanent basis. In some cases, people have fled for political reasons. The United States has immigrants from all over the world and in recent years, many

Cuban, Cambodian and Vietnamese refugees. Thus, linguistic minorities may arise out of a wide variety of historical circumstances, and the latter will largely shape the development of their language habits (Jessel 1978).

While language is ordinarily an essential or ordinary requisite of ethnic group membership, there is no necessary correlation, for peoples readily give up their language under certain circumstances. For example, Whites living among Blacks will ordinarily acquire their speech patterns, and vice versa. Ethnicity may be signalled in some cases by a different language, in others by a different language variety. Both ethnic group boundaries and social class boundaries may serve as barriers to communication. They may also promote certain linguistic attitudes toward one's own speech and that of the out-group. At times language is a more or less incidental difference among groups (e.g. between black and white Americans), whereas in other situations the primary difference is linguistic in nature (e.g. among the French, German, and Italian Swiss), or at least language may be the primary symbol of the difference.

Relations between groups may range from complete harmony to outright warfare. More often than not, the groups have repressed their hostility so as to live in more or less mutually (not necessarily symmetrically) beneficial accomodation. If the differences which separate groups (ethnicity, language, religion, social class) parallel each other rather than cross-cut each other, the friction or conflict may be aggravated, as several differences reinforce each other. It is popularly believed that linguistic differences cause difficulties in communication and that knowing each other's language will help people understand each other better, thus paving the way for more harmonious relations.

Thus, for example, L. L. Zamenhof (1859–1917), a Jewish oculist in Bialystok, Poland, then under Russian rule, believed that the strife among the four ethnic groups of his home town (Russians, Poles, Germans, and Jews) was largely due to the fact that few spoke the languages of the other groups and, hence, misunderstandings developed from the lack of ability to communicate. He believed that interethnic and international relations could be improved if everyone in the world spoke one language in addition to his own, that is, an international auxiliary language. He, therefore, set about to create Esperanto (see section 6.4).

Interestingly enough, another Russian Jewish scholar, living at the same time in the same general area came up with a radically different linguistic solution to the problems of intergroup relations, at least as far as the situation of the Jews was concerned. This man, Eliezer Ben-Yehuda (1858–1922), advocated Jewish settlement in Palestine and believed that the revival of Hebrew as a spoken language was a necessary vehicle for the rejuvenation and creation of a modern Jewish culture there. He believed, furthermore, that Hebrew ought to be the common language of Jews in the Palestine settlements. As a result of his efforts and of others, Hebrew eventually became the predominant language in the Jewish settlements in Palestine and in the state of Israel after 1948.

One of the most difficult of all ethnic groups to define is the Arab. There are peoples from northern Nigeria to Central Asia who call themselves Arabs. Most are Muslim, but many are Christian; yet as a totality, they cannot be said to share the same culture. They do share a common historical background and sense of identity, but more than anything else, they share the Arabic language. This means the written, formal language (normally not spoken), for the dialects vary widely (many are mutually unintelligible). Early in the revival of Arab nationalism, it was fairly well decided that an Arab was anyone who spoke Arabic as his native language and who identified with the Arab nation.

The misunderstanding which occurs among ethnic groups may arise not only from ignorance of the other's language but also from ignorance of the other's sociolinguistic rule system, even when they are speakers of the same language, as for example, whites' negative reaction to black ritual insults such as *sounding*, etc. (see section 9.2). Conversely, conflict may exist even when (or especially when) interlocutors understand each other perfectly well. As Labov (1971a:63–64) notes, "When a southerner insists on calling an older Negro man *boy*, he is using a common cultural symbol to define the status relations once again. Here Negro and white understand each other, even if they are in conflict."

Oftedal (1969:16) defines a linguistic minority as "A group of people whose everyday speech is definitely another language than the language or languages spoken by the majority of the population of the country in which these people live." The difficulty with this definition is that it includes the problematic definition of such terms as group, everyday language, majority, and country. It would also exclude U.S. Blacks from the category of linguistic minority. A linguistic minority may live completely within the boundaries of one country or be divided between two or more contiguous countries, such as, for example, speakers of Frisian, Basque, Kurdish, or Macedonian, who are a majority nowhere. Another group of speakers may be geographically divided into subgroups, separated by other groups of people, such as native speakers of Irish. A group may be a majority in one country but a minority in others. The last possibility is a group delimited socially rather than geographically, such as various tribes of traveling Rom, speaking dialects of Romani, and stationary Yiddish-speaking Jews living among speakers of other languages (Oftedal 1969:18–19).

The Balkan peninsula in southeastern Europe is one of the most ethnically complex areas in the world. The fight for autonomy of many ethnic groups has led to violence and repression for hundreds of years. Linguistic minorities are one of the most commonplace phenomena of the entire area. To gain some idea of the complexity of the situation, a cursory view will be given of Yugoslavia and Greece in this regard.

Except for the Soviet Union, Yugoslavia is probably the most ethnically and linguistically heterogeneous country in Europe. It shares borders with more countries than any other in Europe—seven—with an overlap of minorities on each side of the border. Besides the seven south-Slav ethnic groups (Croats, Serbs, Bosnians, Herzegovinians, and Montenegrins speaking Serbo-Croatian, and Slovenes and Macedonians each speaking their own language, 88 percent of the total), there were, according to the 1961 census: 1,000,000 Albanians; 500,000 Hungarians; 200,000 Turks; 86,000 Slovaks; 63,000 Bulgarians; 61,000 Romanians, and 160,000 Yugoslav Rom. There were also Ukrainians, Vlachs (speakers of local dialects of Romanian), Italians, Greeks, Czechs, Germans, Russians, Negroes (Albanian speaking), and Kalmyks (Lockwood

1975:6). A very few Spanish-speaking and Yiddish-speaking Jews survived the Holocaust.

Despite this tremendous variety of linguistic minorities, most of whom enjoy schooling, newspapers, and other institutions in their own languages, the only really serious politicolinguistic problem is the strong insistence of many Croatian intellectuals and political leaders that Croatian is a separate language, not merely the "Western Variant" of a common Serbo-Croatian language. They insist that, instead of three national languages, there should be four: Serbian, Croatian, Slovenian, and Macedonian, each with equal rights. About forty Croatian signers of a declaration of this effect were either reprimanded or expelled from the Communist Party in 1967 (Spalatin 1970:171–172).

Although Macedonian is regarded as one of Yugoslavia's three official languages, it has no official standing at all in Greece, where efforts have been going on for some time to Hellenize the local Macedonian population, including prohibition of the language and deportations. Officially, they are known as Slavic-speaking Greeks. Briefly in Bulgaria between 1945 and 1948, Macedonian had the status of a minority language. The official Bulgarian position now is that Macedonian is a dialect of Bulgarian (cf. Andonovski 1971; Friedman 1975; Institut za Makedonski Jazik 1978).

In Yugoslavian Macedonia, there are linguistic minorities such as the Albanians, Turks, Vlachs, and Rom. At the present time, mainly Turkish and Albanian are being developed in the region. These minority languages have their own schools, theaters, radio, television broadcasts, and newspapers. Vlachs and Rom are very small in numbers, but their languages are freely used in their private and domestic lives (Markov 1969). Recently a local radio station began broadcasting in Romani.

Although Greece does not recognize the linguistic rights of the Macedonians, it does grant some cultural autonomy to the 110,000 Muslims living in Western Thrace, as a result of the Treaty of Lausanne of 1923. This treaty compulsorily exchanged Turkish citizens of the Greek Orthodox faith residing in Turkey with Greek citizens of the Muslim faith residing in Greece, with the exception of the Muslims of Western Thrace and the Greeks of Istanbul. The Treaty guaranteed certain privileges of religion, and linguistic and educational freedom to the minority in each country. In Western Thrace, Muslim teachers, most of them Turkish citizens or locals trained in Turkey, teach the Islamic religion, Turkish, science, mathematics, and music, while state teachers teach Greek, history, and geography (Ammanatis 1969). Greece also has important Vlach and Albanian minorities, but no special provision is made for their languages, and both groups are becoming Hellenized rather rapidly.

9.1 Ethnic minorities in the United States

While the ethnic situation in the United States has long been touted as a "great melting pot," in actuality, educational and other official institutions have striven to enforce a single cultural standard for all, namely middle-class, white, Anglo-

Saxon, mainly Protestant, culture. The culturally different, for their part, have struggled to retain some measure of cultural autonomy. In recent years, ethnic has become fashionable, and the doctrine of cultural pluralism has almost won the day, but not quite. Perhaps many people still think like President Theodore Roosevelt, who believed that immigrants should give up their native tongues and speak English exclusively. Perhaps many people feel that the minorities have little to contribute and ought to be grateful for the offer of participation in the majority culture which, at times, is made to them. Both of these assumptions are highly questionable. But here we will confine ourselves primarily to a discussion of the _linguistic_ creativity of the minorities, and the extent to which access to control of the majority language has been denied them by our official and unofficial institutions.

One of the tragedies of the current surge of interest in ethnic studies is that a great deal of energy has had to be spent simply affirming the humanity of ethnic minority groups, insisting that they are not really deficient biologically, intellectually, or linguistically but only deprived economically and politically and, in many cases, still deprived of their dignity and rights.

9.2 United States Blacks

The sociolinguistic situation of the black community is diversified, particularly because of internal socioeconomic differences. Yet Blacks, particularly many poor ghetto black children are often said to be very nonverbal, unable to form concepts or convey logical thoughts, confining speech to monosyllables, single words, etc., because of a lack of verbal stimulation in the home. These allegations were derived from observation of children in classrooms, particularly in language testing situations. These claims of psychologists, who know little about language and even less about black children, could not be farther from the truth. The children are strongly inhibited by the school environment testing situation but become very verbal when left alone. Verbal agility is a very highly valued skill in the black community. Verbal acts are continuously practiced, and verbal virtuosi are greatly admired.

There are a number of black verbal arts known in different geographical areas by various names, such as signifying, rapping, sounding, playing the dozens, woofing, marking, loud-talking, shucking, and jiving. These arts are commented on frequently in conversations by Blacks, as they notice the speech used and make judgments of the ability of particular speakers. According to Mitchell-Kernan, (1972:165), "Concern with verbal art is a dominant theme in Black Culture."

Signifying is a tactic employed in verbal dueling but can also refer to a way of encoding messages or meanings in natural conversation in an indirect fashion. This is an alternative message form, selected for its artistic merit which occurs embedded in a variety of discourse. The basic idea is that meaning goes beyond the dictionary entries for words. As Mitchell-Kernan points out, "Complimentary remarks may be delivered in a left-handed fashion. A particular utterance may be an insult in one context and not in another. What pretends to be informative may be intended to be persuasive. Superficially self-abasing remarks are self-praise." The hearer is forced to rely on the given context and his background knowledge of the world, including the interpretation of paralanguage. On the other hand the signifier is rewarded for his cleverness.

Rapping is a "fluent and lively way of talking characterized by a high degree of personal style" (Kochman 1969). The following example represents an interchange between Mitchell-Kernan (R) and three young men in a public park:

I: Mama, you sho is fine.
R: That ain' no way to talk to your mother.
  (Laughter)
I: You married?
R: Um hum.
I: Is you husband married?
  (Laughter)
R: Very.
  (The conversation continues with the same young man doing most of the talking. He questions me about what I am doing, and I tell him about my research project. After a couple of minutes of discussing "rapping," he returns to his original style.)
I: Baby, you a real scholar. I can tell you want to learn. Now if you'll just cooperate a li'l bit, I'll show you what a good teacher I am. But first we got to get into my area of expertise.
R: I may be wrong but seems to me we already in your area of expertise.
  (Laughter)
I: You ain' so bad yourself, girl. I ain't heard you stutter yet. You a li'l fixated on your subject though. I want to help a sweet thang like you all I can. I figure all that book learning you got must mean you been neglecting other areas of your education.
II: Talk that talk!
R: Why don't you let me point out where I can best use your help.
I: Are you sure you in the best position to know?
  (Laughter)
I: I'mo leave you alone, girl. Ask me what you want to know. *Tempus fugit,* baby.
  (Laughter)

(Mitchell-Kernan 1969:106–107)

Marking (related to the standard English word "mocking") is carried out when the narrator, in addition to reproducing the words of individual actors, affects the voice and mannerisms of the speakers, thus offering implicit comment on the speaker's background, personality, or intent. They may mimic someone "trying to talk proper" with a falsetto voice, or an Uncle Tom by a parody of regional black speech. Marking is particularly interesting as a source of information concerning language attitudes and values. Note the following marking of a black company man who is reported as having addressed a company meeting:

S_1: What did he say?

S_2: (Drawling) He said, "Ahm so-o-o happy to be here today. First of all, ah want to thank all you good white folks for creatin' so many opportunities for us niggers, and ya'll can be sho that as soon as we can git ourselves qualified, we gon be filin' our applications. Ya'll done done what we been waiting for a long time. Ya'll done give a colored man a good job with the company.

S_1: Did he really say that?

S_3: Um hum, yes, he said it. Girl, where have you been. (A put down by intimating S_1 was being literal)

S_1: Yeah, I understand, but what did he really say?

S_4: He said, "This is a moment of great personal pride for me. My very presence here is a tribute to the civil rights movement. We now have ample evidence of the good faith of the company, and we must now begin to prepare ourselves to handle more responsible positions. This is a major step forward on the part of the company. The next step is up to us." In other words, he said just what (S_2) said he said. He sold us out by accepting that kind of tokenism.

(Mitchell-Kernan 1972:178)

The dozens or sounding is a verbal contest which takes place in a crowd of boys. It begins by one of the boys insulting a member of another's family, usually the mother, while others spur on the insulted boy to respond with a clever slur on the protagonist's family. There then follows an exchange between the two contenders, which continues until everyone is bored, until one hits the other, or until something else comes up to interrupt the proceedings. These games not only serve to assert the boys' "virility," masculine identity, independence from women, and to release pent-up aggression but also to develop valuable verbal skills which they will need as adults to cope with their environment.

Abrahams (1962:210) gives an example of a possible sequence, which starts with X mentioning the name of A's mother, Constance. Someone in the crowd says:

B: Yeah, Constance was real good to me last Thursday.

A: I heard Virginia's (B's mother) lost her titty in a poker game.

B: 'Least my mother ain't no cake, everbody got a piece.

A: I hate to talk about your mother,
　　She's a good old soul.
　　She's got a ten-ton pussy
　　And a rubber asshole.
　　She got hair on her pussy
　　That sweep the floor.
　　She got knobs on her titties
　　That open the door.

Any number of retorts and counterretorts are then elicited.

When confronting the white man, the establishment, or any authority figure, the Black has learned shucking (or jiving) to avoid difficulty, often most ingeniously. Many black youths cultivate speech behavior which may be successful in manipulating and controlling people and situations. Control of language results in control of people, which makes survival in the ghetto possible. This is a far cry from the stereotype of the nonverbal, "linguistically deprived" ghetto dweller.

Another sociolinguistic phenomenon related to Blacks, which has been of great interest, is a variety of American English associated with Blacks and which has been called by various names: Negro Nonstandard English, Black English, Ebonics, and Black English Vernacular (BEV). This particular variety is not spoken by all Blacks, but practically all persons brought up in the black community understand it. We are not referring here to black slang, which is very changeable, ingenious, much admired, and copied by white speakers. Rather, we are referring to some relatively minor syntactic and phonological differences but which may make cross-ethnic communication difficult.

As a variety of American English, BEV differs from other varieties only in certain features; furthermore, as is the case with closely related varieties, they have very similar, if not identical, underlying structures. That is, the basic linguistic knowledge of all native speakers of American English dialects is fundamentally the same. Their speech differs primarily in outward manifestation of surface structure. Furthermore, no speaker of Black English uses Black English forms exclusively; even where such forms are natural and appropriate in his dialect, he may occasionally or frequently use "standard English" (SE) forms instead. Although Black English speakers use both Black English and "standard" English forms in their speech, that is, they speak a "mixed" dialect, still certain forms can be identified as BEV forms.

Following are some examples of BEV forms, chosen because they represent forms stigmatized by speakers of SE and supposedly representative of "errors" or "ignorance," particularly of logic. BEV shares, with some nonstandard vernaculars, a construction usually referred to as the "double negative." Such forms are socially stigmatized, not because of "illogic" but rather because the people who speak that way are concentrated on the lower echelons of our socioeconomic system. The speech is devalued because the people are. That is true of its origin, but the continuing evaluation is due to the propagation and enforcement of norms by institutions, as well as significant individuals.

Two famous features of Black English which are generally not shared with other dialects of American English are copula deletion (dropping forms of the verb to be) and habitual be. Consider the following sentences, all acceptable in BEV:

1. He crazy.
2. He be sick all the time.
3. I know who he is.

Of these, only 3 is also acceptable in standard English. A common evaluation of 1 and 2 is that many Blacks do not know how to conjugate the copula, that is, the verb *to be*, or else fail to use it at all. But Sentence 2 is an instance of habitual *be*, a particular kind of verbal form which indicates aspect rather than tense and has no parallel in SE. It indicates continuation of an action or a state over time, rather than a temporary condition or action which takes place only once. With regard to Sentence 1, many languages delete the copula in the present tense. For example, the Hebrew equivalent of 1 is

/hu mešuga/ literally, "he crazy"

But sentence 3 shows that BEV speakers not only know how to conjugate the verb, but also do not omit it under all circumstances. Also note that, of the following two sentences showing contraction, the first is acceptable in standard English, while the second is not. The third is unacceptable in *any* dialect.

   1. He's crazy.
*2. I know who he's.
*3. I know who he.

In other words, BEV and SE agree on the unacceptability of contraction or deletion in sentence-final position. The connection seems to be that only where SE permits contraction does BEV permit deletion. The most widely accepted explanation is that both dialects follow the same rules for contraction, but that BEV has an additional phonological rule permitting deletion of the single consonant in that position, so we have also, for example:

SE	BEV
They are crazy.	They crazy
They're crazy.	

Thus, a big difference, absence of the copula, can be explained by a minor phonological rule. Similar rules also found in standard English delete consonants from word-final consonant clusters, for example:

fist fight	⟶	fisfight
hand towel	⟶	hantowel
I worked today	⟶	I work today

On the other hand, for some black speakers "six" and "sick" may be homophonous, for example; or "poor," "poke," and "pope"; or "asks," "ask," and "ass." Final cluster simplification is much more frequent in BEV. Likewise, it has more r-lessness than New York English.

Thus, some differences between SE and BEV can be explained as modifications and extensions of rules found in other dialects. The number of structures unique to BEV is small. It seems unlikely, for example, that they could be responsible for the disastrous record of reading failure in the inner-city schools, which must be attributed to social causes.

BEV in its most characteristic form is spoken mainly by street youth between the ages of about 9 to 18, with a peak use about 15 to 16. It is a relatively uniform dialect which is spoken by most black youth in most parts of the United States today, including most rural areas, but especially in the inner city areas of New York, Boston, Detroit, Philadelphia, Washington, Cleveland, Chicago, St. Louis, San Francisco, Los Angeles, and other urban centers. It is also used in the casual, intimate speech of many adults. Isolated black youths not well integrated in the peer group culture, the so-called "lames," show much more influence from SE, so that rules that are categorical for the core group members are variable for the lames (for example, copula deletion) (Labov 1973a:81).

As the young person loosens his ties with his peer group and moves out into the adult world, his speech is increasingly influenced by SE norms. In fact, many black adults have negative attitudes toward BEV, feeling it has no place at all in the school, that the job of the school is to teach in, and teach standard English. Another possible manifestation of these attitudes is the attention paid to Swahili, in that people regard Swahili as a "real" language, not a product of "ignorance" (Stewart 1969b:221). There are also widespread negative feelings against non-Blacks' attempting to define and institutionalize a black language (Mitchell-Kernan 1969:68). The keynote of the Black Power and other ethnic liberation movements in the United States has been self-definition and self-determination.

In a study of community attitudes toward Black English, Hoover (1978) found black parents favorably disposed toward both the Black English vernacular and standard Black English (basically standard English with a few black syntactic, phonological, and lexical features). The poorer respondents, however, were less favorably disposed toward BEV. They were concerned about their children learning the standard variety, for they were aware of discrimination against the nonstandard speaker. Parents in more affluent homes, that is, those with professional and skilled occupations were less concerned about the BEV which their children were picking up on the street, for their children learned the standard variety at home. While all parents thought it was the business of the school to teach the standard variety, they felt it was also the teachers' duty to be aware of Black English, although it would be patronizing for them to use it.

A number of scholars have criticized the use of the term *Black English*, in that "Black" refers to the total ethnic community, whereas "Black English" refers to the language of a subgroup within that community (Wright 1975:189). It is an open question whether the entire black community possesses an overall gestalt or configuration in its speech, or shares an overall linguistic identity, since we have very little information on the speech of middle-class Blacks.

Because of the still widely held notion that different means inferior, many persons, not linguists, deny any essential differences between white and black speech, saying that all features of the latter originated in British dialects or southern white speech. Some black leaders and parents would prefer that the subject of black speech not be discussed at all, and while some black militants may use black slang in their own speech, none have referred to Black English as their own dialect and one to be proud of. There are, in fact, strong pressures against the recognition, description, or even mention of black speech patterns.

Many teachers, principals, and civil rights leaders wish to deny the very existence of such patterns. Labov (1972b:7) believes, however, that a careful statement of the situation can be made as follows: "Many features of pronunciation, grammar and lexicon are closely associated with black speakers—so closely as to identify the great majority of black people in the northern cities by their speech alone." There is, of course, overlap with other varieties, especially in the South. We are dealing with a stereotype which normally provides correct identification and which forms the social basis of language perception. But variable data are perceived in categorical terms. Almost every feature of BEV can be found among southern white speakers but is more frequent among black speakers.

Similarities between the speech of southern Blacks and Whites may be due more to the influence of Black English on the speech of southern Whites than vice versa. Wolfram (1974b) has shown that in Mississippi, for example, although there are basic distinctions between poor black and poor white dialects, a few white speakers have gained a familiarity with such Black English features as is-deletion and distributive be from their contacts with Blacks. This is understandable, as many white children have been reared by black nursemaids and played freely with black children.

Overfocusing on BEV has led to a misconception about the range of varieties utilized by Blacks as a speech community. The erroneous notion has been promoted that BEV represents the central communication medium for black speakers and that ghetto street talk is the most highly valued language variety for black speakers and supposedly signals one's closeness to "authentic" black culture. BEV is being described against a background of ignorance of white, middle-class speech. There are few substantial linguistic studies of middle-class, suburban Whites. Thus, BEV is being compared with Standard English, rather than with the white vernacular. As Wright (1975:187) notes, "We really do not know what language patterns characterize the speech of middle-class, white children in informal, peer-group contacts. It may be that many of the non-standard patterns of Black children occur with higher frequency in the speech of White children in nonadult dominated situations." Furthermore, even ghetto street adolescents are multistyle speakers, using the appropriate styles at school, church, speaking to adults, etc.

The question of the origins of the Black English Vernacular has attracted a great deal of scholarly attention. The older theories of origin of BEV attributed its special qualities to archaic features derived from East Anglia, which is supposedly the origin of southeastern United States dialects. But in more recent years, the theory of pidgin/creole origins of BEV has received wide support among sociolinguists (see section 6.4).

In Louisiana, African slaves developed a language that has been called Negro French, Creole French, Gombo, or Patois. Thomas (1973:17) calls it Black French. There are at least two other varieties of French in Louisiana: Creole French (or Colonial French), originally the language of the well-educated, wealthy plantation owners of colonial times, and Acadian French (Cajun), originally the language of impoverished refugees from eighteenth-century Canada. In certain areas, Black French and Acadian French are spoken by Blacks and Cajuns alike. The three varieties form a dialect continuum. In colonial and pre-Civil War times, the slave owner's children learned Black French from their nurses, while some slaves were educated in France. More recently Whites have continued to learn Black French from their nursemaids. Black French is undergoing a process of decreolization and increasingly coming to resemble Acadian French, which is the only French dialect now being used to any great extent (Thomas 1973:23).

9.3 United States Hispanics

Hispanic people form the largest linguistic minority in the United States. Within the Hispanic community, the three largest groups are persons of Mexican, Puerto Rican, and Cuban descent, respectively. The various Hispanic groups share many similarities, but there are some important differences, due primarily to the different historical circumstances under which they became incorporated into American society. Some Mexican Americans or Chicanos, as they are usually called nowadays, are descendants of the Spanish-speaking population which was living in the Southwest when it was taken from Mexico as a result of the Texas Annexation (1836), the Mexican War (1848), and the Gadsden Purchase (1859). Most Chicanos, however, are immigrants or the descendants of immigrants who have come from Mexico since that time. Puerto Ricans, as United States citizens, have been moving to the mainland, principally to the large northeastern cities, since the late 1940s. Both Puerto Ricans and Mexican Americans score low on economic, health, and educational indices. They have a high dropout rate from school and are underrepresented in higher education. The Cubans are primarily refugees who have fled Castro's Cuba since the 1960s and until recently were largely middle and upper class in background. They have been the object of very special attention by the United States government, a fact often deeply resented by the neglected American citizens of Mexican and Puerto Rican descent.

All three groups, however, have had to face the language barrier and adjust to an alien culture. Massive bilingual education was first provided for Cubans and then provided on a more limited scale for Puerto Ricans and Chicanos. The most significant problem that has arisen in this regard is that the vast majority of Chicano and Puerto Rican children, if they do speak Spanish, speak a nonstandard variety, often laden with regionalisms, archaisms, and heavy influence from English—in other words, the variety they learned from adults in the community. Whether in a bilingual education program or in an ordinary high-school or college Spanish class, they are very likely to have a Standard Spanish speaking teacher, often a Spaniard, South American, Cuban, or even a non-Hispanic teacher, who may place a very low evaluation on the local vernacular. As more Chicano and Puerto Rican teachers are trained, this problem will be alleviated, but only if these teachers, now having mastered the standard themselves, will be tolerant and understanding of the nonstandard speakers, and treat them as different, not deficient.

Although Spanish is the only language other than English which has been increasing from one decennial census to the next in numbers of mother-tongue claimants, the growth of the Spanish speaking population is the result primarily of continuing immigration rather than intergenerational language maintenance. As a matter of fact, a number of studies show a sharp decrease in Spanish use from one generation to the next (Hernández-Chávez 1978). The grandchildren of Spanish-speaking immigrants have, for the most part, lost active command of the language except along the border with Mexico. As the vast majority of Chicanos are native born of native-born parentage, English is now the most widely used language in the Chicano community. This is less true of the Puerto Ricans who are residentially more segregated and economically more deprived.

There appear to be three major varieties of English spoken in the Chicano community: (1) English indistinguishable from that of Anglos (i.e. white non-Hispanics) (2) English with heavy influence from the speaker's Spanish and (3) a variety of English which shows influence from Spanish, but which is current in the Chicano community and often spoken by Chicano English monolinguals. This latter variety represents not imperfect learning of English but rather the acquisition of a community standard (Metcalf 1979). Similar dialects have been reported for English-monolingual, American Indian communities.

Puerto Ricans living in the ghettos of large northeastern cities, especially in New York, manifest many aspects of nonstandard English which cannot be attributed to the influence of Spanish. Rather, they have been borrowed from the Black English Vernacular. Those Puerto Rican youths having the closest contacts with Blacks have the greatest number of such features in their English (Wolfram 1972).

Besides various varieties of standard and nonstandard Spanish among Chicanos, we find a unique youth jargon, or caló, among delinquent and nondelinquent gangs in the barrios, or ethnic enclaves. Also known in various communities and different times as pachuco or tirilí, etc., this caló originated in the underground of Mexico, with elements traceable back to the speech of gypsies and criminal elements in Spain. It is in part a secret language, and as outsiders learn the meaning of certain words or expressions, they quickly invent new ones. Many of these are calques, or literal translations of English idioms into Spanish, which are understandable only to bilingual persons (and, hence, usually exclude older Spanish monolinguals such as parents, or younger English monolinguals, i.e. the "lames"). They also use extensions of meaning, vague references, or completely invented words. Some caló terms have acquired a more general distribution in the Chicano speech community. Ability to speak caló is a mark of pride among young men, caló being somewhat idealized now by the Chicano movement as a unique ethnic creation.

Perhaps the central feature of Hispanic speech in the United States is language mixture. This takes various forms: the insertion of a single word from one language into a sentence in the other language (usually an English word in a Spanish sentence), with or without phonological or morphological adaptation); intrasentential code switching, where there is a change to the other language in the middle of the sentence; and intersentential code switching, where the change takes place at the end of a sentence.

Bilingual Chicano kindergarten children have been noted to switch to one language or the other, depending on the perceived linguistic capabilities of the child they are speaking with. That is, a child might be talking Spanish but will switch to English if an English monolingual child or English-dominant child enters the play group. Huerta (1978) notes the following brief interchange between an adult and a child:

M: Llévese a esta muchacha terca. ("Take away this stubborn child")
A: I'm not *terca*! ("I'm not stubborn!")

Here, the child emphasizes the denial by quoting the original Spanish word. (Also, *terca* is somewhat stronger than *stubborn*.) Or Huerta quotes a student as saying, "Siempre no voy a la *library*" (I'm not going to the library after all"), where *library* has been inserted in English because the university library is part of the Anglo culture and experienced in English. Nevertheless, the feminine article *la* is used with *library* because its equivalent in Spanish, *biblioteca*, is also feminine.

Switching may also be for the purpose of quoting somebody's exact words, e.g. "Y luego me dijo: Why don't you ever come to see me, Buddy?" ("And then he said to me . . ."). Switching may also be used to mitigate, to soften a request, as in the following sequence cited by Valdés-Fallis (1978):

T. Well right now it's not doin' too good.
N. Why, is it stalling out on you again?
T. Yeah, especially in the morning.
N. Maybe you're not letting it warm up enough?
T. No, lo que necesita es que alguien que sepa de carros me lo chequié. (No, what it needs is for someone who knows about cars to check it for me.)
N. Bueno, pos si quieres que le meta mano, I'll be glad to (O.K., so if you want me to give it a try . . .)

Language mixture, particularly among Chicanos, has been very extensively researched, and a number of conclusions emerge. In the first place, the main motivation is not inability to come up with the right word in a particular language, except among young children or those very weak in the language. Instead, mixture, especially code switching, is a learned skill which demands a high level of bilingualism. It is rule-governed and requires command of the syntactic systems of both languages. It does not indicate a confused mind or deficiencies in cognition. It is normal because it is normal in the community. A person may switch because the situation or the topic has changed, that is, a speaker may switch to Spanish because a Spanish-dominant speaker has joined the conversation or may switch to English to discuss something which is normally experienced in English, such as school or work. The switch may also be metaphorical, that is, the speaker desires to convey something beyond the mere words, such as, for example, ethnic solidarity or evocation of some particular mood, say, nostalgia.

Hispanics have somewhat mixed feelings about language mixture. They are aware that many purists frown on it and that Anglos use a derogatory terminology to refer to this mixed speech, such as "Tex-Mex," or "Spanglish." But the rise of ethnic power movements such as the Chicano movement has done much to rehabilitate the image of mixed speech, *caló*, and the nonstandard varieties which have become for some a mark of ethnic pride. Apparently, however, in the Chicano community attitudes toward nonstandard varieties of Spanish are more positive than attitudes toward Chicano English. It would seem as if Chicanos had absorbed some of the Anglo prejudice toward accented English, a possible barrier to upward mobility. It appears, however, that regardless of whatever changes may take place in educational and immigration policies, distinctive varieties of Spanish and English are likely to flourish for quite some time to come among Americans of Hispanic descent. (For further information on Hispanics, see Attinasi, et al. (1977), Bowen and Ornstein, eds. (1976), Hernández-Chávez et al., eds. (1975), Peñalosa (1980), and Teschner et al., eds. (1975).

9.4 Social class, ethnicity and education

The main function of traditional educational systems was the training of priests and civil servants in a classical language, as, for example, Latin in Western Europe, Sanskrit in northern India, or Arabic in the Islamic countries. Since scholars possessed a common language, diplomatic intercourse was facilitated over large areas of linguistic diversity. Scholars studied a body of scripture the very existence of which conserved a classical form of the language as the spoken varieties of it were diverging more and more from the original language of the scriptures. Only a tiny elite was thus able to master the mysteries of education.

In modern societies, education is more broadly available, and language is still generally one of the most, if not the most, important of the subjects taught. To a certain extent, the school is teaching a standard language, to a certain extent it is engaged in creating it. Much depends on the linguistic background of the teachers. If United States teachers were socialized in a middle-class environment, for example, very likely they came to their schooling already in possession of the standard variety, but if their background was lower class, then they learned the school language as a second variety. If, furthermore, they were insecure in this situation, they may have attempted to overcorrect and to bring this hypercorrect attitude to their later teaching and pass it on to their students. Undoubtedly some of the departures from earlier English have been brought about by the insecurities of school teachers about their own language. The fact that the bulk of elementary teachers in the United States have been traditionally recruited from the upper reaches of the working class, rather than from the middle class proper lends some credence to these suggestions (cf. phenomenon of hypercorrection in section 8.5).

Largely unacquainted with the point of view and findings of modern linguistics, teachers generally have been intolerant of nonstandard forms. Enforcement of a single standard, of course, facilitates the job of teaching, while the facilitation of communication among diverse groups is also unquestionably an advantage. Similarly, teachers may consider bilingualism of linguistic minorities as a "problem," although, paradoxically, they may approve of the teaching of foreign languages. But some "foreign" languages are not really foreign at all, for example, Spanish. As Spanish is indigenous to the United States Southwest, it is not really a foreign language there, though it is foreign to most students. On the other hand, French is foreign to the Southwest but not to Louisiana or parts of New England.

The linguistic situation in the United States is patently not at all parallel to that of such countries as bilingual Belgium (French or Dutch) or quadrilingual Switzerland (German, French, Italian, Romantsch). In any case, teaching their own language to an ethnic minority is a very different matter from teaching the same language to a group to whom the language is completely foreign. This fact has often been lost sight of, as when, for example, the same teaching materials which were developed to teach Spanish to English-speaking students are also used to teach Americans who are native speakers of Spanish, even though they may in many cases speak a dialect different from that taught in the schools, often by a teacher of non-Hispanic origin. This situation has been the setting for a significant conflict between Chicano students and Anglo teachers which has had important reverberations throughout the Chicano community for many years.

Concerned educators meeting at the Tucson Conference of 1966 called for bilingual education programs for Mexicans in the Southwest. The growing Chicano movement, the education lobby in Washington, and other groups put pressure on Congress that led to the Bilingual Education Act of 1968. This act saw bilingual education as the means of solving the problems of speakers with limited English skills. The policy of the Federal government was to help with the planning, financing, and evaluation of bilingual education programs. The decision rendered in 1973 by the United States Supreme Court in the case of Lau versus Nichols, 1973, permits citizens to petition local school boards for instruction in the native language of the children. Programs are now available in French, Portuguese, Chinese, Samoan, Navaho, and other languages, in addition to Spanish, in different parts of the country. Bilingual education is the first major breakaway from the melting pot idea, and a possible avenue for equalizing educational opportunity between the affluent and the dispossessed. (For a recent world-wide survey of bilingual education, see Fishman 1976; for a recent survey of policy issues in United States bilingual education, see Padilla; ed. 1979).

One of the functions of the school has traditionally been to confer prestige upon those who already speak or learn to speak and write those languages or language varieties deemed prestigious by the schools. Thus, the school provides its graduates with certain linguistic skills useful in competing in social and economic life. But as individual mobility may be promoted by the school, so may the school contribute to the continuation of existing patterns of stratification by stressing certain language varieties.

Whatever social inequalities exist in a society are likely to be perpetuated by its educational system. Education is, except in a few instances, not an autonomous institution but, rather, a tool of the most powerful groups in the society. Their assumptions regarding the nature of society, education, social justice, and language are the governing ones as far as the structure and administration of the school systems are concerned. Among these are assumptions regarding the nature of language, and the linguistic characteristics and needs of the country.

The elite, exercising their power through governmental structures, establishes language policy which then is carried out by the public school system. Where minority groups speaking different languages are present, their relative political strength will be reflected in the degree of attention paid to their special needs by the educational authorities. But it is also doubtful that even an enlightened language policy will level either social class or language differences (Smith and Lance 1979).

In standardized testing of school children in modern industrial societies, the aspects of the child's performance which are being measured reflect the values of the testers who, in turn, express the values of a competitive, technologized society. The test is administered in the dialect and interaction style of the dominant group. Consequently, children not from the dominant group are baffled and insecure when confronted by the linguistic and communicative demands of these tests (John 1973:230–231). They may respond with defensive, monosyllabic behavior.

Thus has arisen the myth of the linguistically deprived child which labels, for example, some Chicano bilingual children as "alingual" or labels speakers of the Black English Vernacular as having "no language at all." This deficit hypothesis has led to various types of compensatory education programs where the supposed linguistic deficiency would be remedied. The fact, however, is that what was generally taught were middle-class speech patterns rather than "language" as such (see section 8.4). As a result of these theories, compensatory education programs had been instituted, in part to "compensate" for the "deficient" language of the poorer classes. The erroneous nature of the theories foredoomed these efforts. Dittmar (1976:80) has clearly pinpointed the reasons:

> The basic idea of compensatory education is not to blame the miseries of the lower class on the social system with its norms and principles of unequal distribution of poverty and wealth but rather to make the lower class itself the scapegoat of its own condition. It is thus a requisite of compensatory education that the poor performance and inability of the lower classes should be proved. Once this has been achieved (the representatives of the Deficit Hypothesis are trying to do just this) the State can intervene (with compensatory programmes) to try and adapt the lower class to the norms of the middle class. Although these programmes are claimed to be charitable measures designed to create equality of opportunity, they provide in fact the foundation for mobilizing the work forces which have become necessary to maintain the processes of production.

The failure of the compensatory education programs, such as "Head Start," thus points up the erroneous nature of the deficit hypothesis on which they were based. But advocates have insisted that learning was destroyed by the "bad" teaching which followed, or else they claim that the home environment was so bad that Head Start could not possibly have overcome it. The children, not the theory, are blamed.

Of course, middle- and lower-class speech are different from each other, but they can perform the same functions. The forms of the standard language can be learned, too, but in an accepting and linguistically sophisticated environment. Some steps have already been taken in this direction. In 1974, the National Council of Teachers of English affirmed students' rights to their own language: "to the dialect that expresses their family and community identity, the idiolect that expresses their unique personal identity . . ." (Marckwardt 1976). Unfortunately, not all teachers have accepted this position.

Reactions of teachers to children's speech may be part of a self-fulfilling prophecy syndrome. They expect less from nonstandard speakers, and the pupils generally respond to the teacher's expectations. Teachers' attitudes toward the child are thus an important factor contributing to his success or failure. The classical study of the effects of teachers' expectations on pupil's performance (Rosenthal and Jacobson 1968) drew a 20 percent sample of pupils by a table of random numbers. Teachers were then told that these students would be fast bloomers, that is, experience an unusual spurt in academic performance. Eight months later these "unusual" children showed significantly greater gains in I.Q. (intelligence quotient) than did the remaining children who had not been singled out for the teachers' attention. The results of this study have been challenged on the basis of defective statistical methodology by a number of scholars, but the authors insist their results are valid (Elashoff and Snow 1971). Certainly they are consistent with other studies of the self-fulfilling prophecy.

Middle-class bias against lower- or working-class speech is reflected in the assumption that the correlation between lower socioeconomic status and school failure necessarily results from cognitive deficiency stemming from linguistic deprivation. Teachers are supposed to accept the student where he is, but unfortunately they lack the training to know where the student is linguistically and how he got there. Children's language may be stigmatized as not being language at all, or as nonlogical, because it differs from the teacher's middle-class dialect. In a threatening situation, the child is unable to display his normal verbal virtuosity, such as his bilingualism and code-switching abilities, which are not prized by the school. Hence, he may be labelled as "alingual" or "verbally deprived." Prejudice against lower-class or ethnic minority children may be rationalized in linguistic terms.

Labov found no connection between linguistic skill in the vernacular and success in reading. As he points out ". . . . the major causes of reading failure are political and cultural conflicts in the classroom, and dialect differences are important because they are symbols of this conflict" (Labov 1972b:xiv).

While the problem faced by the bidialectal black speaker is similar to that of his bilingual classmates of immigrant background, the latter are more likely to be regarded by the teacher as speaking "real" languages, rather than being just "careless" and "stubborn" in their speech.

Some linguists and educators have advocated teaching black ghetto youth to read using vernacular texts that systematically move from the syntactic structures of the ghetto community to those of the standard-English speaking community. Such teaching should give credence to the child's speech and thus support his ego and give him a chance to experience success in school (Baratz 1969:114). But whatever method is utilized, the study of social dialects can make an important contribution to changing teachers' attitudes.

Taking a different tack, Sledd (1969, 1972) has questioned the inevitability of language prejudice and the necessity of formulating educational goals so as to accommodate it. Rather than fomenting bidialectalism, Sledd believes we should attack the negative language attitudes of powerful individuals in the mainstream of society. Some black scholars see racial prejudice on the part of the white society as the real problem and the focusing on the language question as something of an attempt to dodge the real issue (Wolfram and Fasold 1974:181–182). Obviously, either to eradicate black dialect or to promote bidialectalism, or simply to teach standard English all involve serious problems, and no matter what tack is taken, substantial numbers of Blacks will be antagonized. What is certain, however, is that the ultimate decision will have to be made by the black community itself.

Meanwhile an important decision has been rendered by the United States Distict Court for Eastern Michigan, a decision which has widespread implications for all linguistic minorities. The court ruled that not only was Black English a rule-governed and systematic variety of English but also that treatment of the children's language variety as an inferior system by insensitive teachers can be educationally damaging. The decision ordered the Ann Arbor School District to help its teachers to recognize the children's home language and to use that knowledge in teaching the reading of standard English. The school district is now implementing a plan to carry out the court's order (Center for Applied Linguistics 1980; Wolfram 1979).

Discussion Questions

1. Discuss the relationship between ethnicity and language. To what extent does one determine or shape the other?
2. How does ethnic and linguistic diversity in Yugoslavia differ from that in the United States?
3. Discuss the types and functions of the different forms of black verbal arts.
4. What are some of the ways in which the Black English Vernacular differs from other varieties of English? What is the social significance of the differences?
5. What are some of the criticisms directed against the concept of Black English?
6. How does the sociolinguistic situation of United States Hispanics differ from that of United States Blacks?
7. What varieties of speech are found in the Chicano and other Hispanic communities in the United States?
8. Discuss the failure of the public school system in dealing with the linguistic differences in the student population.
9. How does the school district with which you are best acquainted deal with linguistic differences?

10

Nationalism, colonialism and culture contact

The modern world capitalist system first emerged in the early sixteenth century in western Europe with the production of agricultural commodities for sale on a world market (Wallerstein 1974, 1979). A number of factors accounted for the emergence of the world system at that time, one of the most important of which was the colonization of the Americas, later of parts of Africa, Asia, and Oceania. The colonized areas became the periphery of the system, as they supplied raw materials to the core countries (the colonizers) and the latter provided them with manufactured goods in return. It was the first phase of the world system, agricultural capitalism, which paved the way for industrial capitalism. The industrial revolution was largely financed by the gold, siver, and other commodities plundered from Mexico, Peru, and other peripheral areas.

It is noteworthy that the rise of capitalism gave rise to the modern phenomena of nationalism, strong centralized political states, colonialism, racism, and standard languages. The importance of the latter was emphasized in a classic statement of Lenin:

> Throughout the world, the period of the final victory of capitalism over feudalism has been linked with national movements. For the complete victory of commodity production, the bourgeoisie must capture the home market, and there must be politically united territories whose populations speak a single language, with all obstacles to the development of that language and to its consolidation in literature eliminated. Therein is the economic foundation of national movements. Language is the most important means of human intercourse. Unity and unimpeded development of language are the most important conditions for genuinely free and extensive commerce on a scale commensurate with modern capitalism, for a free and broad grouping of the population in its various classes and lastly for the establishment of a close connection between the market and each and every proprietor, big or little, and between seller and buyer. Therefore, the tendency of every national movement is towards the formation of *national states*, under which the requirements of modern capitalism are best satisfied. (Lenin 1947:8–9).

Of course, the final victory of capitalism over feudalism took place at different times in different places, thereby accounting for the emergence of national languages in each case.

While linguistic unity strengthened the core countries of the system, use of their languages in peripheral areas retarded the linguistic as well as the economic development of the exploited colonies. Continuing use of English, French, etc. as "languages of wider communication" in the Third World is related to the continuing domination of the world economy by the United States and the European Common Market countries (along with Japan, which has had little linguistic impact on the rest of the world.).

10.1 Nationalism

A nationality may have all or some of the following characteristics: common descent, territory, political entity, customs and traditions, religion, or language. Some nationalities, like the Swiss, however, have no language of their own; others, like the Norwegians, had no true language of their own until after they had achieved nationality. Ideas of nationality and ethnocentrism have been related to language differences ever since ancient times. The Greek word for barbarian, *barbaros,* was originally akin to the Sanskrit *barbara,* which meant "stammering" or "non-Aryan," whereas the Slavs called the Germans *nemtsi* or "mutes" since they could not make themselves understood.

In the Middle Ages, no one thought to compel others in linguistic matters. The people of that time did not think in terms of nationality. They did not impose languages but, instead, religious creeds (Kolarz 1946:10). With the Renaissance and Reformation and the introduction of printing and the spread of education to the middle and lower classes, the general population began to participate in national politics. As a consequence, there was a development of language loyalty and its expression in the politics of nationalism. Some Romantic thinkers thus came to believe that language is the most important identifying characteristic of peoples and, therefore, should serve as the criterion of political boundaries, ignoring the vast complexities in the relationship between language and political community.

Before the rise of nationalism, language was rarely stressed as a factor on which the power and prestige of a group depended. Modern nationalism's concern with languages as an index of authenticity was first stressed by Johann Gottfried Herder (1744–1803), who developed the view that the mother tongue expressed a nationality's soul or spirit. He viewed language as the best way to safeguard or recover a national heritage. He believed also in the desirability of diversity in language and in culture. In Herder's words:

"Has a nationality anything dearer than the speech of its fathers? In its speech resides its whole thought domain, its tradition, history, religion and basis of life, all its heart and soul. To deprive a people of its speech is to deprive it of its one eternal good... With language is created the heart of a people" (quoted by Fishman 1972a:1). Another German thinker, Johann Fichte, 1762–1814, expressed a prevalent attitude when he said, "Wherever a separate language is found, there is also a separate nation which has the right to manage its affairs... and to rule itself" (quoted by Inglehart and Woodward 1972:358).

This particular attitude is not a universally accepted one, although the relationship between language and nationalism has been at the heart of a number of sociolinguistic and ideological issues. The identification of language with nationality undoubtedly contributed to the growth of fullfledged written languages in Europe (Deutsch 1968:599–600), as witnessed by the following figures:

Year	Number of Written Languages
950	6
1250	17
1809	16
1900	30
1937	53

On the other hand, nationalism and ethnicity do not always go hand in hand. For example, the ethnically and linguistically German people of French Alsace-Lorraine were opposed to annexation by Germany in 1871, for they wished to remain politically French. Even today they consider themselves German-speaking Frenchmen, rather than Germans living under French rule (Kohn 1965:61). An obvious counter example is the Arab nationality, based primarily on language, rather than race, culture, or territory.

Even more striking were the various nineteenth century "pan" movements which were based on the premise that linguistic similarity could serve as the basis for far-flung territorial states encompassing, for example, all the speakers of German, Turkish, or Slavic languages, as in the so-called pan-German, pan-Turkish, or pan-Slavic movements. Yet, it is not necessarily the case that linguistic and ethnic affinity results in cultural and ideological affinity and thus in the desire for union. There was, in effect, no cultural affinity among the various Slavic speaking peoples. Polish civilization had less in common with Russian civilization than with that of Catholic Europe. Contrary to pan-Slav theory, Slavic peoples frequently felt more bitter hostility against each other than against non-Slavic peoples, such as Poles against Russians, Ukrainians against Poles, or Serbs against Bulgars. In effect, these movements proclaimed the affinity of various peoples, in spite of differences of political citizenship and historical background, of civilization and religion, solely on the strength of an affinity of language.

Cultural and linguistic differences do not always lead to demands for recognition and political autonomy, as in Cyprus or Belgium. Differences may not be noted, or if noted not ideologized—that is, not made the source of divisiveness, as in Switzerland. In recent decades, suitability for science and technology is demanded of new languages; suitability for governmental and literary use, as before World War I, is no longer sufficient. Hence, the linguistic component of nationalism is weaker than it once was. Technology necessarily has a uniformizing tendency, and, hence, is inherently nonethnic. Only two or three science/technology languages are needed at the international level, so that diglossia at the national level becomes imperative. Thus, a national language may be used for ordinary, literary, and governmental affairs but an international language like English or French for science, technology, and diplomacy (Fishman 1968a:44–47).

Nationalism seems to occur in two principal forms, sometimes called "ethnic" and "political" nationalism. In the first type, a local ethnic group in a multinational state is asserting its identity and demanding self-determination, including in some cases its own nation-state. In the second type, an ethnically and linguistically diverse overseas colony (usually of a European power) is demanding cultural and political independence. In this type, there is likely to be a broader concept of ethnicity or nation, encompassing, as it might, ethnically diverse groups. This is the case, for example, in almost all of the former African colonies. In almost all cases of nationalism (not true, for example, of the nationalism of the American colonies in 1776), there is a marked language difference between the submerged nation and its master(s). In the case of ethnic nationalism, there is usually only one language, which is the language of the oppressed. In multilingual nations like Nigeria or Kenya, on the other hand, the voice of the submerged nation had to express itself in English, even to its own supporters, or to use a native trade lingua franca like Swahili. Nationalism and socialism in Angola and Mozambique are expressed in Portuguese.

The concept of nation as a people, as above, must not be confused with the concept of the nation-state, which is a political entity having sovereignty and a separate physical existence. In other words, we must distinguish political community and sociological community, each of which may have language needs unrecognized by the other. Present-day nationalism involves both modernization and authentication, and these two goals can easily be in conflict. For the nation, the major problems center around language maintenance and enrichment, but for the nation-state, they center around political, social, and economic integration in the context of national and international problems (Fishman 1968a:39–43).

Ethnic nationalism has flourished in eastern Europe, where it has been difficult for territoriality to be the basis of nationhood. There is a lack of segregation of nationalities, as there are very few clear-cut geographic boundaries between the ethnic groups. Throughout eastern Europe, during the past few centuries, the most powerful groups subjugated the less powerful ones, and the upper classes of the oppressed often adopted the language and culture of their conquerors. Thus, they changed their nationality, so that the masses of the people were deprived of their own upper classes and were reduced to the condition of serfs, as they continued to speak their vernacular (Kolarz 1946:13). For example, in Poland and Lithuania, White Russian and Ukrainian nobles changed to Polish nationality, and in Hungary, the Slovak and Romanian nobles were Magyarized. The people emerged from their long silence after the emancipation of serfs in Russia in 1861 and Austria in 1848, and the gradual disappearance of Ottoman rule from the Balkans. These emancipated people began to form the new middle class of the towns and to reverse the assimilation process.

Religious consciousness may, in some cases, be related to national and linguistic identification. For example, when Greek-speaking Muslims on Crete had to decide whether they would be Greeks or Turks at the time of the 1923 exchange of populations, they chose to be Turks and were repatriated to Turkey. At the same time, 100,000 Turkish-speaking members of the Greek Orthodox Chruch living in Anatolia chose to be Greeks and to be repatriated to Greece (Kolarz 1946:20–21).

In the eighteenth century, the Romanians lived under Turkish or Hungarian rule, were Greek Orthodox, and used the Cyrillic alphabet. They were hardly conscious of the Latin origin of their language. When some Romanian priests joined with Rome and established a Romanian Uniate Church, they introduced the Latin alphabet and emphasized the Latin origin of their language. This Roman origin made the Romanian people feel superior over the other Balkan peoples, such as Magyars, Slavs, Turks, and Greeks. They felt themselves to be an outpost of Roman civilization in the East. The various Romanian provinces were politically united in 1918, the final outcome of what had started as historical and cultural research (Kohn 1965:47–48).

Since particular alphabets have been connected with certain creeds, to change an alphabet has been at times practically tantamount to a change of religion. In 1863, for example, the Czar decreed that the Lithuanians had to use the Cyrillic alphabet, but the people preferred to give up literary activity rather than to use the symbol of the Russian Orthodox Church. The Latvians, Estonians, and Czechs rejected the Gothic alphabet of their German overlords. In Albania, there was a battle of the alphabets, where the Greek alphabet was used by the Orthodox, the Arabic alphabet by Muslims, and the Latin alphabet by the modern nationalist movement. In 1913, there was a public burning of Albanian books printed in the Arabic script.

Eastern European ethnic cultural nationalism, which emphasized a culturally homogeneous state protecting cultural authenticity, can be contrasted with nationalism of the Western European variety. The latter can be characterized as liberal nationalism. It has emphasized the state as the provider of universal institutions, civil rights, and social services. Contemporary African and Asian nationalists have been more influenced by the Western European than the Eastern European type of nationalism (Fishman 1972a:117).

Linguistic nationalism may be expressed in a number of different forms, as indicated by Kloss (1967). It may give rise to an urge to adopt or expand a second language or to reject one foreign language in favor of another. In some multiethnic nation-states (e.g. Belgium or Finland), two or three languages may enjoy full equality of status, or one language is selected for national purposes (e.g. Urdu in Pakistan), but otherwise all languages are treated as equal. There are still other cases where the state in theory makes all languages equal but in practice discriminates among them (e.g. the Soviet Union).

10.2 Imperialism

Imperialism, like nationalism, is a term difficult to define with any kind of scientific objectivity, laden as it is with all sorts of ideological impedimenta. Academic sociologists in the past have rarely discussed the subject, and it has been only in recent years, with the growth of the radical movement in sociology, that the influence of ideas such as those contained in V. I. Lenin's *Imperialism* has reached any currency in standard sociological contexts.

Taken at its simplest, imperialism can be understood to mean the domination or the attempted domination of one nation by another. It need not involve direct administration, as in the case of colonialism. The form of domination may be political, economic, cultural, or even linguistic. It may involve domination of nations or areas of nations overseas, or it may involve contigous conquest, as in the nineteenth-century drive to the Pacific (from opposite directions) by the Americans and Russians, the former proclaiming their "Manifest Destiny" in subjugating the Indians and Mexicans in their path, the latter, embodying Czarist imperialism, more frankly proclaiming their superiority over the Asiatic peoples they subjugated.

Linguistic imperialism can be understood as the linguistic domination of one nation by another. In its noncontiguous form, except in cases of outright colonialism, it sometimes involves consent on the part of the dominated. A developing nation may have a need for certain products, such as military hardware, agricultural implements, or factory machinery, which need special training for their use and a continuing supply of replacement parts. Natives of the developing country are sent to the supplying nation for training in use of the new equipment and, perforce, must learn the language of the industrialized country. They return to their own country to use the equipment but now must deal with the supplying country on a continuing basis as old machinery or parts have to be replaced. As they do so, they carry on correspondence in the language of the supplying country. The developing country, however, now has a nucleus of persons trained in that language and undoubtedly has begun, if it had not already done so, to teach the language in some of its institutions. Because of this and because of contacts previously established, particularly if these contacts have been satisfactory, the next time a need arises which can be satisfied by an industrialized nation, whether it be industrial equipment or perhaps some specialized kind of training such as nursing or agriculture, there will be a natural tendency to consider seeking the services of the same country, rather than turning to a different country for which natives would have to be prepared in a new language. If they do resort to the same country, their technological, economic, and linguistic dependence on that country is strengthened to the point where it becomes almost impossible to break away. Frequently, the linguistic dependence is further strengthened by the supplying country's providing either free or heavily subsidized language instruction, in either of the two countries.

Economic and technological imperialism is not necessarily always accompanied by linguistic imperialism if, for example, the language of the supplying country is "difficult" or "exotic," particularly if it has a different, difficult writing system. For example, Japanese suppliers do not ordinarily expect to do foreign business in Japanese. Rather, they conduct it in a language of international scope, such as English. The Japanese cannot reasonably expect any significant proportion of the staffs of Toyota or Datsun agencies abroad to learn Japanese.

In a very different situation, Israel extends technical aid to developing nations, not so much to dominate these countries but to garner friends in its struggle for the right to exist. Training courses for foreign technicians are sometimes given in Hebrew, more often in English or French. Israel itself has heavily depended on English and French, but French influence has been on the wane, as France ceased being Israel's principal arms supplier after the 1967 war. Use of English has been on the increase, as Israel has ended up with a single ally and principal supplier, the United States. The extent to which Israel's continued existence depends on the United States' good will and aid is matched by the position of English as the unquestioned second language of Israel and as dominant in certain fields. For example, the work of chief pharmacists in large Israeli hospitals is almost entirely in English, and both textbooks and libraries at the university level are about 80–90 percent in English, the humanities excepted.

It would be a mistake to assume that the situations just discussed work only to the disadvantage of the less developed country; on the contrary, many advantages are obtained. On the other hand, it must be emphasized that the spread of English throughout the world has been a direct result of the influence of British and American economic and military dominance.

10.3 Colonialism

In recent years, the similarities have been stressed between external and internal colonialism, that is, between overseas colonies and subjugated ethnic groups, such as American Indians, Blacks, and Chicanos in the United States. There is certainly little difference ordinarily in the linguistic results. The language of the colonized is restricted in its use and development and has invariably less prestige, frequently even in the minds of its own speakers. Both types of colonized groups appear to suffer the consequences outlined by Blauner (1969): displacement, deculturation, deautonomization, and subjugation, as well as racism.

Under colonialism, a people is not in full control of its own institutions. Fundamental policies are decided elsewhere, and the colonized must accommodate as best they can. Because of limitations on freedom as well as finances, the colonized have to make the best of whatever kind of school system, if any, is provided by the colonial masters. Decisions concerning linguistic matters will be undertaken with the general goals of colonialist policy in mind. In other words, language is made to play the part of an instrument of colonial policy.

As is the case with all decisions, rationalizations are always readily forthcoming, some of them justified. Thus, a colonial language like English or French, for example, is a key to understanding industrial civilization and reaching out to the broader world. At the same time, it facilitates the colonialist's task if the colonized learn his language rather than vice versa, particularly if in a multilingual society. What then happens is that those who master the colonialist's language tend to become intermediaries between rulers and ruled, and to become the nucleus of a new native elite. They may further become the source of ideas from the outside such as anticolonialism and nationalism.

Different colonial powers have imposed different language policies. In Africa and Asia, the British and Germans tended to use local languages, whereas the

French and Portuguese diffused their own languages. French has remained an element of social prestige for the opportunities it offered. Parents of children in some missionary schools in Africa have even demanded that mission schools stop teaching local languages and teach in French. However, the Islamized populations in Africa showed some opposition to French schools, since they seemed to threaten the teaching of Arabic. As a result, at times sons of slaves or pagans were sent to fill school quotas and acquired a French education that enabled them later on to overthrow the power of the Muslim elites (Alexandre 1972:78). French policy was cultural imperialism, but it was also ethnocentric nationalistic humanitarianism, for the French felt they were giving the best culture which mankind had to offer.

Much of the world has been decolonialized, but the legacy of the colonial period remains to plague the countries of the Third World as they struggle to modernize, industrialize, and liberate themselves from Western economic domination. Some linguistic aspects of this struggle are discussed in Chapter 11.

10.4 Culture contact

When persons from different cultures come into contact, we may speak of the process as *culture contact.* This can extend from very casual encounters to two peoples living side by side for centuries. When people who speak different languages come into contact, they may communicate either through gestures or through some common third tongue. More drastic solutions are either to learn the other people's language or to construct a new one, a simplified version of one of their languages with features of the second, such as a pidgin.

The degree of intensity and length of contact are important variables in predicting the amount of mutual influence that is likely to take place. Thus, merchants, missionaries, travellers, or colonial administrators who, individually or in small groups, visit foreign cultures are likely to learn the local languages but unlikely to have very much impact on them or to spread their own language among the people. On the other hand, a large influx of colonists or traders or the setting up of extensive institutions such as schools to serve the people is likely to result in much linguistic influence. Coterritorial habitation between two linguistically different groups may result in the production of some bilingualism in both groups. The bilinguals may then serve as the medium of transmission of forms or features from one language to the other, as well as cultural exchange.

Changes in the size or composition of a population by virtue of different fertility, mortality, or migration rates can have important effects sociolinguistically. If the subcomponents of the population are characterized by different languages or different language varieties, the languages themselves and the attitudes toward them may change. This is particularly true in countries with a delicate ethnic balance between two different language communities with different population growth rates, as, for example, the French/Dutch split in Belgium, the French/English split in Canada or the English/Afrikaans split in

South Africa. In such cases, the group which is increasing is likely to demand more language rights, that is, that the language be made official in more circumstances and that it achieve full equality with the other language if this has not already been achieved. On the other hand, a group diminishing in size may have to fight vigorously for retention of the language rights it already has, which, however, may be conceded by the other group as a matter of political expediency. Just as members of a society or subsociety with a disappearing indigenous culture may start a nativistic movement to protect and perpetuate their culture, so may a group be especially motivated to perpetuate or revive their ancestral tongue. In some cases, they may establish language academies or schools, urging or encouraging scholars to write grammars or dictionaries of their languages.

Lewis (1972b:11–12) points out that in the Soviet Union, high fertility rates are helping to maintain local languages, even when the language community is losing its importance in numerical terms relative to Russian. In the Soviet Union, as in most developing countries, bilingualism is almost always a characteristic of the male population. The women not only are conservative linguistically but also are far more restricted in their social and intercultural contacts.

Conquests, invasions, deportation, and mass immigration often result in the extinction, superposition, or merger of whole languages. Four types of results can be distinguished: (1) the language of the conquered people all but disappears, as in the case of African slaves taken to the New World, (2) the conquerors adopt the language of the conquered, as in the case of the Norman invasion of England, (3) two populations mingle with wholesale borrowing of vocabulary by one of the languages, as in the case of the Arab conquest of Persia, or (4) varying degrees of societal bilingualism, as in much of the world. In attempting to analyze reasons for the different results, we must not lose sight of the fact that languages do not come into contact under neutral emotional conditions but always produce significant attitudinal reactions. Both social-structural and social-psychological variables must be taken into consideration, especially in dealing with the processes of acculturation and assimilation.

10.5 Acculturation and assimilation

Culture contact almost invariably results in some degree of acculturation, that is, persons of each culture take on some traits, however modified or reinterpreted, from the other culture. The process is rarely symmetrical. Usually one party to the transaction adopts more than the other. That is true in general and also is true of linguistic acculturation specifically. If acculturation of immigrants to the culture of a host society reaches the point where the immigrants (or their descendants) are indistinguishable in behavior and attitudes from the natives, we may say that assimilation has taken place. While it is not unusual for individuals to reach this stage, it has been rather exceptional in modern times for a whole immigrant community to become assimilated and thus virtually disappear as a separate entity, a process sometimes referred to as amalgamation. Thus, although assimilation is perhaps the limiting case, we may speak of varying degrees of acculturation.

Language plays a most important role in these processes. Not only is language (that of the host society) the most important vehicle for acquiring the new culture, it may be the most important element of the culture being acquired. The extent to which immigrants retain their original language is a matter dealt with in maintenance/shift (see section 10.6). One universal feature of certain stages of the linguistic assimilation process is bilingualism, characterized by large-scale language mixture and code switching. Some linguistic minorities in Europe, such as Basques in France and Spain or German speakers in Belgium are indigenous, whereas Turkish and Yugoslav *Gastarbeiter* (migrant workers) in Western Europe are immigrant minorities. Most linguistic minorities in the United States are immigrant groups.

Factors promoting or retarding the linguistic acculturation of indigenous minorities or of individual immigrants and of immigrant groups as a whole are several. For example, similarities of the two languages, particularly the difficulty of the new language as perceived by those who must learn it must be considered. Likewise, immigrants or other minorities must have opportunities to learn the new language. Thus, an oft-cited reason for the relatively low degree of linguistic acculturation of the Mexican immigrant community in the United States is the fact that Mexicans were imported to do hot, heavy, and dirty work in groups isolated from the outside society, working in mines and fields and living in company housing. Their immediate supervisors were ordinarily bilingual Chicanos, thus obviating the necessity of learning English for mere survival. When they brought their families, they were housed in segregated neighborhoods and attended segregated schools and churches. This isolation was to the detriment of the workers' acquisition of English but to the advantage of the employers, some of whom are now feeling the repressed hostility of generations as expressed through César Chávez' United Farm Workers Union. Once the Mexican workers did learn English, however, they became better apprised of the nature of United States society and began demanding further rights and benefits. This then created a need for the employers to import additional workers from Mexico, who were more docile and unsophisticated, which led to the continuing influx of *braceros*, green-card holders, and undocumented workers all competing with native workers (largely Chicanos) for the scarce, low-paying jobs. In all of this, language has unquestionably played an important part.

As immigrants who live under highly segregated conditions find it difficult to learn the language of the host country, so conversely immigrants who come as individuals and live among the natives (particularly if they marry one) ordinarily learn the language very quickly. Age is another important factor. Small children learn a new language in a matter of months. In a study done by the writer in Israel, immigrants who came in their teens or early twenties had all become very fluent in Hebrew in a few years, whereas of those immigrating after age 35, very few had developed any real facility in Hebrew at all. (For further discussion of linguistic assimilation see section 10.6.)

10.6 Language maintenance and language shift

In multilingual situations, under what conditions does a group strive to retain use of its own language, that is, manifest language loyalty, and under what conditions is a group likely to adopt the language of another group? These are the matters dealt with in the study of language maintenance and language shift, where we observe the relationship between degree of change or stability in language usage patterns, and ongoing psychological, cultural, or social processes. Such study focuses particularly upon situations involving bilingualism without diglossia. Such situations are inherently unstable. There may be different reactions in the spoken and written realms. Where people have become literate before acquiring their second language, reading and writing in the mother tongue will be more likely to be maintained.

Fishman (1972b) indicates that there have been five major language shifts in modern times, namely the adoption of the vernacular for governmental, technical, educational, and cultural activity in Europe; the wholesale adoption of European languages by the native populations of the Americas; the spread of English and French as languages of wider communication for elites throughout the world; the Russification of non-Russian Soviet peoples; and the displacement of imported languages by native languages in much of Africa and Asia.

Fishman (1966) classifies the languages of the United States into indigenous languages (languages of the American Indians); colonial languages, that is, the languages of the European colonizers who settled territories that later became part of the United States (English, Spanish, French, and German, which did survive, and Russian, Swedish and Dutch, which did not); and immigrant languages, those of the immigrants to the United States during the past two centuries, especially during the mass immigration of 1880 to 1920.

Compared with most nations of the world, an astounding number of immigrants and their descendants in the United States have given up their languages and shifted to a new mother tongue. Over 20 million immigrants between 1840 and 1924 were native speakers of some other language. Except for the speakers of colonial languages in the Southwest, in New England, and the Louisiana Bayous, the shift to English mother tongue was quick and free of intergroup conflict, although there has been conflict between generations within each immigrant group. Extraordinary language loyalty has been manifested by Mexicans and Puerto Ricans in the United States, but these communities are constantly being reinforced by new immigrants from Mexico and Puerto Rico (see section 9.3). As a result, Spanish is the only major language in the United States, other than English, whose speakers are increasing in numbers.

The United States has put comparatively few restrictions on the public and private use of foreign languages. Nevertheless, foreign languages have shrivelled in its free atmosphere, whereas they had flourished under adverse conditions in Europe. So something other than freedom is operating, as all languages are reduced to the same sad state. Their newspapers die, the schools close, the organizations shift to English, and only a small dedicated group tries to keep the language alive (Glazer 1966:361). Faced with mass education, mass culture, and the demands of the economy, the immigrants lost the natural supports for language use, except the family, or in some instances, the Church. As the language begins to disappear, public support is sought.

As one ethnic leader expressed the matter, "Now the question no longer is: how shall we learn English so that we may take part in the social life of America and partake of her benefits; the big question is: how can we preserve the language of our ancestors here, in a strange environment and pass on to our descendants the treasures which it contains?" (Trond Bothne, Professor at Luther College, 1898, quoted by Fishman, ed. 1966, flyleaf).

The functions of English as a lingua franca among the different immigrant groups has been an important factor in English acquisition. Those unable to speak English were more likely to be employed in occupations with low income or high unemployment rates (Lieberson and Curry 1971:132). Widespread education has been the most significant factor in acquisition of English by the second generation. Those more segregated were less likely to learn English.

However, the causes of mother-tongue shift need not be the same as the causes of bilingualism. The first is most likely to occur where there is greater linguistic diversity. Frequency of bilingualism in the first generation affects shift in the second. In a pluralistic society, language maintenance can be promoted by such factors as religious and social isolation of the group from the majority society, fostering of schools, and preimmigration experience with language maintenance. Those promoting shift can include military service, intermarriage, compulsory universal education, physical and social mobility, and prestige of certain languages (Lieberson 1970:13–14). It is not necessarily the case that urban dwellers are more inclined to language shift than are rural dwellers. What is true is that cities are generally the place where social movements originate, and depending upon circumstances, the urban environment may promote either language maintenance or language shift (Fishman 1972b:126).

It is similarly not always true that the less prestigious language is replaced by a more prestigious language, unless we define prestige solely as the measure of a language's value in social advance. The definition of social advance is, of course, in itself a knotty problem. But there are numerous cases where a nonstandard dialect has replaced a standard one, for example, the displacement of Lithuanian by a German dialect in East Prussia before World War I, although many Lithuanians spoke Standard German. Similarly in an area of Schleswig, Standard German displaced Danish, only to be displaced, in turn, by a Low German dialect. In another case, Jewish elites in Eastern Europe before and after World War I shifted from a dependence on Russian, Polish, or German to bilingualism with Yiddish. Part of the problem in interpreting such cases is that we know very little about the relationships between language attitudes and language use.

Religion has been a potent factor in the maintenance of Welsh, of French in Canada, of Afrikaans in the Republic of South Africa, of Flemish in Belgium, and Irish in Ireland. The relationship of religion and the maintenance of the vernacular has often been extremely close. Religion normally fosters traditionalism and thus slows down the assimilation process leading to ultimate monolingualism.

Language policy obviously affects language maintenance. Take, for example, the case of Basque, spoken on both sides of the Pyrenees and linguistically unrelated to either Spanish or French (or to any other language, as far as we know). A few centuries ago Basque was much more extensively spoken on the French side of the border than on the Spanish side. Nowadays, the area of Basque speech is much smaller in France than it is in Spain. The apparent reason for the change is the difference in language policy of the two countries. The Spanish government (except during the short-lived Republic and since the accession of King Juan Carlos in 1975) has consistently discouraged, if not tried to obliterate, non-Spanish languages, prohibiting their use for many purposes and hindering their development. One reaction of the Basque people has been a strong nationalistic feeling and pride in their distinct language. In France, on the other hand, a laissez-faire policy has prevailed; since to the government the virtues of French were self-evident, if some people have some other language, that was their loss. The French simply ignored other languages, neither hindering nor helping their development. Therefore, there was no nationalistic reaction of any strength, only a reciprocity of the toleration. Assimilation into the national culture and language was expected because of its self-evident political and economic usefulness (Engerrand 1956). The situation is parallel to the oft-noted function of anti-Semitism in the development of strong Jewish communities and the gradual assimilation of Jews (especially through intermarriage) where anti-Semitism is negligible, as in present-day Scandinavia. (Some doubt is thrown on the above remarks concerning French language policy by the 1978 bombing of the Versailles Palace by Breton nationalists.)

While repression of Basque or Catalan nationalism in Spain may help explain language maintenance among these peoples, it is difficult to sort out cause and effect. The repression of their nationalism has been caused in part at least by the stubborn refusal of these people to become linguistically assimilated to Castilian. It should be pointed out that in the Spanish situation, what is being rejected by the nationalists is not Castilian as such but Castilian monolingualism. They are fighting for a situation of stable bilingualism with diglossia. It may be that the 1975 decrees of King Juan Carlos, legalizing the minority languages, may help bring this about.

In cases where language shift does take place, there is always an intermediate stage of bilingualism as the group passes from monolingualism in one language to monolingualism in the other. There have been, of course, innumerable historical instances of language shift, but what we are witnessing in so many parts of the world today is this transitional situation.

Language shift in immigrant populations, at least in the United States, ordinarily takes place over a period of three generations, unless some very strong factors promoting language maintenance are involved. That is, the first, immigrant generation ordinarily learns the language of the host country to some extent. In the United States, for example, the second generation is usually bilingual, speaking the immigrant language (or both languages, and/or a mixture of the two) at home and in the ethnic neighborhood but speaking English in school and in dealing with members of other groups.

When members of the second generation grow up, they usually speak English to each other and later to their children. The latter, the third generation is thus usually monolingual in English. What is true of language is generally true of the immigrant culture as well, except that one frequently observes the so-called "return of the third generation." This term refers to the situation where the second generation, in its eagerness to become American, rejects the language and culture of the first generation. The third generation, however, sensing the loss of the ethnic language and culture wishes to return to them but generally is able to do so only in a symbolic way (Nahirny and Fishman 1965). To a certain extent the "return of the third generation" has been a strong component in the student demand for language and ethnic studies in the United States, on the part of, for example, Chicano or Asian-American students, most of whom by now are, indeed, of the third generation.

Studying the incidence of language shift of German speakers in Belgium, Luxembourg, and Alsace-Lorraine, Verdoodt (1972:376) concluded that a community can best resist language shift when it can maintain a diglossic functional differentiation between its own language (or languages) and that of the majority. This is most likely to be the case when an indigenous minority has attained legal and economic protection before tendencies to shift gather momentum.

Weinreich (1953a:98) points out that the absence of sociocultural divisions, such as ethnicity, religion, race, age, social status, etc., to reinforce differences in mother-tongue, not only facilitates language shift, but it probably also weakens resistance to interlingual influence.

The factors promoting language shift are not always easy to perceive. It soon becomes obvious to an immigrant, under ordinary circumstances, that he must learn the language of the host country in order to survive. It is not equally obvious to him why his children or grandchildren find it equally necessary or desirable to cast off the immigrant tongue. Sometimes the process starts in the first generation, particularly under conditions of endemic xenophobia. The immigrant himself may overemphasize his allegiance to his new country. Sometimes an immigrant will refuse to speak his own language to his children in the usually mistaken belief that this will facilitate their acquisition of the other language. In such cases it would seem that the immigrant has internalized the host country's antiforeign attitudes and racism, and promoted his own self-hatred. Or children may refuse to speak the ethnic tongue and poke fun at their elders speaking the host language. There is also the phenomenon of the *passive bilingual,* who understands the parents' tongue but cannot (or will not) speak it, and the *covert bilingual,* who speaks the language but refuses to admit it, ashamed as he is of its foreign association (Sawyer 1977). The ethnic's consciousness of this socially generated self-hatred has been a strong factor in the movements for ethnic pride and ethnic self-determination.

In considering conditions under which shift is likely to occur, one has to deal with both linguistic and nonlinguistic factors. Among the latter, the most important would appear to be the nature of the relationship between the speakers of the two languages in question, that is, between which the shift is taking place. Thus, for example, consider the situation of military conquest. Often the prestige of the conquerors, their language, religion, and culture is such, and the advantages of assimilating to the conquerors' language so obvious and so great, that the subjugated population rushes headlong into a language shift. Witness the rapid shift to Arabic, originally the language of the Arabian Peninsula only, taking place throughout the Middle East and North Africa after the great Islamic conquests started by the Prophet Muhammad in the seventh century. However, Arabic supplanted the local languages generally only when those languages were closely related to and thus similar to Arabic, as Aramaic in Syria and Iraq, Coptic in Egypt, and various Berber languages in North Africa. All of these languages are members of the Afro-Asiatic family (often called by the earlier term Semitō-Hamitic). The Iranians, Kurds, Afghans, all speaking Indo-Iranian languages unrelated to Arabic, did not shift to Arabic, though they adopted the Arabic alphabet and a massive infusion of Arabic loanwords. The Spaniards, likewise, did not give up their language during seven centuries of Islamic occupation, although Spanish (and Portuguese, too) adopted thousands of Arabic words. There was also some writing of Spanish in Arabic script (*aljamía*). Similarly, Arab conquests in sub-Saharan Africa, India, and the Malayo-Indonesian area did not result in a shift to Arabic, although again the peoples who accepted Islam also adopted the Arabic alphabet and many Arabic loanwords, all the way from West Africa to the Philippines.

A similar instance is that of the Sephardic Jews, expelled from Spain in 1492 and dispersed throughout the Mediterranean region. They have retained their Spanish to this day in the Balkans and Turkey, but in Italy they quickly shifted to the closely related Italian. On the other hand, there has been a large-scale shift (but not very rapid, considering a time span of almost five centuries) to Arabic in the Arabic-speaking countries (except Egypt, where French has been the language of the Jewish home). Because of these variations, obviously nonlinguistic as well as linguistic factors have to be taken under consideration. Thus, the persistence of Yiddish among Eastern European Jews for almost a millennium is perhaps best explained by their geographical, cultural, and social isolation from the surrounding societies, an isolation much greater than that of Jews in the Arab societies. Perhaps linguistic assimilation of the Jews has been roughly inversely correlated with the degree of anti-Semitism. Thus, Yiddish is virtually dying out in the United States, whereas it flourishes, relatively, in the Soviet Union, despite official repression. The Jews are the only ethnic group in the Soviet Union which has no territorial base and for which no provision is made for the education of their children in their own vernacular, that is, Yiddish. There is, however, no educational discrimination of this sort in the case of Russian-speaking or Tadjik-speaking Jews, etc.

An important language shift to Hebrew has been taking place among the multilingual population of pre-1948 Palestine and in the present-day state of Israel. By 1913, Hebrew had become the language of instruction at all levels in Jewish Palestine. At first the revival of and shift to Hebrew was based on beliefs and ideology but more recently based on the functions of instrumentality and private need. Acquisition of Hebrew has become a means toward private ends, rather than expression of an ideal (Hofman and Fisherman 1971:343–344).

At times a language or local dialect becomes extinct or dies out. Denison (1977) prefers the term "language suicide" to "language death" because, in most instances, people voluntarily give up speaking a language and teaching it to their children. (It is a delicate matter to identify a dying language because its speakers will ordinarily be offended by this prognostication and will vociferously proclaim that the language is alive and well.) On the other hand, some American Indian communities have asked linguists to record their languages before they are completely lost. Of course, under conditions of genocide, a language may disappear along with the people who spoke it, as happened in the case of the Tasmanians and of some Amerindian peoples. There is also the phenomenon of *linguicide,* whereby there is a deliberate effort to kill off the language, although not its speakers, as the attempt to wipe out Ukrainian in Czarist Russia.

Where the dominant language and the minority tongue are closely related, the dominant group may try not to blot out but to *dialectize* the minority tongue. Thus, for example, the Bulgarians regard Macedonian as a dialect of Bulgarian, not as a separate language, as do the Serbs. The Serbs, on the other hand, treat Croatian as a "variant" of Serbo-Croatian, not as a separate language, as Croatian nationalists insist.

Most usually, a language dies because children no longer learn it. Only the elderly still speak it fluently, whereas middle-aged and younger people may be only semispeakers. As the old people die off one by one, the language goes as well. But in these final stages of transition from bilingualism and/or diglossia to monolingualism and monoglossia, the disappearing language undergoes important changes, including varying degrees of relexification and phonological and syntactic influence from the dominant language. As the domains of use continue to shrink, styles are lost, and speakers end up with a monostylistic language, used in a single domain, the intimate one. As its functions shrink, so do its forms, and the end result may be a pidgin-like language. In other words, a dying language goes through the same stages, but in reverse order, as a pidgin does on its way to becoming a creole, that is, expansion of forms, functions and styles. In both cases also, the pidgin stage is correlated with low social status. Pidgin speakers may continue bilingualism, develop a creole, or adopt a mainstream language. Speakers of the dying langauge, however, abandon their bilingualism and become monolingual speakers of the mainstream language.

Discussion questions

1. Discuss the relationship between the emergence of the world capitalist system and the origin of modern standard languages.
2. Discuss the relationship between language and nationalism in its "ethnic" and "political" varieties.
3. Describe the linguistic results of colonialism and culture contact.

4. What types of social conditions promote assimilation and language shift on the one hand and cultural retention and language maintenance on the other?
5. Describe the generational differences among immigrant populations with reference to language maintenance/shift.
6. What sorts of conditions lead to the disappearance of a language?

11

Language policy
and language conflict

11.1 Industrialization and modernization

There are a number of interrelated sociocultural and economic changes which
the industrialized countries of the world underwent a hundred and fifty or so
years ago and which the so-called developing countries of the Third World are
undergoing today. The conceptualization of these processes is somewhat of a
theoretical and ideological controversy at the present time in sociology. Those
who use the *development model* envision the Third World nations evolving into
societies which are reasonable approximations to the societies of Western
Europe; to them, *modern* means "Western." One of the characteristics which
these societies are said to be acquiring then is *modernization,* which is usually
defined in terms of an increase in such factors as literacy, urbanization, per capita
income, areal mobility, exposure to communication, industrialization, and
political participation. One important aspect of modernization is *social mobilization,* the process by which hitherto isolated sectors of the population are drawn
into fuller participation in public life. This is accomplished by opening channels of
communication from centers of political control, economic power, and innovation to outlying areas and groups. The basis for such communication lies in widely
circulating mass media, increased literacy, and a general educational system.
Those directing the social mobilization process in developing countries not only
must decide what language to choose but also how to carry out the standardization process.

The processes of modernization and industrialization do not in themselves
necessarily lead either to uniformation or diversification of languages. In fact,
both may go on simultaneously. While new languages or varieties (for example,
languages of wider communication) may be introduced from the outside, others
may spread by means of educational or other institutions over wider areas and
displace certain varieties. At the same time, old and new varieties may interact to
produce new hybrid varieties. The status of some varieties is lowered at the same

time that the status of others is elevated. For example, in Yugoslavia, Macedonian has achieved the status of a full-fledged language, at the same time that Yiddish has been almost completely obliterated in Eastern Europe. The American experience is atypical, in that the various ethnic populations in contact with each other are all dislocated populations. Dislocation often leads to cultural and ethnic assimilation, as is happening in the Soviet Union and in much of postwar Europe.

In Europe and North America, industrialization preceded urbanization, and (particularly in Eastern Europe) ethnic nationalism preceded political nationalism. Furthermore, the first set of phenomena preceded the second. In the Third World today, however, we seem to be witnessing the reverse of these sequences, that is, nationalism there is preceding urbanization which, in turn, is preceding industrialization. Third World elites are de-emphasizing language issues of a local or regional nature at the same time that they are favoring continued use of supraregional and colonial languages as an aid in the modernization and industrialization processes (Fishman 1972b:125).

Those who prefer the *liberation model*, rather than the development model, envision Third World societies as liberating themselves both from the traditions of a feudal-like society, as well as from the shackles of colonialism and neocolonialism. Regardless of the conceptualization involved, it is apparent that the changes these societies are undergoing are directly related to language problems. In the first place, the former colonized areas are faced with the legacy of colonialist language policy. In most cases, the natives learned Western technology, organization, and culture through the medium of a Western language, hence their own languages did not have adequate opportunity to develop their lexicons to meet these needs. They were even compelled to think in the Western language in dealing with technologies, organizational structures, and other cultural systems imported from, and imposed on them, from the West (cf. section 10.2).

With the achievement of independence in the former colonies, many desired that modern science, technology, and civic life be the patrimony of the entire nation, not just of a privileged elite. This meant that the people would have to receive a modern education in their own, or a closely related, vernacular. This involves the question of language development, how a language can be expanded and adapted to a radically new kind of technological and social order. That it can be done is proven, for example, by the cases of English and Japanese, which changed to meet the needs of an industrial society, although they had a century or more in which to do it. The developing nations, however, cannot wait a hundred years for their languages to catch up with their technology through "natural," that is, unplanned change. Change must be rapid, and it must be planned.

There are similarities between economic development and language development. In neither respect are the non-Western nations likely to follow in the steps of the developed Western nations. The former are much poorer now than were the rich countries of today in their developing periods. The Third World countries have an unfavorable balance of resource exploitation, and they do not have the ready markets for the sale of their wares at advantageous prices, the emigration outlets, nor the cheap sources of raw materials that the Western nations had when they industrialized in the eighteenth and nineteenth centuries. Just as the Western nations have pre-empted markets and raw materials, so have they pre-empted the language field. European languages are those through which most future technical, political, and social changes will reach the indigenous language communities, and the most likely languages through which locals can leave the indigenous language community (Fishman 1973a:28–29).

A further problem of the Third World nations is that their political boundaries correspond rather imperfectly to pre-existing ethnic boundaries. Although this was also true of the new nations of Eastern Europe after World War I, the latter had for decades engaged in nationalistic activity, which lead to a high degree of cultural consolidation and integration before the achievement of nationhood. On the other hand, in the new nations of Africa especially, political independence was achieved far in advance of unification around a set of national symbols. Hence, language may become a symbol not of ethnic but of national identity, except for those ethnic groups who resist fusion into the larger nationality. In addition to these problems of cultural legitimacy and authenticity, the new nations have been confronted with language problems revolving around efficiency and instrumentality. That is, the countries are faced not only with ideologies and symbolization and unification but with solving practical problems, in business, government, education, etc. In much of the Third World, the symbolic goals may have to give way to the immediate operational needs of the country. Some language or multiple languages may have to be recognized. For example, a common solution is the use of local languages for elementary schooling but a European language for government activity and higher education. In the newly emergent countries of Africa and Asia, the demand for literate education comes from those classes which especially see themselves at an economic disadvantage without it. They do not see education as a means of developing an integrated personality but as the only way to get ahead economically. Vernacular education may not necessarily be in the best interest of these people's ambitions. Education in a world language may promote more opportunity for social mobility, but cultural estrangement may be the price for economic advance.

Ferguson (1968a:28) identifies three dimensions of language development, namely graphization (reduction to writing), standardization, and intertranslatability with the languages of the industrialized, secularized, and structurally differentiated modern societies. A language may be considered modernized when it has become the equal of other developed languages as an appropriate vehicle of modern forms of discourse. The process of modernization includes the expansion of the lexicon, as well as the development of new styles and forms of discourse.

Some nation-states are more homogeneous linguistically than others, and this seems to favor development and modernization. Fishman (1968c:60) has claimed that linguistically homogeneous countries are usually economically and educationally more advanced, and politically more modernized and stable than the heterogeneous ones. On the average, the more homogeneous countries are also richer. He concludes that while language diversity may hinder, language unity helps development. When there is a diversity of language, political section-alism may be aggravated, which hinders cooperation among groups and regions, as well as impeding political stability and political participation. Language diversity also slows economic development, by reducing occupational mobility and the number of people available for mobilization into the modern sector of the economy. It is, furthermore, difficult to diffuse innovative techniques to the polyglot population. In a study of the interrelationships of these factors, Pool (1972) concluded that a country can have any degree of language uniformity or fragmentation and still be underdeveloped. On the other hand, a highly linguistically homogeneous state can be anywhere from very rich to very poor. "But a country that is linguistically highly heterogeneous is always under-developed or semi-developed, and a country that is highly developed always has considerable language uniformity. Language uniformity, then, is a necessary but not sufficient condition of economic development..." (There are individual exceptions, such as Switzerland, for example.)

11.2 Language policy

Language politics can be defined as the struggle to influence or participate in the formulation of and implementation of policy regarding the uses to which certain languages and language varieties will be put, as well as whom these policies will favor and whom they will affect adversely. Such policies are often formulated "for the common good," though in a linguistically diverse state, any linguistic policy is likely to discriminate. For example, it is not economically or otherwise feasible to set up school instruction in everybody's vernacular. Complete equity rarely results because such matters are decided not by humani-tarians and scholars but by practical politicians responsible to powerful leaders and constituencies for the solution of practical problems.

Kloss (1968) has identified a series of stages of government attitudes toward language. A particular language may be recognized as any one of the following:

1. Sole official language (e.g. French in France)
2. Joint official language (e.g. French and Flemish in Belgium)
3. Regional official language (e.g. Ibo in eastern Nigeria)
4. Promoted language: lacks official status but used by government in deal-ings with public (e.g. Spanish in Southwestern United States)
5. Tolerated language (e.g. Basque in France)
6. Discouraged language (e.g. Macedonian in Greece)

Among the human rights which all people should be able to enjoy are language rights. There are language rights which are promotion-oriented, that is, where public authorities make use of the foreign language in their own activities; and there are toleration-oriented language rights, that is, those which allow the minorities the right to use the language in domains where the citizens them-selves, not the authorities, become active. A common position is that the acquies-cent rights should be granted whenever a group is willing and able to make the necessary exertions, but that linguistic minorities can lay no claim to promotion-oriented rights (Kloss 1971).

There is no universal consensus that immigrants, for example, necessarily and automatically are entitled to language rights. There are arguments both for and against granting such rights. Usually the dominant group feels that the immi-grants ought to give up their language as soon as possible. One argument is that immigrants, by the very fact of immigration, have tacitly agreed to adapt themselves to the new country. Yet, many came to the New World to escape minority status abroad and, under certain conditions, were able to cultivate their languages more vigorously in the Americas, for example, Albanian, Lithuanian, Ukrainian, Yiddish, and Syrian Arabic. Another argument claims immigrants ought to assimilate because of the economic benefits they have gained but fails to take into account the economic contributions of the immigrants themselves as producers and consumers. Finally, the dominant group may be afraid of the formation of new ghettoes and the threat to national unity if language rights are granted.

On the other hand, Article 27 of the Covenant on Civil and Political Rights adopted by the United Nations on December 18, 1966, and Article 5 of the Convention Against Discrimination in Education, adopted by UNESCO on December 14, 1960, recognize that ethnic groups have the right to maintain their languages. A more specific argument is that parents have the right to choose the type of education they prefer for their children and to have them study any branch of learning they choose. It is furthermore advantageous to the state to have a reservoir of bilingual citizens who may serve as bridges between countries. But perhaps the strongest argument is the cultural enrichment which state and society derive from the presence of a variety of languages and language-based cultural traditions.

Language rights can be based on either the principle of territoriality, in which case the language used in a given situation will depend solely on the territory in question, e.g. a particular province, or on the principle of personality, in which case language use will depend on the linguistic status of the person or persons concerned, e.g. membership in a particular ethnic group. In the first instance, use is determined by community membership. In the latter case, the basis for classification may be either objective or subjective, that is, determined by either ethnic sentiment or a preference for one of the languages the individual knows (McCrae 1975:33, 44–41). In the case of the application of the territoriality principle, a minority within the designated territory may have to make some concessions, depending on whether the policy instituted is unilingual or bilingual, and of what sort.

The linguistic policy of newly independent countries is normally affected by such factors as: the length of the period of colonial rule, and whether during that period there was more than one colonial power in possession; the amount of education provided by the colonial rulers, for what classes, to what level, and in what language; the manner of achieving independence, and relations subsequently with the former colonial power and its allies (Le Page 1964:45).

Rulers of multilingual states have followed three types of language policies in order to promote a particular language over all the others. Interestingly, each one of these policies has been followed at one time or another in Russia or the Soviet Union. In the first type, the language of the most powerful nationality is imposed upon the other nationalities, and the use of their language is prohibited. This was Czarist policy and the policy in Hungary after Magyar replaced Latin. In the second type, a supranational legitimacy is conferred on one language derived from religious, cultural, or ideological considerations, as in the case of Soviet policy, and that of Ottoman Turkey, the Hapsburg Empire, and the British colonies in India and Africa. The third type of policy is to create new languages by the elevation of local dialects or variants so as to ensure the supremacy of a favored language. This policy has been carried out in places like Yugoslavia, where creation of the Macedonian literary language has neutralized the competing political claims of Serbians and Bulgarians on the Macedonians. Divisiveness has been promoted among the Turkic dialects of Soviet Asia so as to guarantee the supremacy of Russian.

Pre-World War I multilingual empires, like the Austro-Hungarian Monarchy, the Russian Empire, and the Ottoman Empire, generally followed repressive policies toward their minorities in language, as in other areas. Hungarian administration in their half of the Dual Monarchy was particularly oppressive, as the Magyars tried to transform their ancient multinational kingdom into a Magyar national state. In 1833, the official language was changed from Latin to Magyar. The resulting Magyarization of governmental administration aroused the deep resentment of Slovaks, Croats, Serbs, and Romanians. The Magyar nationalists had demanded constitutional reforms, liberal legislation, and independence from the Hapsburgs. But the "liberation" of the Magyars meant the "oppression" of the non-Magyar peoples within Hungary itself (Kohn 1965:49).

Some of the modern states which succeeded the multilingual empires after World War I have been even less liberal toward the minor ethnic groups. In the Soviet Union, language equality is nominal rather than real. For example, a Ukrainian or Latvian who migrates to Siberia is expected to send his children to a Russian school, but a Russian who moves to Riga or Odessa is not expected to send his children to a Latvian or Ukrainian school (Kloss 1967).

Soviet language policy elevated the importance of Russian among the non-Russian peoples by elevating dialects into languages so as to prevent the formation of large blocks of homogeneous language speakers, e.g. Turkish, which might oppose Russian dominance. The divide-and-conquer policy was never so successfully applied to language problems, as minor dialectal differences were exaggerated by enlarging on them. The development of a possible regional non-Russian language was effectively blocked. Russian necessarily became the lingua franca of the entire country. The teaching of Russian in all non-Russian schools became compulsory in 1938. Also the late 1930s saw the shift from the Latin to the Cyrillic alphabet for non-Russian languages, except for those well-established, literary languages which had their own non-Cyrillic scripts such as Armenian, Finnish, Georgian, Yiddish, and the Baltic languages. The Soviet government at that time released an undisguised Russification program, in the interests of promoting the learning of Russian and the spread of Russian culture. Peoples wishing to develop the resources of their own languages rather than borrowing Russian words or international words in their Russian form, or Muslim peoples who wanted to borrow from Arabic, Turkish or Persian, were condemned as "local bourgeois nationalists" (Goodman 1968:725–728).

In Central Asia, in pre-Soviet times, the use of the Arabic alphabet had facilitated the borrowing of Persian and Arabic words among Turkic speakers and encouraged multilingual scholarship. The Arabic alphabet tended to obscure differences among dialects because vowels were not written. Turkic speakers, thus, could learn fairly easily to read writings in other dialects and Turkic languages including Ottoman. The Arabic alphabet was the symbol of religious and cultural ties with the larger Islamic world (Bacon 1966:190).

Around 1923, that is, after the Russian Revolution, an improved Arabic alphabet was introduced for Uzbek, Kazakh, and Kirghiz. The Soviet government, however, was finding that it was having to impose its rule by force and began to see the danger inherent in the continued use of an alphabet that separated the Central Asians from the Russians and maintained a common mode of expression with Muslims outside of the Soviet Union, some of whom had voiced Pan-Turkic sympathies. Therefore, a unified Latin alphabet was officially introduced in 1928 for use in writing Central Asian languages. As a matter of fact, in the late twenties there were even powerful spokesmen for the idea of Latinizing Russian itself. But this radically cosmopolitan idea died out with the rebirth of Russian nationalism in the 1930s (Weinreich 1953b). Central Asian scholars did not strongly oppose the move, because it provided a common script for all Turkic speakers, was better adapted to the Turkic phonetic system than was the Arabic alphabet, and turned out to be almost identical to the Latin alphabet adopted in November 1928 in Turkey under Atatürk. Tadjik scholars were less pleased because the Latin script emphasized dialectal differences between Tadjik and standard Persian. Linguistic considerations were not uppermost, for, in the Soviet view, "Every script is not only a technique of writing but also its ideology" (Weinreich 1953b:48). By 1930, all the languages of Central Asia had been provided with Latin alphabets, and hundreds of thousands of adults and children became literate.

But Turkey's adoption of a similar Latin alphabet aroused the fear in Soviet leaders that a new Pan-Turkic literature might develop in the Latin alphabet and attract the Central Asian peoples toward Turkey and away from Russia. Therefore, in 1940, the Latin alphabet for the Central Asian languages was replaced by a series of modified Cyrillic alphabets (not a single unified alphabet this time), which emphasized grammatical and phonological differences by creating certain special letters for each of them. The purges of 1932–1938 had liquidated many of the scholars who would have opposed this second transition.

Minorities speaking related languages are thus hindered in reading each other's newspapers and books because of alphabets that they have been forced to use which deliberately contrive to exaggerate small differences among the languages. For example, they may represent the same sound in two different but closely related languages by two different alphabetic characters. In the more liberal atmosphere of the 1970s, some Soviet scholars have come out in favor of reform and unification of the different Cyrillic alphabets used for writing the various Turkic languages. However, after three decades of using these writing systems, the people are quite used to them, and reform would, therefore, probably prove to be very difficult, even if Soviet authorities should approve of the effort (Henze 1977).

Soviet policy has been not only to establish Russian as a second native language throughout the non-Russian areas, but also to transform tribal and community languages into developed national languages with a rich modern vocabulary. These aims may prove to be contradictory since, in fact, Russian is considered a superior language; therefore it is doubtful if any of the local languages will ever become completely adequate as educational media. Nevertheless, it should be pointed out that Soviet policy differs from Czarist, in that dozens of languages not permitted by the Czarist regime are used today in education and publishing, although some languages have been banned: Arabic, Hebrew, Chechen, Ingush, Kalmyk, German, and virtually Yiddish as well. In the Soviet Union, the schools work in more than 70 languages of instruction, and literature and textbooks are published in all of them (Serdyuchenko 1962:23).

The Soviets rather than excluding the minority languages from certain functions have been Russifying them. Central Asian scholars have been accustomed to translate concepts introduced by the Russians into more familiar Turkic, Persian, or Arabic words. This practice has been discouraged and virtually overcome by constant reiteration of the Russian terms in school, speeches, and newspapers. At the same time, the use of Cyrillic script has facilitated the direct adoption of Russian words. Another advantage of the Cyrillic alphabet for the non-Russian languages is that the children do not have to learn two alphabets, since they will study Russian, in any case.

Linguistic research and publishing in the Soviet Union is carried out on a scale unequalled in any other country. Its object is to bring the various languages of the country into line with Soviet political, technical, and cultural requirements, especially by "enriching" and "developing" existing languages, particularly by means of massive infusing of elements of the Russian language.

In addition to the massive infusion of Russian words into the minority languages, the Russian language has penetrated the minority languages in two other ways, namely by the actual movement of Russian populations into minority areas and by the substitution of Russian for national languages among large numbers of people because of its usefulness as a lingua franca.

Despite a high level of forced, planned, and voluntary migration from European to Asian regions of the U.S.S.R., people of the latter regions have been able to achieve a high degree of language maintenance, especially in the rural areas. This has been in the face of the ideological movement toward the "merging" of the nations and their cultural traditions. Ethnic groups have been redistributed for purposes of administration such that groups of one nationality may be separated from their conationals and administered with groups of another nationality with whom they have little ethnic or linguistic affinity, with adverse effect on language maintenance (Lewis 1972a:316–317).

In contrast to the Soviet Union, in Yugoslavia current government policy emphasizes economic decentralization, regional, and national autonomy. This policy has helped to promote the autonomy of languages and language variants, which, in turn, however, may provide a linguistic cover for interethnic disputes.

Thus, the Serbs believe that the desire of the Croats to maintain and reinforce their variant of Serbo-Croatian is parochial and potentially separatist, while Croats see Serbian efforts to promote their variant as arrogant. The Croats are fewer but better organized, and their Latin alphabet more widely used, for example, in all telephone books and neon signs throughout Yugoslavia. In the army, the Latin alphabet is used exclusively (Magner 1967).

With the overthrow of the military dictatorship in Greece in 1975, the new government of Constantine Karamanlis instituted sweeping reforms to introduce dhimotiki as the sole language of education up to the university level and of government administration; and by 1980, it was to have become the language of university education, as well (on Greek diglossia see also section 7.3). In 1928, dhimotiki had been introduced as a subject into the first four grades, but katharevousa was used in all higher grades, except Greek literature classes, since most of the twentieth century Greek writers have written in dhimotiki. Only a handful of highly educated Greeks ever mastered the complex orthography and grammar of katharevousa. Many educated in it continue to use it, but it will die off as the older generation does (Karanikolas 1979). At the same time that the diglossic struggle has been going on between the partisans of the two varieties of Greek, Greeks have shown little concern for the sociolinguistic situation of their Slavic-speaking minority, although their Turkish-speaking minority has received special consideration. While Macedonian has been elevated to the status of a full-fledged language in Yugoslavia, its very existence has been denied in Greece. As Lunt explains, "The Greeks violently object to having any Slav referred to as a Macedonian, on the grounds that by historical right only a Greek can be a Macedonian. They ignore the overwhelming evidence that the countryside right down to Salonika was almost completely Slavicized by the eighth century" (Lunt 1959:25, n.2).

The policy of the French government has always been to teach the national language in the schools, which everyone was expected to understand and speak, but to allow linguistic freedom for the entire population and to grant, for example, freedom to religious practitioners to preach and teach religion in whichever language they choose. Above all, the government's policy is not to discriminate against populations which speak some other language or dialect. The French have not considered instituting bilingual education, for none of the indigenous minority languages (except for German, which is taught in Alsace-Lorraine) have attained a cultivated, literary form (Dauzat 1940:118). This policy ignores the needs of the children of immigrant workers from Italy, Turkey and other countries, as well as native Basque and Breton speakers.

King Juan Carlos's decree of November 15, 1957 legalized the regional languages of Spain and gave Basques, Catalans, Galicians, and Valencians (about one-third of the country's population) the right to use their native languages for the first time since Franco's ascension to power in 1938. The languages can now be used in official and other public events and taught in the public schools. In his first message to Parliament, King Juan Carlos had said, "A just order, equal for all, permits recognition of regional characteristics, the expression of the varied nature of the peoples which make up the sacred reality of

Spain. Within the unity of the realm and the state, the king wishes to be the king of every citizen, each in his own culture, history and tradition" (Leslie 1975).

Although almost the entire population of Somalia speaks Somali as their first language, there is no officially sanctioned orthography, so that Italian, English, and Arabic are used as written languages by shopkeepers, policemen, and members of Parliament, although shopkeepers and policemen deal with the public in Somali, and parliamentary debates are carried on in Somali. Only a small proportion of the population has mastered any of the three written languages (Heine 1970).

In India, the Hindi elite, which wields strong influence in literature, publishing, and government, has interpreted language reform and development to mean classicalization, that is, the adoption of words from Sanskrit in place of popular words of foreign origin, that is, Persian, Urdu, or English. This policy has resulted in a widening of the gap between literary Hindi and the spoken language of the masses, and an advantage in the educational system for the middle and upper classes. This conception of language planning is aimed more at expressing the "genius" of Hindi than at mobilization of the masses. Thus, expressive rather than instrumental values are served (Gumperz 1971:134–143).

Seemingly, of all social institutions, the one which is most intimately connected with and related to the questions dealt with in the sociology of language is education (see also section 9.4). Next to the family, where one's first language is learned, the school is of central importance in the use of and teaching about language, with vast implications for and impact on the rest of society. As noted above, one of the major reasons for the recent emergence of our field of study has been the confrontation in school systems of language-related, educational questions, particularly those related to minority groups. Elite education had few problems to contend with. In modern mass education, on the other hand, the great sociocultural and linguistic heterogeneity of the students has led to massive failure in the teaching of reading and other language-based skills (Spolsky 1974:2028).

The vernacular language is the child's own, which he has acquired in informal ways; in school, he acquires a standard and/or a classical language. Paradoxically, there are no real problems connected with the acquisition of classical languages, for they are normally either taught to select elites or taught in the context of a flourishing religious system. Both teachers and students accept the fact that learning a classical language is not simple, for it is a new language for the student; but in the case of standard languages, there has been an unawareness of the relationship between the student's vernacular and the standard language taught in the school. Teachers assume that everyone speaks the standard language or dialect, or that he will soon pick it up easily. Those who do not conform to these assumptions may be classified as stupid when they fail intelligence tests given in a language they don't know or continue to speak a dialect which differs from the standard. The resolution of the problem of the nonstandard speaking child can go to, at least, two extremes. One is the elimination of nonstandard speech; the other (perhaps utopian) is to promote society-wide appreciation for nonstandard dialects, so they will be acceptable in all contexts. A middle-of-the-road policy favored by many linguists is bidialectalism, featuring context-relevant code switching. In any case, solution of the problem must take into account the functions of language, not just for communication but also as a symbol of group identity and solidarity. Bidialectalism may, of course, lead in time to monodialectalism.

Whereas in traditional societies teachers may be considered elite guardians of an esoteric body of knowledge and a secret language, teachers in the mass education systems of modern societies are usually members of the upwardly mobile, lower middle class. They see as one of their most important tasks to teach the linguistic and other social mannerisms to be acquired by those who wish to move upwardly socially (Labov 1969). The teachers may be native speakers either of the child's language or of the school language, which will affect what methods they choose and how effective they are.

In some countries, the Ministry of Education resolves linguistic problems by issuing decisions which the schools controlled by the ministry must accept, such as lexical, grammatical, and spelling questions. Such decisions, of course, have an effect far beyond the confines of the schools themselves. Other countries, notably France, have language academies whose decisions are widely accepted. Interestingly enough, there has never been any such official or semiofficial authority in either Great Britain or the United States, and no ministry or department of education intervenes in such matters.

A much more controversial and emotionally-charged issue concerns the matter of the language of instruction to be used in the schools because of the different advantages for different students. Studies have shown quite consistently that where students are taught the first year or two in their native language and then switch to the official language for instruction in the third year, or where education is bilingual from the first year, they do better scholastically, emotionally, and socially than those who receive instruction in the official language only (John and Horner 1970). In some bilingual programs, one language is used for some purposes, the other language for other purposes, that is, there is functional separation of domains. Any such programs must take into consideration the child's situation, as well as the objectives of the community. Vernacular education has resulted in better self-images, greater ease and spread of expression and learning, as well as retention of subject matter and greater creativity. But what is best for the child may not necessarily be the best for the adult or best for the society. In multilingual countries, the social cost of providing vernacular education for all may be prohibitive. No country, certainly not a poor one, can afford to maintain schools, textbooks, and teacher training in dozens of different vernaculars.

In some cases, parents do not wish their children to be educated in the vernacular. For example, the Turkish minority in western Iran wishes their children to be educated in Persian, which they consider more prestigeful and useful. Likewise, speakers of varieties of Creole English in the West Indies do not wish to have their children educated in the vernacular, which is symbolic of low status and poverty. They want their children schooled in standard English, which symbolizes higher status and which opens up opportunities for upward mobility.

As far as the United States is concerned, in few of the education statutes passed in the nineteenth century was there any mention of English as the *only* language of instruction (Macías 1979). But in 1868, a Federal law was passed regarding American Indians, which set the policy of taking children off the reservation and placing them in boarding schools where they would learn English (being forbidden to speak their native languages) and be assimilated into the mainstream culture. In 1891, a law was passed requiring English to be taught in New Mexico. By 1923, some 34 states had statutes stipulating English as the sole language of instruction (Stoller 1976). There are now five or fewer states with such a statute, as bilingual education has spread to more and more areas.

In some cases, the language of instruction in the governmental school system may be native to none, or virtually to none, of the students. In some colonial societies, the language of the colonial administration, rather than any vernacular language of the colonialized natives, was used. Such was the general policy of the French in their colonies in all parts of the world, whereas the British attempted to develop the use of the vernacular whenever possible. American colonial policy likewise has generally followed the French colonial model in its colonialized or formerly colonialized territories of Puerto Rico, Hawaii, the Philippines, Alaska, Samoa, and Micronesia, not to speak of the internally colonialized American Indian reservations. Now, however, Alaska and Hawaii are populated by a majority of native speakers of English, and the Indians of necessity must deal with an English-speaking society. There seemed to be much less excuse for continuing the policy of instruction in English only in Puerto Rico (up until the 1940s) where the entire population is Spanish-speaking, or in the Philippines where the students spoke many different languages, but where Spanish had been entrenched as the language of instruction for three and a half centuries. The American administration, thus, replaced one colonial language with another. Although the Philippines have been independent since 1945, the legacy of colonialism has left in its wake the use of English as the principal language of instruction from the third grade through the university level. Local vernaculars are used in the first two grades, and Pilipino, the national language based on Tagalog, is taught at all levels of the school system. Although Tagalog is not spoken natively by a majority of Filipinos (although it is spoken by a majority as a second language), it is the language of the politically dominant Manila region. Had it not been for the intrusion of Spanish or English, Tagalog might have become the principal language of instruction throughout the Philippine school system. This would have worked to the detriment of speakers of other Philippine languages, although at least they would be using a native, rather than a colonial, language. Conversely, a number of recently decolonialized peoples have chosen to retain the language of their former colonial masters, rather than one of their own languages. This step may have been taken either to avoid a choice among the languages of a number of rival and competitive ethnic groups, or else because in no local language were adequate teaching materials available, or no one had been trained to teach in any of the native languages. Therefore, the former colony may find it easier, or more expeditious, to continue to use French or English, for example.

Once a language of instruction has been decided on, or if there is, for all practical purposes, one language in the country or region, the variety to be used for instructional purposes must still be chosen. Ordinarily this variety is that of the educated middle class, although, incipiently, it may have been the language of a powerful elite. In some cases, the variety chosen may not be a spoken one at all, the most notable case being that of Arabic. In the Arab countries, modern written Arabic, which is essentially the classical Arabic of the Koran with a modernized lexicon, is the medium of instruction at all levels, although the vernacular is sometimes used by the students or by the teacher by way of explanation of the classical forms.

In a real sense, the school language is no one's vernacular. For example, in the United States, no one quite speaks the same way outside of school as he does inside except, of course, some of the teachers, and for this they may well be ridiculed. Furthermore, standards of "correctness" may be based on consideration of the written language and hence be quite irrelevant to the spoken language. These standards are enforced on the spoken language of the students while in school, only to be ignored by them once they are beyond its confines.

Another set of decisions relates to which foreign languages should be taught. In some cases, it will be a former colonial language, like English or French in Africa, a language of religion such as Arabic in the non-Arab Islamic countries, a language of cultural prestige like French in Portugal, or a language to facilitate communication with the broader world outside, particularly its allies, as in the case of English in Israel. In countries where the official language has a very small number of speakers, say Hebrew in Israel or Icelandic in Iceland, it is not economically feasible to produce textbooks and stock libraries in the national language in adequate variety for the needs of higher education. Hence, it is necessary for students to learn some language of world importance, such as French, English, Spanish, or Russian in order to pursue their education at the university level. Sometimes this situation has prolonged a colonial situation or outlived the dismemberment of multinational empires. German is still widely used in Eastern Europe and the Balkans; contrariwise, there are virtually no vestiges of the use of Turkish in territory formerly administered by the Ottomans, that is, outside of Turkey itself. This points up the very different functions of Turkish in the old Ottoman Empire, used primarily as a language of administration, whereas German in the old Austro-Hungarian Empire was used in many different spheres of life, particularly education.

Which foreign languages are taught at any particular period of a country's history are indicative of certain prevailing cultural attitudes and values, at least those of the dominant classes. Thus, in the Western world a hundred years ago, a knowledge of Greek and Latin was considered part of the intellectual equipment of every educated person. A generation ago in United States universities, French and German were the intellectuals' languages, their knowledge being an absolute prerequisite for entrance into a Ph.D. program. Thus, high schools generally offered French and German, and usually Latin as well, in the more academically oriented schools. In more recent years, as a result of the Good Neighbor policy of World War II days, increasing tourism with Mexico, and increased interest in and by our Spanish speaking citizens, the teaching of Spanish has spread, and in much of the country is the most widely taught language. As a result both of the Cold War and a result of the realization of Soviet scientific and technological achievements, Russian has become increasingly popular. Ethnic languages have long been taught in either private and/or public schools where large numbers of ethnic people resided, as for example, Italian, Polish, Chinese, Japanese, or Hebrew. Increasing ethnic consciousness has increased the demand for the teaching of ethnic languages, particularly Spanish for the Chicano, Cuban, and Puerto Rican population, but also Swahili for Blacks. Overall, however, foreign language enrollments in the United States have been declining.

The only international languages of technical and scientific cultures are French, English, Russian, and German, and any scientist who wants to keep up with what is going on in his field probably ought to know at least two of these languages. By an accident of history, two of these languages, English and French, have diffused over much of modern Africa. In terms of political utility, the independent African states will probably find it in their interest to develop this positive aspect of their colonial legacy. A class structure seems to be emerging in Africa which is based on linguistic factors. The majority of the population speaks only African languages and has to use the mediation of an educated minority to communicate with the modern economic world. This minority is separated from the majority by its class-specific monopoly of the use of French and English. It is communication through these languages which makes possible the organization of the entire modern sector of production and distribution of goods (Alexandre 1972:86).

The agencies of mass communication are concerned with language, and their policies and activities have a far-ranging impact on language and language-related social phenomena. Much like the educational institutions, the agencies of mass communication must establish policy, such as determining, for example, the language or languages to be used in broadcasting. In autocratic states, this will be decided by the government; in places like the United States, by private corporations; but in Great Britain or Israel, by public broadcasting corporations. In any case, the decision has to be made. Considerations include the desire to emphasize or promote a particular language, as over against the size of particular populations desiring radio or television broadcasts in their own language. In capitalist countries, this is likely to be decided on the basis of the commercial returns to be expected from advertising in various languages but in the socialist countries to be decided on the basis of accepted governmental policies.

Not only language but language variety has to be decided upon, as well as style, for the various programs. Thus, for example, in the Arab countries classical Arabic is generally used in broadcasting, except for informal conversation, comedy, and soap operas. Where there are several competing ways of pronouncing a language, one particular way must be chosen. The announcers over Israel radio, for example, use a type of pronunciation (for Hebrew) used nowhere else. They make fine distinctions of sounds found in no native speaker and ignored even in academic Hebrew.

When we consider broadcasting in the United States, we are surprised at the homogeneity of pronunciation to be found throughout the country. Regional speech patterns are not ordinarily reflected by local announcers, at least not on network stations. This situation has led to the coining of the term network English to refer to this supposedly regionless variety of American English. While radio and television "personalities" have their own regionally-affected speech patterns, there is a general lack of regionalism in the speech of announcers.

One is also conscious of the lack of ethnic accents among broadcasters of ethnic origin. In the United States, there are now newscasters of Black, Chicano, Chinese and Japanese extraction. Their impeccable "network" English, however, shows almost without exception no traces of an ethnic intonation, at least to the untrained ear. The message being conveyed, in not too subtle a manner, to the minority groups, is that you, too, can become a television announcer, as long as no one can tell from your speech what your ethnic and class background is.

11.3 Language planning

Language treatment includes the many different kinds of attention which people give to language problems, that is, social problems in which language aspects are pre-eminent. Most of these problems are concerned with which language or which variety of a particular language ought to be used on which occasions by which people. These problems appear to grow out of socioeconomic shifts, such as those caused by population growth and migrations, or rapid industrialization, or new group identifications and political processes. The most important type of language treatment is language planning. Das Gupta (1973:157) defines language planning as "a set of deliberate activities systematically designed to organize and develop the language resources of the community in an ordered schedule of time." Fishman (1973a:24–25) defines it as "the organized pursuit of solutions to language problems, typically at the national level." It can, at one extreme, refer to individuals who give some thought and perhaps some action to language problems. In an intermediate position, we find private bodies, such as language academies, which may or may not operate with government recognition and support. Finally, there is direct pursuit of language planning by official governmental agencies.

Choice of a national language will, of course, be related to the monolingual or bilingual nature of the country. There is a very important difference between countries with minorities and those without a majority at all. The language chosen may even be that of a small minority, e.g. Irish Gaelic 3 percent or Pakistani Urdu 7 percent. In Israel, Hebrew had practically no native speakers at the time it was chosen as the national language. On the other hand, in Indonesia Javanese was spoken by 40 percent of the population, but Bahasa Indonesia, a pidginized variety with no native speakers, was chosen. Bangladesh is an example of a linguistic minority (Bengali speakers within the former Pakistan) recently successful in breaking away and setting up their own separate nation-state.

Some languages are a problem because they are unwritten, while others are written but not standardized, or else still others have practically no written literature in the language. Whether the elite wishes to keep power or to democratize the state, it still has to make language policy decisions. Choice of a former colonial language as official may benefit the elite, but it also puts speakers of all native languages at the same disadvantage and, hence, is "neutral" in that respect, e.g. English in Anglophone West Africa or Portuguese in Angola.

In order to carry out language planning, it is essential to be well appraised of the sociolinguistic situation in the country. Surveys may be needed to establish what languages and language varieties are actually spoken by what numbers of people. This is important whether we are talking about language choice in a Third World country or setting up a bilingual education program in the United States. Good research methods must be used to gather and interpret language use data.

Choice of language or language variety involves questions such as at what levels of the school system particular languages will be taught or used as the medium of instruction. After a particular language or language variety has been chosen, changes may be planned for that language, for example, expansion of the lexicon to incorporate needed terms for science, industry, commerce, administration, and other activities with which the language had not previously dealt adequately. Or a writing system may have to be chosen for, devised for, adapted to, or reformed for the language.

There are two approaches to language planning—the policy approach which includes selection of the national language, standardization, literacy, and orthographies, and the cultivation approach which deals with questions such as correctness, efficiency, and linguistic levels fulfilling specialized functions and problems of style. Generally speaking, we find the policy approach in the less developed speech communities, whereas the cultivation approach is found in modern industrialized societies (Rubin 1973b:3–4).

Planning by the state is no guarantee that the planning will succeed. For example, in Norway, the ruling socialists have been quite unsuccessful in pushing the actual spoken and written standard in the direction of more non-Danish forms, but the most famous failure is that of Gaelic in the Irish Republic. In the Soviet Union, the fumbling methods of the authorities is illustrated by the choice of the Uzbek literary language, where the phonological system was standardized in 1923, but radically revised in 1927, and again in 1937 and 1940 (Bennigsen and Quelquejay 1961:55).

On the other hand, planning can be successful at the international level. Malaysia and Indonesia have cooperated to develop a spelling system which can be used for their two closely related national languages, Bahasa Malaysia and Bahasa Indonesia, which had quite different orthographies, influenced by English and Dutch spelling, respectively. The long-awaited system was decreed as the official system of spelling in both countries concerned in 1972, with a five-year phasing-in period. They planned to have time to produce textbooks using the new system and to familiarize school children with it (Omar 1975:77–78). The new orthography will particularly facilitate the sale of textbooks in the other country. Indonesia has the more developed language of the two, and Malaysia will be greatly aided in standardizing its own language and incorporating scientific terminology because of the agreement.

At the opposite extreme, a single person may exert tremendous effect on the language planning process, as exemplified by Ivar Aasen on Norwegian, Adamantios Korais on Greek, Vuk Karadžić on Serbo-Croatian or Blaže Koneski on Macedonian. The most famous individual language planner, however, is probably Eliezer Ben Yehuda. Fellman points out that Ben Yehuda himself undertook seven steps in order to implement his vision of the revival of Hebrew, namely: setting up of the first Hebrew-speaking household; a call to the Jews in Palestine and abroad for assistance and advice; founding of Hebrew-speaking societies; setting up classes in which Hebrew was learned through the medium of Hebrew; publishing a modern Hebrew newspaper; compiling a dictionary of ancient and modern Hebrew; and the formation of a Language Council. These various steps had differing degrees of effectiveness in the total revival process, which could not have been successful without the cooperation of a host of other people, some working with Ben Yehuda, some independently of him, but all inspired by his charismatic leadership. Furthermore, a fertile ground for language revival lay waiting. As Fellman notes, "Hebrew at the time was not a dead language which had to be artifically revived by Ben Yehuda and his followers but was in fact a flexible instrument of expression for many purposes, including even some topics of everyday conversation. . . . The linguistic situation before the revival, especially among those European Jews who came to Palestine, was such that the speaking of Hebrew, *once begun,* was *almost* natural." As Rabin points out, "Hebrew was on the threshold of speech. . . . For one whose entire intellectual life took place in that language, speaking it offered no difficulty" (quoted by Fellman 1974:427–428).

Although writing is, in essence, a secondary linguistic phenomenon originally based on speech, it also has somewhat of an independent existence. Since its origins some five thousand years ago, writing and speech have continued to influence each other. Because the earliest developed writing systems were so cumbersome and required lengthy training for their mastery, literacy was from the beginning confined to a small class of specialists who tended to exaggerate the importance, even sacred character, of the written word. A certain reverence for the printed word has survived down to our time. Similarly, books were viewed with great respect, if not awe, before the invention of the printing press because of the enormous expense involved in the hand-copying of manuscripts. Because of the reverence for the written word, because of the vested interest of those who have expended great efforts learning to write, the written language is generally more conservative than the spoken language.

Before the invention of writing, all societies were, of course, preliterate. Societies since that time which have no means of writing are referred to as nonliterate, whereas those societies with writing systems have varying proportions of their population which can be characterized as literate or illiterate. A significant social change takes place when a previously homogeneous preliterate society develops a cleavage in its population between the literate and the illiterate as a result of the introduction of writing, either in their own language or some other.

Almost all new writing systems adopted or suggested in recent years have been alphabetic. A new alphabet may be demanded in three different types of situations: (1) to create a standard alphabet when the language in question has not yet been written, (2) to provide auxiliary alphabets for languages which already have a nonalphabetic script, such as roman script for Chinese (pinyin), or transcriptions for linguistic studies and textbooks (for example, for colloquial Arabic); (3) to replace an older, inadequate alphabet with a more phonemic one, that is, spelling reform.

For a new alphabet to be successful, it must not only represent the language economically, consistently, and unambiguously but also facilitate learning to read and write and be suited to the needs of modern techniques of printing and typewriting (Berry 1968:737–738). It must furthermore not go against strongly entrenched attitudes, like the desire to have a "modern-looking" alphabet or one which resembles that of some prestigious language with which the people also identify.

In the matter of orthographies, social considerations loom large, as different writing systems have symbolic significance related to group loyalty and group identity, as well as to significant reference groups. Utilizataion, imposition, or abolition of alphabets such as the Latin, Cyrillic, or Arabic is directed at far-reaching social and cognitive-emotional reorganization which also will have practical consequences for the relevance of the skills maintained by traditional elites. It is necessary to consider how the new skills and the new statuses deriving from the use of the new alphabet will be allocated. Such momentous matters often arouse the greatest passions, either in the transition from preliterate to literate society or in the substitution of one alphabet for another.

The introduction of writing (*graphization*) adds another variety of language to the community's repertoire. Eventually the belief develops that the written language is the "real" language and that speech is a corruption of it. This widespread belief limits the kind of conscious intervention in the form of language planning that the community will conceive of or accept. They frequently believe that to change the writing is to change the language.

Alphabetic writing systems, when first devised for or applied to a particular language, generally try to achieve a one-to-one correspondence between phoneme and letter, and most have been initially quite successful in this respect. However, if the writing system remains static while the language undergoes widespread phonological change, the orthography becomes of historic value rather than reflecting how the language is actually pronounced. This is strikingly the case in such languages as English or French. Here, the more or less separate existence of the written language becomes a major social issue, as demands for spelling reform, that is, closer correspondence between letters and sounds, are heard. A host of arguments are sometimes heard why it is difficult, costly, or even downright impossible to phonemicize the writing system. There is a tremendous waste of effort spent by children studying an archaic spelling system (if any actually master it), effort that could be spent much more profitably elsewhere in this age of the knowledge explosion. Nevertheless, there is no effective spelling reform movement anyplace in the English-speaking world. In defense of the conservative position, however, it should be pointed out that, should English be written as it is spoken, there would be as many written varieties as there are spoken varieties, thereby impeding written communication among the enormously variegated speakers of English throughout the world. Nevertheless, there is still much that could be done, for example, dropping letters that *nobody* ever pronounces, as for example:

(p)sychology   throu(gh)   (k)nife

Spelling reform strongly affects the already literate and reveals the societal network, ramifications, and linguistic adjustments which are apparently only technical in nature. Yet, spelling reform does represent departure from established written tradition and therefore must deal with its guardians, the authors, priests, professors, and the institutions they serve (Fishman 1972b:181).

Some writing systems are obviously better suited to the languages they represent than others, that is, it is relatively easier for the native speaker to learn to read and write in his own language with one system than with another. For example, the Cyrillic alphabet is more suitable for Russian than the Roman alphabet is for English, while the latter is more efficient than the use of Chinese characters for writing Japanese or Chinese. On the other hand, this system has some advantages which would be lost if alphabetic writing were adopted, for example, the distinguishing of homophonous words, and the facilitating of written communication among widely separated and nonmutually intelligible dialects. Advantages such as these are often cited by those opposed to reform of writing systems. Thus, people rightly point out that, were English to be written phonetically, we could no longer distinguish in writing between "no" and "know," or between "fair" and "fare," although each of the latter also contains a subset of homophonous words. But conservatives, and others, rarely argue issues solely on their merits alone. Rather, there is an emotional and ideological attachment to those things which one defends. This is just as true of the defense of existing writing systems as it is of any other cause, for writing systems come to have symbolic value. They may come to have a sacred or semisacred character if revered religious texts are written in them, particularly if that language is no longer spoken.

It would seem as if extensive spelling reform is carried out only under extraordinary social and political conditions, perhaps most effectively under a well-organized dictatorship, for example, spelling reforms in Russia after the Bolshevik takeover, the substitution of the Roman for the Arabic alphabet in Turkey under Atatürk, or current efforts in China to simplify the writing of the millennia-old Chinese ideographic system.

There is no near parallel any place in the world to the massive, planned language change taking place now in China. Hundreds of simplified characters are now in regular use, and *putonghua* (common speech) is spreading rapidly among the 30 percent of the Chinese population which speak dialects not mutually intelligible with *putonghua*. Romanized spelling is extending to other uses, and changes are progressing toward the ultimate goal of replacing both traditional and simplified characters (Ferguson 1975:6). The mainland Chinese,

普通话

at least, have given up for the time being, however, any major effort to replace their traditional logographic characters with a phonemic alphabet; rather, they have decided to concentrate on the simplification of traditional writing. Thus, the goal also of separate, written, phonetic languages for the regional dialects has also been given up. Phonetic writing (*pinyin*) is used as an aid in pronouncing characters in textbooks, in library filing, in the navy and fishing fleet, in many of the railroads, and for other largely auxiliary purposes. (DeFrancis 1972:450–461)

11.4 Social and language conflict

Next to change, perhaps the most pervasive feature of human societies is conflict, between individuals, between individual and group, and between groups. While poor communication between groups may result in conflict, more generally the roots of conflict lie in the competition for power, privilege, and prestige, or simply to gain certain basic rights. Conflict may range in intensity from verbal abuse to physical violence, resulting in the destruction of life and property. At other times, the conflict may be muted and subtle, as in ridicule of a person's manner of speech.

The most important type of social conflict, in the context of the sociology of language, is conflict over language rights. Violence may occur because people are not allowed to speak or write their own language, or because a particular language has been chosen for official governmental use, so that speakers of other languages are at a disadvantage in competition for civil service jobs. Witness the notorious language riots in India, in which numerous persons were killed or injured, or note South Africa's worst racial violence in its history in June 1976, resulting in hundreds of persons being killed. This was triggered by black high school students' protesting the government requirement that they be taught half their classes in Afrikaans, the language of the dominant Boers, which was to them a symbol of white oppression. Half of the classes were in English, which they preferred and regarded as a progressive language, a bridge to the outside world. The government eventually rescinded the order.

Where languages are of officially equal status, as in Switzerland, and upward mobility is not blocked by an elite language group, language differences are not divisive, and individuals can seek to climb the class ladder. Where mobility is blocked by the recognition of one preferred language, as in Belgium or Canada, language differences are ordinarily politically divisive; the individual must unite with members of his language group to raise the group as a whole, through political action. In India, English is less divisive than Hindi as an official language because it is a second language for almost the entire population and an equal handicap for them. Inglehart and Woodward (1972:366) believe that, if upward social mobility is not a normal expectation, there is less likelihood of language differences leading to political conflict. Official status of languages is critical in newly industrializing countries because government jobs provide the chief avenue for upward mobility.

Languages are not intrinsically a cause for conflict but rather may become symbols of or focal points of a political cause, such as revolt against a foreign government, as was the case of Magyar in the eighteenth century and Gaelic and Catalan in the nineteenth. These languages were dying out before they were revived by intellectuals and political leaders partly to provide an audience and a constituency (Inglehart and Woodward 1972:372–373; Dauzat 1953:177). Kelman (1971:36) notes that "Assuming that the major impetus for major linguistic conflicts is an instrumentally based grievance—a response by the weaker language group to discrimination, to exclusion, and to denial of its rightful share of power and resources—the conflict readily becomes intensified by sentimental elaborations. Since language is so closely tied to group identity, language-based discrimination against the group is perceived as a threat to its very existence as a recognizable entity and as an attack on its sacred object and symbols." Wherever language conflict has become an explosive issue, the aggrieved group tends to be less economically developed and limited in its access to opportunities for participation and mobility. Political and economic power are concentrated in the hands of those who speak the favored language. These hypotheses are among the potentially most explosive in the entire sociology of language. The continuing industrialization and modernization of increasingly wider areas of the world will only make their relevance more apparent.

Discussion questions

1. Compare language modernization/development with social modernization/development.
2. What is meant by language policy? What are some of the issues with which it deals?
3. Identify the language policies of your local governmental and educational institutions.
4. What language rights should be granted to all populations? Explain the rationale for your answer.
5. How has language policy been used to "divide and rule"?
6. Compare the language policies of three or four different countries, indicating the types of issues dealt with in each.
7. Discuss the pros and cons of bilingual education. If there is a bilingual education program in your community, interview the parents of students enrolled for their opinions of its effectiveness.
8. What are some of the problems that must be faced in teaching children in their own vernacular?
9. With what types of activities is language planning concerned?
10. Discuss the major issues involved in orthographic reform.
11. Under what conditions may language questions become the motivation for social conflict?

A note on phonological transcriptions

The symbols used are those customary in linguistic work. Most of them represent the same values as their counterparts in ordinary spelling. Those which do not or which may present difficulties for the uninitiated are presented below. The equivalences are broadly practical, rather than strictly scientific.

/a/   *a* as in Spanish *cama*
/æ/   *a* as in English *cat*
/aw/ *ou* as in English *shout*
/ay/ *i* as in English *nice*
/č/   *ch* as in English *church* or Spanish *chico*
/ə/   *a* as in English *about* or *sofa*
/ɛ/   *e* as in English *pet*
/e/   *e* as in Spanish *pena*
/ey/ *ai* as in English *bait*
/g/   *g* as in English *get*
/h/   *h* as in English *hill*
/i/   *i* as in Spanish *pico*
/ɪ/   *i* as in English *sit*
/iy/ *ee* as in English *beef*
/ǰ/   *j* as in English *jewel*
/ŋ/   *ng* as in English *sing*
/ɔ/   *aw* as in English *awful*
/o/   *o* as in Spanish *mono*
/ow/ *o* as in English *broke*
/r/   *r* as in Spanish *pero*, *madre*
/š/   *sh* as in English *hash*
/u/   *u* as in English *full* or *ou* as in French *fou*
/v/   *v* as in English *very*
/x/   *j* as in Spanish *caja* or *ch* in German *Achtung*
/y/   *y* as in English *yes*
/z/   *z* as in English *zero*
/ž/   *s* as in English *pleasure* or *j* in French *jamais*

Bibliography

Abrahams, Roger D.
  1962   "Playing the Dozens," *Journal of American Folklore* 75:209–220.
  1974   "Black Talking in the Streets,"pp. 240–262, in Bauman and Sherzer, eds.
Alatis, James E., ed.
  1969   *Linguistics and the Teaching of Standard English to Speakers of Other Languages or Dialects.* Washington, D.C.: Georgetown University Press.
  1978   *International Dimensions of Bilingual Education.* Washington, D.C.: Georgetown University Press.
Alatis, James E. and G. Richard Tucker, eds.
  1979   *Language in Public Life.* Washington, D.C.: Georgetown University Press.
Alexandre, Pierre
  1972   *An Introduction to Languages and Language in Africa,* tr. by F.A. Leary. London: Heineman.
Alleyne, Mervyn C.
  1971   "Acculturation and the Cultural Matrix of Creolization," pp. 169–186, in Hymes, ed.
Allsopp, R.
  1958   "The English Language in British Guiana," *English Language Teaching* 12, no. 2:59–66.
Altona, Salih J.
  1970   "Language Education in Arab Countries and the Role of the Academies," *Current Trends in Linguistics* 6:690–720. Also in Fishman, ed., 1974.
Ammanatis, Adamandios.
  1969   "The Moslem Minority in Greece," pp. 94–100, in Holmestad and Lade, eds.
Andonovski, Hristo
  1971   *Egejska Makedonija.* Skopje: Misla.
Anttila, Raimo
  1972   *An Introduction to Historical and Comparative Linguistics.* New York: Macmillan Co.
Attinasi, John, *et al.*
  1977   "Language Policy and the Puerto Rican Community," *Bilingual Review* 5, nos. 1–2:1–39.
Austin, John L.
  1962   *How to Do Things with Words.* Cambridge: Harvard University Press.
Bach, Emmon
  1968   "Nouns and Noun Phrases," pp. 90–122, in Bach and Harms, eds.

Bach, Emmon and Robert T. Harms, eds.
    1968   *Universals in Linguistic Theory.* New York: Holt, Rinehart and Winston.
Bacon, Elizabeth E.
    1966   *Central Asians under Russian Rule.* Ithaca, N.Y.: Cornell University Press.
Bailey, Charles-James N.
    1973   *Variation and Linguistic Theory.* Arlington, Va.: Center for Applied Linguistics.
    1975   "The New Linguistic Framework and Language Planning," *International Journal of the Sociology of Language* 4:153–157.
Bailey, Charles-James N. and Roger W. Shuy, eds.
    1973   *New Ways of Analyzing Variation in English.* Washington, D.C.: Georgetown University Press.
Bales, Robert F.
    1950   *Interaction Process Analysis; a Method for the Study of Small Groups.* Cambridge, Mass.: Addison-Wesley Press.
Baratz, Joan C.
    1969   "Teaching Reading in an Urban Negro School System," pp. 92–116, in Baratz and Shuy, eds.
Baratz, Joan C. and Roger W. Shuy, eds.
    1969   *Teaching Black Children to Read.* Washington, D.C.: Center for Applied Linguistics.
Bartsch, Renate and Theo Vennemann
    1975   *Linguistics and Neighboring Disciplines.* Amsterdam: North-Holland Publishing Co.
Baskakov, N.A.
    1960   *The Turkic Languages of Central Asia: Problems of Planned Culture Contact.* Oxford: Central Asian Research Centre.
Bauman, Richard and Joel F. Sherzer, eds.
    1974   *Explorations in the Ethnography of Speaking.* London: Cambridge University Press.
Bell, Roger T.
    1976   *Sociolinguistics: Goals, Approaches, Problems.* New York: St. Martin's Press.
Bellugi, Ursula and Roger Brown, eds.
    1964   *The Acquisition of Language.* Chicago: University of Chicago Press.
Bennigsen, Alexandre and Chantal Quelquejay
    1961   *The Evolution of the Muslim Nationalities of the U.S.S.R. and Their Linguistic Problems,* tr. by Geoffrey Wheeler. London: Central Asian Research Center.
Berger, Peter L. and Thomas Luckmann
    1967   *The Social Construction of Reality: A Treatise in the Sociology of Knowledge.* New York: Anchor Books.
Berlin, Brent and Paul Kay
    1969   *Basic Color Terms: Their Universality and Evolution.* Berkeley: University of California Press.
Bernstein, Basil
    1972   "Social Class, Language and Socialization," pp. 157–178, in Giglioli, ed.
Bernstein, Basil, ed.
    1971–75 *Class, Codes and Control.* Vol. 1. *Theoretical Studies Towards a Sociology of Language.* Vol. 2. *Applied Studies Towards a Sociology of Language.* Vol. 3. *Towards a Theory of Educational Transmissions.* London: Routledge & Kegan Paul.
Bernstein, Basil and Dorothy Henderson
    1972   "Social Class Differences in the Relevance of Language to Socialization, v. 2, pp. 126–149, In Fishman, ed.
Berry, J.
    1968   "The Making of Alphabets," pp. 737–753, in Fishman, ed.

Bickerton, Derek
    1975   *Dynamics of a Creole System.* London: Cambridge University Press.
Birdwhistell, Ray L.
    1970   *Kinesics and Context: Essays on Body Motion Communication.* Philadelphia:
            University of Pennsylvania Press.
Blakar, Rolv Mikkel
    1975   "How Sex Roles are Represented, Reflected and Conserved in the Norwegian
            Language," *Acta Sociologica* 18, nos. 2–3:162–173.
Blanc, Chaim
    1960   "Stylistic Variations in Spoken Arabic: a Sample of Interdialectal Educated
            Conversation," in Ferguson, ed.
    1964   *Communal Dialects in Baghdad.* Cambridge: Harvard University Press.
Blauner, Robert
    1969   "Internal Colonialism and the Ghetto Revolt, *Social Problems* 16:393–408.
Blom, Jan-Petter and John Gumperz
    1972   "Social Meaning in Linguistic Structures: Code Switching in Norway," pp. 407–
            434, in Gumperz and Hymes, eds.
Bloomfield, Leonard
    1933   *Language.* New York: H. Holt.
Blount, Ben G.
    1975   "Studies in Child Language: an Anthropological View," *American Anthropolo-
            gist* 77:580–600.
Blount, Ben G., ed.
    1974   *Language, Culture and Society: a Book of Readings.* Cambridge: Winthrop
            Publishers.
Blount, Ben G. and Mary Sanches, eds.
    1977   *Sociocultural Dimensions of Language Change.* New York: Academic Press.
Blumer, Herbert
    1969   *Symbolic Interactionism: Perspective and Method.* Englewood Cliffs, N.J.:
            Prentice-Hall.
Boas, Franz
    1911   "Introduction" to the *Handbook of American Indian Languages.* (Bulletin of the
            Bureau of American Ethnology, 40, pt. 1). Washington, D.C.: Government Print-
            ing Office. Also in Blount, ed., 1974.
Bodine, Ann
    1975   "Androcentrism in Prescriptive Grammar: Singular 'they', Sex-Indefinite 'he'; and
            'he or she'," *Language in Society* 4:129–146.
Boggs, Stephen and Laura Lein
    1978   "Sequencing in Children's Discourse: Introduction," *Language in Society* 7:293–
            297.
Boulton, Marjorie
    1960   *Zamenhof, Creator of Esperanto.* London: Routledge and Kegan Paul.
Bowen, J. Donald and Jacob Ornstein, eds.
    1976   *Studies in Southwest Spanish.* Rowley, Mass.: Newbury House.
Bram, Joseph
    1955   *Language and Society.* New York: Random House.
Bright, William, ed.
    1966   *Sociolinguistics: Proceedings of the UCLA Sociolinguistics Conference, 1964.*
            The Hague: Mouton.
Broadrib, Donald
    1970   "Esperanto and the Ideology of Constructed Languages," *International Lan-
            guage Reporter* 16, no. 56:1–9.

Brouwer, Dédé, Marinel Gerritsen, and Dorian de Haan
   1979   "Speech Differences between Women and Men: On the Wrong Track?" *Language in Society* 8:33–50.
Brown, Roger W.
   1958   *Words and Things*. New York: Free Press. (Reprinted in 1968).
   1973   *A First Language: the Early Stages*. Cambridge: Harvard University Press.
Brown, Roger W. and Marguerite Ford
   1961   "Address in American English," *Journal of Social Psychology* 62:37–385. Also in Moscovici, ed.
Brown, Roger W., Bruce Fraser and Ursula Bellugi
   1964   "Explorations and Grammar Evaluation," in Bellugi and Brown, eds.
Brown, Roger W. and A. Gilman
   1960   "The Pronouns of Power and Solidarity," in Sebeok, ed., 1960. Also in Giglioli, ed. and Fishman, ed., 1968.
Bruner, Jerome S.
   1975   "The Ontogenesis of Speech Acts," *Journal of Child Language* 2:1–19.
Bull, William E.
   1964   "The Use of Vernacular Languages in Education," pp. 527–533,in Hymes, ed.
Burling, Robbins
   1964   "Cognition and Componential Analysis: God's Truth or Hocus-Pocus?" *American Anthropologist* 66:20–28.
   1970   *Man's Many Voices: Language in its Cultural Context*. New York: Holt, Rinehart and Winston.
   1973   *English in Black and White*. New York: Holt, Rinehart and Winston.
Callary, Robert E.
   1975   "Syntax and Social Class," *Linguistics* 143:5–16.
Campbell, Robin and Roger Wales
   1970   "The Study of Language Acquisition," pp. 242–260, in Lyons, ed.
Capell, A.
   1969   "The Changing Status of Melanesian Pidgin," *La Monda Lingvo-Problemo* 1:107–115.
Casagrande, Joseph B.
   1966   "Language Universals and Anthropology," in Greenberg, ed.
Cazden, Courtney B.
   1970   "The Neglected Situation in Child Language Research and Education," pp. 81–101, in Williams, ed.
   1972   *Child Language and Education*. New York: Holt, Rinehart and Winston.
   1973   "Language Socialization," in Shuy, ed.
   1977   Review of Francis 1975, *Language in Society* 6:417–420.
Cazden, Courtney B., Vera P. John, and Dell Hymes, eds.
   1972   *The Functions of Language in the Classroom*. New York: Teachers College Press.
Center for Applied Linguistics
   1980   *The Ann Arbor Decision: Memorandum Opinion and Order & the Educational Plan*. Arlington, Va.: Center for Applied Linguistics.
Cherry, Colin
   1961   *On Human Communication: a Review, Survey and a Criticism*. New York: Science Editions.
Chomsky, Noam
   1957   *Syntactic Structures*. The Hague: Mouton.
   1964   "A Review of B.F. Skinner's *Verbal Behavior*," pp. 547–578, in Fodor and Katz.
   1965   *Aspects of the Theory of Syntax*. Cambridge: MIT Press.
   1972   *Language and Mind*. Enlarged ed. New York: Harcourt Brace Jovanovich.

Christian, Chester
  1972   "Language Functions in the Maintenance of Socioeconomic Hierarchies,"
          pp. 181–191, in Ewton and Ornstein, eds.
Cicourel, Aaron
  1970   "The Acquisition of Social Structure: Towards a Developmental Sociology of
          Meaning," in Douglas, ed., and in his *Cognitive Sociology.*
  1974a   *Cognitive Sociology: Language and Meaning in Social Interaction.* New York:
          Free Press.
  1974b   "Ethnomethodology," *Current Trends in Linguistics* 12:1563–1605.
  1978   "Sociolinguistic Aspects of the Use of Sign Language," pp. 271–313, in
          Schlesinger and Namir, eds.
Cohen, Marcel
  1956   *Pour une sociologie du langage.* Paris: Albin Michel.
Cohen, Percy S.
  1968   *Modern Social Theory.* New York: Basic Books.
Cook, Jenny A.
  1973   "Language and Socialization, a Critical Review," v. 2, pp. 293–341, in Bernstein,
          ed.
Cook-Gumperz, Jenny
  1973   *Social Control and Socialization: a Study of Class Differences in the Language of
          Maternal Control.* London: Routledge and Kegan Paul.
  1975   "The Child as Practical Reasoner," pp. 137–162, in Sanches and Blount, eds.
Cooper, Robert L. and Joshua A. Fishman
  1974   "The Study of Language Attitudes," *International Journal of the Sociology of
          Language* 3:5–19.
Corrigan, P.
  1975   Review of Mueller 1973, *Sociological Review* 23:455–461.
Corsaro, William
  1975   "Sociolinguistic Patterns in Adult-Child Interaction." Paper presented at annual
          meeting of American Sociological Association.
  1977   "The Clarification Request as a Feature of Adult Interactive Styles with Young
          Children," *Language in Society* 6:183–207.
Coulter, Jeff
  1973   "Language and the Conceptualization of Meaning," *Sociology* 7, no. 2:173–189.
Craig, Dennis R.
  1976   "Bidialectal Education: Creole and Standard in the West Indies," *International
          Journal of the Sociology of Language* 8:93–134.
Crosby, Faye and Linda Nyquist
  1977   "The Female Register: an Empirical Study of Lakoff's Hypotheses," *Language in
          Society* 6:313–322.
Crystal, David
  1971   *Linguistics.* Harmondsworth: Penguin Books.
Current Trends in Linguistics
  1971+   Ed. Thomas A. Sebeok. The Hague: Mouton.
Curtiss, Susan
  1977   *Genie: a Psycholinguistic Study of a Modern-Day "Wild Child."* New York:
          Academic Press.
Curtiss, Susan, *et al.*
  1974   "The Linguistic Development of Genie," *Language* 50:528–554.
Das Gupta, Jyotirindra
  1970   *Language Conflict and National Development: Group Politics and National
          Policy in India.* Berkeley: University of California Press.
  1973   "Language Planning and Public Policy: Analytical Outline of the Policy Process
          Related to Language Planning in India," pp. 157–165, in Shuy, ed.

Dauzat, Albert
    1940   L'Europe linguistique. Paris: Payot.
Davis, Kingsley
    1947   "Final Note on a Case of Extreme Social Isolation," American Journal of
              Sociology 52:432–437.
De Camp, David
    1971   "Introduction: The Study of Pidgin and Creole Languages," pp. 13–39, in Hymes,
              ed.
    1972   "Hypercorrection and Rule Generalization," Language in Society 1:87–90.
De Francis, John
    1972   "Language and Script Reform," Current Trends in Linguistics 2:130–150. Also in
              Fishman, ed., 1972.
De Laguna, Grace Andrus
    1927   Speech, Its Function and Development. Bloomington: Indiana University Press.
              Reprinted 1973.
Denison, Norman
    1969   "Sociolinguistic Aspects of Plurilingualism," pp. 255–278, in International Days
              of Sociolinguistics.
    1977   "Language Death or Language Suicide?" International Journal of the Sociology
              of Language 12:13–22. (Also in Linguistics 191:13–22).
Denzin, Norman K.
    1972   "Genesis of Self in Early Childhood," Sociological Quarterly 13:291–314.
Deutsch, Karl W.
    1966   Nationalism and Social Communication: An Inquiry into the Foundations of
              Nationality. Second Edition. Cambridge: MIT Press.
    1968   "The Trend of European Nationalism—the Language Aspect," pp. 598–606, in
              Fishman, ed.
Deutscher, Irwin
    1975   Review of Cicourel 1974, American Journal of Sociology 81:174–179.
Diebold, A. Richard
    1964   "Incipient Bilingualism," pp. 495–508, in Hymes, ed.
Dillard, J. L.
    1972   Black English: its History and Usage in the United States. New York: Random
              House.
Dittmar, Norbert
    1973   Sociolinguistik. Frankfurt: Fischer Athenaeum.
    1975   Review of Labov 1972.
    1976   A Critical Survey of Sociolinguistics: Theory and Applications. New York: St.
              Martin's Press.
Douglas, Jack, ed.
    1971   Understanding Everyday Life: Toward the Reconstruction of Sociological
              Knowledge. Chicago: Aldine.
Dreitzel, H. P., ed.
    1970   Recent Sociology no. 2: Patterns of Communicative Behavior. New York:
              Macmillan.
Dressler, Wolfgang and Ruth Wodak-Leodolter
    1977   "Language Death: Introduction," International Journal of the Sociology of
              Language 12:5–11. (Also in Linguistics 191:5–11).
Dubois, Berry Lou and Isabel Crouch
    1975   "The Question of Tag Questions in Women's Speech: They Don't Really Use
              More of Them, Do They?" Language in Society 4:289–294.
Dulling, G. K.
    1968   "The Turkic Languages of the U.S.S.R.: A New Development," Central Asian
              Review 16:97–109.

Duncan, Starkey
    1972   "Some Signals and Rules for Taking Speaking Turns in Conversation," *Journal of Personality and Social Psychology* 23:283–292.
Edelsky, Carole
    1979   "Question Intonation and Sex Roles," *Language in Society* 8:15–32.
Edwards, A. D.
    1976   "Social Class and Linguistic Choice," *Sociology* 10:101–110.
Efron, David
    1972   *Gesture, Race and Language.* The Hague: Mouton.
Elashoff, Janet D. and Richard E. Snow
    1971   *Pygmalion Reconsidered: A Case Study in Statistical Inference: Reconsideration of the Rosenthal-Jacobson Data on Teacher Expectancy.* Worthington, Ohio: Charles A. Jones Pub. Co.
Elgin, Suzette Haden
    1973   *What is Linguistics?* Englewood Cliffs, N.J.: Prentice-Hall.
Engerrand, George D.
    1956   Personal Communication.
Erickson, Frederick
    1975   Review of Cook-Gumperz 1973, *Language in Society* 4:110–113.
Ervin, Susan
    1964   "Imitation and Structural Change in Children's Language," in Lenneberg, ed.
Ervin-Tripp, Susan
    1971   "Sociolinguistics," vol. 1, pp. 15–91, in Fishman, ed.
    1972   "On Sociolinguistic Rules: Alternation and Co-Occurrence," pp. 213–250, in Gumperz and Hymes, eds.
    1976   "Is Sybil There? The Structure of Some American English Directives," *Language in Society* 5:25–66.
Ervin-Tripp, Susan and Claudia Mitchell-Kernan, eds.
    1977.   *Child Discourse.* New York: Academic Press.
Eterovich, Francis and Christopher Spalatin, eds.
    1970   *Croatia: Land, People and Culture.* Toronto: University of Toronto Press.
Ewton, Ralph W., Jr. and Jacob Ornstein, eds.
    1972   *Studies in Language and Linguistics 1972–73.* El Paso, Texas: Texas Western Press.
Farb, Peter
    1974   *Word Play: What Happens When People Talk.* New York: Alfred A. Knopf.
Fasold, Ralph W.
    1975   Review of Dillard. *Language in Society* 4:198–221.
Ferguson, Charles A.
    1959   "Diglossia," *Word* 15:325–340. Also in Hymes, ed., 1964 and Giglioli, ed.
    1968a   "Language Development," pp. 27–35, in Fishman, Ferguson and Das Gupta, eds.
    1968b   "Myths about Arabic," pp. 375–381, in Fishman, ed.
    1971   *Language Structure and Language Use.* Stanford: Stanford University Press.
    1973   "Language Problems of Variation and Repertoire," *Daedalus* 102:37–46.
    1975   "Linguistics Serves the People: Lessons of a Trip to China," *Items* 29, no. 1:5–8.
    1976   "The Structure and Use of Politeness Formulas," *Language in Society* 5:137–151.
Ferguson, Charles A., ed.
    1960   *Contributions to Arabic.* Cambridge: Harvard University Press.
Fellman, Jack
    1974   "The Role of Eliezer Ben Yehuda in the Revival of the Hebrew Language: An Assessment," pp. 426–455, in Fishman, ed.

Fillmore, Charles J.
  1973   "A Grammarian Looks to Sociolinguistics," pp. 273–287, in Shuy, ed.
Firth, J. R.
  1970   *The Tongues of Men and Speech.* London: Oxford University Press.
Fishman, Joshua A.
  1960   "A Systematization of the Whorfian Hypothesis," *Behavioral Science* 5:323–339.
  1968a   "Nationality-Nationalism and Nation-Nationism," pp. 39–51, in Fishman, Ferguson and Das Gupta, eds.
  1968b   "Sociolinguistics and the Language Problems of the Developing Countries," pp. 3–16, in Fishman, Ferguson and Das Gupta, eds.
  1968c   "Some Contrasts Between Linguistically Homogeneous and Linguistically Heterogeneous Polities," pp. 53–68, in Fishman, Ferguson and Das Gupta, eds.
  1970   *Sociolinguistics: A Brief Introduction.* Rowley, Mass.: Newbury House.
  1972a   *Language and Nationalism: Two Integrative Essays.* Rowley, Mass.: Newbury House.
  1972b   *The Sociology of Language: An Interdisciplinary Social Science Approach to Language in Society.* Rowley, Mass.: Newbury House.
  1972c   "The Sociology of Language," pp. 45–58, in Giglioli, ed.
  1973   "Language Modernization and Planning in Comparison with Other Types of National Modernization and Planning," *Language in Society* 2:23–44.
  1976   *Bilingual Education: An International Sociological Perspective.* Rowley, Mass.: Newbury House.
Fishman, Joshua A., ed.
  1966   *Language Loyalty in the United States: The Maintenance and Perpetuation of Non-English Mother Tongues by American Ethnic and Religious Groups.* The Hague: Mouton.
  1968   *Readings in the Sociology of Language.* The Hague: Mouton.
  1971–72   *Advances in the Sociology of Language,* vols. 1–2. The Hague: Mouton.
  1974   *Advances in Language Planning.* The Hague: Mouton.
  1977   *Advances in the Creation and Revision of Writing Systems.* The Hague: Mouton.
Fishman, Joshua A., Charles A. Ferguson, and Jyotirindra Das Gupta, eds.
  1968   *Language Problems of Developing Nations.* New York: Wiley & Sons.
Fishman, Joshua A. et al.
  1971   *Bilingualism in the Barrio.* The Hague: Mouton.
Fodor, Jerry A. and Jerrold J. Katz
  1964   *The Structure of Language: Readings in the Philosophy of Language.* Englewood Cliffs, N.J.: Prentice-Hall.
Francis, H.
  1975   *Language in Childhood: Form and Function in Language Learning.* New York: St. Martin's Press.
Fraser, Bruce
  1973   "Optional Rules in Grammar," pp. 1–15, in Shuy, ed.
Frazer, Sir James
  1922   *The Golden Bough.* Abridged ed. New York: Macmillan.
Freedle, Roy, ed.
  1977   *Discourse Production and Comprehension.* Norwood, N.J.: Ablex Publishing Corp.
  1979   *New Directions in Discourse Processing.* Norwood, N.J.: Ablex Publishing Corp.
Fremder, Robert and Wallace E. Lambert
  1973   "Speech Style and Scholastic Success: The Tentative Relationships and Possible Implications for Lower Class Children," pp. 237–271, in Shuy, ed.

Friedman, Victor A.
1975   "Macedonian Language and Nationalism," *Balkanistica* 2:83–98.
Gál, Susan
1978   "Peasant Men Can't Find Wives: Language Change and Sex Roles in a Bilingual Community," *Language in Society* 7:1–16.
Gardner, R. A. and Beatrice T. Gardner
1969   "Teaching Sign Language to a Chimpanzee," *Science* 165:664–672.
Gardner, Robert C. and Wallace E. Lambert
1972   *Attitudes and Motivation in Second Language Learning.* Rowley, Mass.: Newbury House.
Garvin, Paul L.
1969   "The Prague School of Linguistics," pp. 229–230, in Hill, ed.
1973   "Some Comments on Language Planning," pp. 24–33, in Rubin and Shuy, eds.
Garvin, Paul L. and Madeleine Mathiot
1968   "The Urbanization of the Guaraní Language: A Problem in Language and Culture," pp. 365–374, in Fishman, ed.
Ghosh, Samir K., ed.
1972   *Man, Language and Society: Contributions to the Sociology of Language.* The Hague: Mouton.
Giglioli, Pier Paolo, ed.
1972   *Language and Social Context: Selected Readings.* Harmondsworth: Penguin Books.
Giles, Howard, ed.
1977   *Language, Ethnicity and Intergroup Relations.* New York: Academic Press.
Giles, Howard and Robert N. St. Clair, eds.
1979   *Language and Social Psychology.* Oxford: Basil Blackwell.
Glazer, Nathan
1966   "The Process and Problems of Language Maintenance: An Integrative Review," pp. 358–368, in Fishman, ed.
Gleason, Jean Berko and Sandra Weintraub
1976   "The Acquisition of Routines in Child Language," *Language in Society* 5:129–136.
Godard, Danielle
1977   "Same Setting, Different Norms: Phone Call Beginnings in France and the United States," *Language in Society* 6:209–219.
Goffman, Erving
1959   *The Presentation of Self in Everyday Life.* Garden City, N.Y.: Anchor Books.
1967   *Interaction Ritual: Essays on Face-to-Face Behavior.* Garden City, N.Y.: Anchor Books.
1971   *Relations in Public: Microstudies of the Public Order.* New York: Harper & Row.
1978   "Response Cries," *Language* 54:787–815.
Goldstein, Bernie Z. and Kyoko Tamura
1975   *Japan and America: A Comparative Study in Language and Culture.* Rutland, Vt.: Charles E. Tuttle Co.
Goodman, Elliot R.
1968   "World State and World Language," pp. 717–736, in Fishman, ed. Reprinted from *The Soviet Design for a World State.* New York: Columbia University Press (1960), 264–284.
Goody, Jack
1968   "Introduction," pp. 1–26, in Goody, ed.
Goody, Jack, ed.
1968   *Literacy in Traditional Society.* London: Cambridge University Press.

Goody, Jack and I. Watt
1972   "The Consequences of Literacy," in Giglioli, ed. Reprinted from *Comparative Studies in Society and History* 5 (1962–3), 304–345.
Greenberg, Joseph H.
1966   "Some Universals of Grammar with Particular Reference to the Order of Meaningful Elements," in Greenberg, ed.
Greenberg, Joseph H., ed.
1966   *Universals of Language.* Second ed. Cambridge, Mass.: MIT Press.
1978   *Universals of Human Language.* Vol. 1. Theory and Method. Vol. 2. Phonology. Vol. 3. Word Structure. Vol. 4. Syntax. Stanford, Calif.: Stanford University Press.
Greenberg, Joseph H. *et al.*
1970   *Linguistics in the 1970s.* Washington, D.C.: Center for Applied Linguistics.
Greenfield, Lawrence and Joshua A. Fishman
1972   "Situational Measures of Normative Language Views in Relation to Person, Place and Topic among Puerto Rican Bilinguals," pp. 64–86, in Ghosh, ed.
Gregory, Michael and Susanne Carroll
1978   *Language and Situation: Language Varieties and Their Social Context.* London: Routledge & Kegan Paul.
Grimshaw, Allen D.
1969   "Language as Obstacle and as Data in Sociological Research," *Items* 23, no. 2:17–21.
1971   "Sociolinguistics," vol. 1, pp. 92–151, in Fishman, ed.
1973   "Rules, Social Interaction and Language Behavior," *TESOL Quarterly* 1:99–115.
1973–74 "On Language and Society," Parts I and II, *Contemporary Sociology* 2, no. 6:575–583; 3, no. 1:3–11.
Grimshaw, Allen D. and Leah Holden
1976   "Postchildhood Modifications of Linguistic and Social Competence," *Items* 30:33–42.
Gruber, Frederick C., ed.
1961   *Anthropology and Education.* Philadelphia: University of Pennsylvania Press.
Gumperz, John
1968   "Types of Linguistic Communities," pp. 460–472, in Fishman, ed.   *134 – 143*
1971   *Language in Social Groups.* Stanford: Stanford University Press.   *14 – 15*   *184 – 185*
1972a   "The Communicative Competence of Bilinguals: Some Hypotheses and Suggestions for Research," *Language in Society* 1:143–154.
1972b   "The Speech Community," *International Encyclopedia of the Social Sciences,* New York: Macmillan (1968), pp. 381–386. Reprinted in Giglioli, ed.
1975   "Foreword," pp. xi–xxi, in Sanches and Blount, eds.
Gumperz, John and Eleanor Herasimchuk
1973   "The Conversational Analysis of Social Meaning: A Study of Classroom Interaction," pp. 99–134, in Shuy, ed.
Gumperz, John and Eduardo Hernández-Chávez
1972   "Bilingualism, Bidialectalism and Classroom Interaction," pp. 84–109, in Cazden, John and Hymes, eds.
Gumperz, John and Dell Hymes, eds.
1972   *Directions in Sociolinguistics: The Ethnography of Communication.* New York: Holt, Rinehart and Winston.
Haas, Mary R.
1964a   "Interlingual Word Taboos," pp. 489–494, in Hymes, ed.
1964b   "Men's and Women's Speech in Koasati," pp. 228–233, in Hymes, ed.
Hagopian, V. H.
1907   *Ottoman-Turkish Conversation Grammar.* Heidelberg: J. Groos.

Hall, Edward T.
  1959   *The Silent Language.* New York: Doubleday.
  1969   *The Hidden Dimension.* Garden City, N.Y.: Anchor Books.
Hall, Robert A.
  1960   *Linguistics and Your Language.* Second, rev. ed. Garden City, N.Y.: Anchor
           Books. First issued, 1950.
  1972   "Pidgins and Creoles as Standard Languages," pp. 142–153,in Pride and
           Holmes. eds.
Halle, Morris
  1962   "Phonology in a Generative Grammar," *Word,* 18:67–72.
Halliday, M. A. K.
  1968   "The Users and Uses of Language," pp. 140–165,in Fishman, ed.
  1970   "Language Structure and Language Function," pp. 140–165, in Lyons, ed.
  1973   *Explorations in the Functions of Language.* London: Edward Arnold.
  1974   Review of Shuy, ed., 1971.
  1975   *Learning How to Mean: Explorations in the Development of Language.* London:
           Edward Arnold.
Hammarström, Göran
  1976   "Towards More Exhaustive Descriptions of Languages," *International Journal of
           the Sociology of Language,* 9:23–41.
Hancock, Ian F., ed.
  1979   "Romani Sociolinguistics." (Entire issue of *International Journal of the Sociology
           of Language,* 19.) The Hague: Mouton.
Hasan, R.
  1973   "Code, Register and Social Dialect," vol. 2, 253–292, in Bernstein, ed.
Haugen, Einar
  1956   *Bilingualism in the Americas: A Bibliography and Research Guide.* University:
           University of Alabama, Press.
  1966a   *Language Planning and Language Conflict: The Case of Modern Norwegian.*
           Cambridge: Harvard University Press.
  1966b   "Linguistics and Language Planning," pp. 50–70, in Bright, ed.
Heine, Bernd
  1970   *Status and Use of African Lingua Francas.* New York: Humanities Press.
Henley, Nancy and Barrie Thorne
  1977   "Womanspeak and Manspeak: Sex Differences and Sexism in Communication,
           Verbal and Nonverbal," pp. 201–218, in Sargent, ed.
Henson, Hilary
  1974   *British Social Anthropologists and Language: A History of Separate Develop-
           ment.* London: Oxford University Press.
Henze, Paul B.
  1957   "Alphabet Change in Soviet Central Asia and Communist China," *Royal Central
           Asian Society Journal* 44:125–126.
  1977   "Politics and Alphabets in Inner Asia," pp. 492–511, in Fishman, ed.
Herman, Simon R.
  1968   "Explorations in the Social Psychology of Language Choice," pp. 492–511, in
           Fishman, ed.
Hernández-Chávez, Eduardo
  1978   "Language Maintenance, Bilingual Education and Philosophies of Bilingualism in
           the United States," in Alatis, ed.
Hernández-Chávez, Eduardo, Andrew D. Cohen and Anthony F. Beltramo, eds.
  1975   *El Lenguaje de los Chicanos: Regional and Social Characteristics of Language
           Used by Mexican Americans.* Arlington, Va.: Center for Applied Linguistics.

Hertzler, Joyce O.
 1953 "Toward a Sociology of Language," *Social Forces* 32:109–119.
 1965 *A Sociology of Language.* New York: Random House.
Hewes, Gordon W.
 1973 "Primate Communication and the Gestural Origin of Language," *Current Anthropology* 14:5–24.
 1978 "The Phylogeny of Sign Language," pp. 11–56, in Schlesinger and Namir, eds.
Heyd, Uriel
 1954 *Language Reform in Modern Turkey.* Jerusalem: Israel Oriental Society.
Hill, Archibald A., ed.
 1969 *Linguistics Today.* New York: Basic Books.
Hockett, Charles F.
 1966 "The Problems of Universals," in Greenberg, ed.
Hoffer, Bates and Betty Lou Dubois
 1977 Southwest Areal Linguistics Then and Now. (Proceedings of the Fifth Southwest Areal Language and Linguistics Workshop.) San Antonio, Texas: Trinity University.
Hofman, John E. and Haya Fisherman
 1971 "Language Shift and Maintenance in Israel," *International Migration Review* 5:204–226. (Also in Fishman, ed. (1972), vol. 2, pp. 342–364.)
Hoijer, Harry
 1954 "The Sapir-Whorf Hypothesis," pp. 92–105, in Hoijer, ed.
 1969 "The Origin of Language," pp. 50–58, in Hill, ed.
Hoijer, Harry, ed.
 1954 *Language in Culture: Conference on the Interrelations of Language and Other Aspects of Culture.* Chicago: University of Chicago Press.
Holmestad, Einar and Arild Jostein Lade, eds.
 1969 *Lingual Minorities in Europe: A Collection of Papers from the European Conference of Lingual Minorities in Oslo.* Oslo: Det Norske Samlaget.
Hoover, Mary Rhodes
 1978 "Community Attitudes Toward Black English," *Language in Society* 7:65–87.
Huerta, Ana
 1978 "Code Switching: All in the Family," Paper presented at the National Conference on Chicano and Latino Discourse Behavior, Educational Testing Service, Princeton, N.J., April 17–19, 1978.
Hymes, Dell
 1961 "Functions of Speech: An Evolutionary Approach," pp. 55–83, in Gruber, ed.
 1971 "Preface," pp. 3–11, in Hymes, ed.
 1972a "Editorial Introduction," *Language in Society* 1:1–14.
 1972b "Foreword," pp. v–x, in Swadesh.
 1972c "Introduction," pp. vii–lvii, in Cazden, John and Hymes, eds.
 1972d "Models of the Interaction of Language and Social Life," pp. 35–71, in Gumperz and Hymes, eds.
 1973 "Speech and Language: On the Origins and Foundations of Inequality in Speaking," *Daedalus* 102:59–85.
 1974a "Anthropology and Sociology: An Overview," *Current Trends in Linguistics* 12:1445–1475.
 1974b *Foundations in Sociolinguistics: An Ethnographic Approach.* Philadelphia: University of Pennsylvania Press.
Hymes, Dell, ed.
 1964 *Language in Culture and Society.* New York: Harper & Row.
 1971 *Creolization and Pidginization of Language.* London: Cambridge University Press.

Ibrahim, Muhammad Hasan
  1973   *Grammatical Gender: Its Origin and Development.* The Hague: Mouton.
Inglehart, R. and M. Woodward
  1972   "Language Conflicts and the Political Community," pp. 358–377, in Giglioli, ed.
           (Reprinted from *Comparative Studies in Society and History,* 1967 10:27–45.)
Institut za Makedonski Jazik
  1978   *About the Macedonian Language.* Skopje: I.M.J.
International Days of Sociolinguistics, Rome
  1969   *Giornate internazionali di sociolinguistica.* Second International Congress of
           Social Sciences. Roma: Istituto Luigi Sturzo.
Itard, Jean Marc Gaspard
  1962   *The Wild Boy of Aveyron,* tr. by George and Muriel Humphrey. New York:
           Appleton-Century-Crofts.
Jakobson, Roman
  1968   *Child Language, Aphasia and General Sound Laws.* Tr. Keiler. The Hague:
           Mouton.
Jespersen, Otto
  1925   *Mankind, Nation and Individual from a Linguistic Point of View.* Cambridge:
           Harvard University Press.
Jessel, Levic
  1978   *The Ethnic Process: An Evolutionary Concept of Languages and Peoples.* The
           Hague: Mouton.
John, Vera P.
  1973   "Sociolinguistic Perspectives and Education," pp. 223–235, in Shuy, ed.
John, Vera P. and Vivian M. Horner
  1970   "Bilingualism and the Spanish Speaking Child," pp. 140–152, in Williams, ed.
Johnson, Samuel
  1755   *A Dictionary of the English Language.* London: Printed by W. Strahan, for J. and
           P. Knapton.
Joos, Martin
  1962   *The Five Clocks.* New York: Harcourt, Brace & World.
Karanikolas, Alexandros
  1979   "The Evolution of the Greek Language and its Present Form," pp. 78–85, in Alatis
           and Tucker, eds.
Katz, Jerrold and Jerry A. Fodor
  1964   "The Structure of a Semantic Theory," pp. 479–518, in Fodor and Katz, eds.
Kay, Paul
  1975   "Synchronic Variability and Diachronic Change in Basic Color Terms" *Language
           in Society* 4:257–270.
  1977   "Language Evolution and Speech Style," pp. 21–33, in Blount and Sanches, eds.
Kaye, Alan S.
  1975   "More on Diglossia in Arabic: Review Article," *Journal of Middle Eastern Studies*
           6:325–340.
Kelman, Herbert C.
  1971   "Language as an Aid and Barrier to Involvement in the National System," pp. 21–
           62, in Rubin and Jernudd, eds.
Kess, Joseph F.
  1976   *Psycholinguistics: Introductory Perspectives.* New York: Academic Press.
Key, Mary Ritchie
  1975a   *Male/Female Language.* Metuchen, N.J.: Scarecrow Press.
  1975b   *Paralanguage and Kinesics.* Metuchen, N.J.: Scarecrow Press.
Kiparsky, Paul
  1968   "Linguistic Universals and Linguistic Change," pp. 171–204, in Bach and Harms,
           eds.

Kjolseth, Rolf
  1972a   "The Development of the Sociology of Language and its Social Implications,"
           Sociolinguistics Newsletter 3, no. 1:7–10.
Kloss, Heinz
  1967   "Bilingualism and Nationalism," *Journal of Social Issues* 23, no. 2:39–47.
  1968   "Notes Concerning a Language—Nation Typology," pp. pp. 69–85, in Fishman,
           Ferguson and Das Gupta, eds.
  1971   "Language Rights of Immigrant Groups," *International Migration Review* 5:250–
           268.
  1977   *The American Bilingual Tradition.* Rowley, Mass.: Newbury House.
Kochman, Thomas
  1969   "Rapping in the Black Ghetto," *Trans-Action* 6, no. 4:26–34.
  1972   "Black American Speech Events and a Language Program for the Classroom,"
           pp. 211–261, in Cazden, John and Hymes, eds.
Kohn, Hans
  1944   *The Idea of Nationalism: A Study of its Origin and Background.* New York:
           Macmillan.
  1965   *Nationalism: Its Meaning and History.* Rev. ed. Princeton, N.J.: D. Van Nostrand.
Kolarz, Walter
  1946   *Myths and Realities in Eastern Europe.* London: Lindsay Drummond.
  1967   *Russia and Her Colonies.* Hamden, Conn.: Archon/Shoestring.
Labov, William
  1969   *The Study of Non-Standard English.* Champaign, Ill.: National Council of
           Teachers of English.
  1971a   "The Place of Linguistic Research in American Society," pp. 41–70, in Greenberg
           et al.
  1971b   "The Study of Language in its Social Context," vol. 1, pp. 152–216, in Fishman,
           ed.
  1972a   "Hypercorrection by the Lower Middle Class as a Factor in Linguistic Change," in
           Labov 1972g. (Reprinted from Bright, ed.)
  1972b   *Language in the Inner City: Studies in the Black English Vernacular.* Philadel-
           phia: University of Pennsylvania Press.
  1972c   "The Logic of Non-Standard English," pp. 179–215, in Giglioli, ed.
  1972d   "On the Mechanism of Linguistic Change," pp. 512–538, in Gumperz and
           Hymes, eds.
  1972e   "The Reflection of Social Processes in Structures," pp. 110–121, in Labov,
           1972g.
  1972f   "The Social Stratification of (r) in New York City Department Stores," pp. 43–69,
           in Labov, 1972g.
  1972g   *Sociolinguistic Patterns.* Philadelphia: University of Pennsylvania Press.
  1973   "The Linguistic Consequences of Being a Lame," *Language in Society* 2:81–116.
Labov, William and David Fanshel
  1977   *Therapeutic Discourse: Psychotherapy as Conversation.* New York: Academic
           Press.
Lakoff, Robin
  1972   "Language in Context," *Language* 48:907–927.
  1975   *Language and Woman's Place.* New York: Harper and Row.
Lambert, Wallace E. and G. Richard Tucker
  1972   *The Bilingual Education of Children: The St. Lambert Experiment.* Rowley,
           Mass.: Newbury House.
Lambton, Ann K. S.
  1953   *Persian Grammar.* Cambridge: Cambridge University Press.

Langendoen, D. Terence
  1968   *The London School of Linguistics: A Study of the Linguistic Theories of B. Malinowski and J. R. Firth.* Cambridge: MIT Press.
Lavern, John and Sandy Hutcheson, eds.
  1972   *Communication in Face-to-Face Interaction.* Baltimore: Penguin Books.
Leach, Edmund
  1954   *Political Systems of Highland Burma.* Cambridge: Harvard University Press.
Lee, Mary Hope
  1977   Review of Mueller 1973, *Language in Society* 6:94–95.
Leech, Geoffrey
  1974   *Semantics.* Harmondsworth: Penguin Books.
Lehmann, Winfred P., ed.
  1975   *Language and Linguistics in the People's Republic of China.* Austin: University of Texas Press.
Lehmann, Winfred P. and Yakov Malkiel, eds.
  1968   *Directions for Historical Linguistics: A Symposium.* Austin: University of Texas Press.
Lenin, V. I.
  1947   *The Right of Nations to Self-Determination.* Moscow: Progress Publishers.
Lenneberg, Eric H.
  1968   "A Biological Perspective of Language," pp. 32–47, in Oldfield and Marshall, eds.
Lenneberg, Eric H., ed.
  1964   *New Directions in the Study of Language.* Cambridge: MIT Press.
Le Page, Robert
  1964   *The National Language Question: Linguistic Problems of Newly Independent States.* London: Oxford University Press.
Leslie, Jacques
  1975   "Mayor's Death Hints New Spain Terror," *Los Angeles Times,* Nov. 25, 1975.
Lewis, Bernard
  1968   *The Emergence of Modern Turkey.* Second ed. London: Oxford University Press.
Lewis, E. Glyn
  1972a   "Migration and Language in the U.S.S.R." In Fishman, ed., (Reprinted from *International Migration Review,* 1971, 5:147–179.)
  1972b   *Multilingualism in the Soviet Union: Aspects of Language Policy and its Implementation.* The Hague: Mouton.
Lieberson, Stanley
  1966   "Language Questions in Censuses," pp. 262–279, in Lieberson, ed.
  1970   *Language and Ethnic Relations in Canada.* New York: John Wiley.
Lieberson, Stanley, ed.
  1966   "Explorations in Sociolinguistics," *Sociological Inquiry,* Spring, 1966, Vol. 36, no. 2.
Lieberson, Stanley and Timothy J. Curry
  1971   "Language Shift in the United States: Some Demographic Clues," *International Migration Review* 5:125–137.
Linder, Eugene
  1976   *Apes, Men and Language.* Harmondsworth: Penguin Books.
Lockwood, William G.
  1975   *European Moslems: Economy and Ethnicity in Western Bosnia.* New York: Academic Press.
Luckmann, Thomas
  1975   *The Sociology of Language.* Indianapolis: Bobbs-Merrill.
Lunt, Horace G.
  1959   "The Creation of Standard Macedonian: Some Facts and Attitudes," *Anthropological Linguistics* 1, No. 5:19–26.

Lyons, John
    1963   *Structural Semantics.* Oxford: Blackwell.
Lyons, John, ed.
    1970   *New Horizons in Linguistics.* Harmondsworth: Penguin Books.
Macías, Reynaldo F.
    1979   "Language Choice and Human Rights in the United States," pp. 86–101, in Alatis and Tucker, eds.
Mackay, Robert W.
    1973   "Conceptions of Children and Models of Socialization," pp. 22–43, in Dreitzel, ed. Also in Turner, ed.
Mackey, William F.
    1967   *Bilingualism as a World Problem.* Montreal: Harvest House.
    1968   "The Description of Bilingualism," pp. 554–584, in Fishman, ed.
    1972a   *Bilingual Education in a Binational School: A Study of Equal Language Maintenance in a Binational School.* Rowley, Mass.: Newbury House.
    1972b   "Concept Categories as Measures of Cultural Distance," pp. 134–168, in Ghosh, ed.
Macnamara, John
    1967a   "The Bilingual's Performance—A Psychological Overview," *Journal of Social Issues* 23, no. 2:58–78.
    1967b   "Introduction: Bilingualism in the Modern World," *Journal of Social Issues* 23, no. 2:1–7.
    1973   "Attitudes and Learning a Second Language," pp. 36–40, in Shuy and Fasold, eds.
Macnamara, John, ed.
    1967   "Problems of Bilingualism," *Journal of Social Issues* 23, no. 2.
Magner, Thomas
    1967   "Language and Nationlism in Yugoslavia," *Canadian Slavic Studies* 1:333–347.
Malinowski, Bronislaw
    1956   "The Problem of Meaning in Primitive Language," pp. 296–336, in Ogden and Richards.
Marckwardt, Albert H.
    1976   "The Professional Organization and the School Language Program," *International Journal of the Sociology of Language* 11:107–123. (Also in *Linguistics* 189:107–123.)
Markov, Boris
    1969   "Language Minority Problems in Macedonia," pp. 86–93, in Holmestad and Lade, eds.
Mathiot, Madeleine and Paul L. Garvin
    1975   "Functions of Language: A Sociocultural View," *Anthropological Quarterly* 48:148–156.
Maurer, David W.
    1939   "Prostitutes and Criminal Argot," *American Journal of Sociology* 44:546–550.
    1950   "The Argot of the Dice Gambler," *Annals of the American Academy of Political and Social Science* 269:114–133.
    1955   *Whiz Mob: A Correlation of the Technical Argot of Pickpockets with Their Behavior Patterns.* (Publications of the American Dialect Society, No. 24.) Gainesville, Fla.: American Dialect Society.
Mazrui, Ali A.
    1971   "Islam and the English Language in East and West Africa," pp. 179–197, in Whiteley, ed.

McClure, Erica
    1978   "Aspects of Code Switching in the Discourse of Bilingual Mexican American
            Children." Paper presented at the National Conference on Chicano and Latino
            Discourse Behavior, Educational Testing Service, Princeton, N.J., April 17–19,
            1978.
McNeill, David
    1970   The Acquisition of Language: The Study of Developmental Psycholinguistics.
            New York: Harper and Row.
    1971   "Are There Specifically Linguistic Universals?" pp. 530–535, in Steinberg and
            Jakobovitz, eds.
McQuown, Norman A.
    1964   "A Planned Auxiliary Language," pp. 555–563, in Hymes, ed.
McCrae, Kenneth D.
    1975   "The Principle of Territoriality and the Principle of Personality in Multilingual
            States," International Journal of the Sociology of Language 4:33–54.
Mead, George Herbert
    1934   Mind, Self and Society. Chicago: University of Chicago Press.
Meillet, Antoine
    1921   Linguistique historique et linguistique générale. Paris: Société Linguistique de
            Paris.
Metcalf, Allan A.
    1979   Chicano English. (Language in Education: Theory and Practice, 21). Arlington,
            Va.: Center for Applied Linguistics.
Miller, Wick and Susan Ervin
    1964   "The Development of Grammar in Child Language," pp. 9–34, in Bellugi and
            Brown, eds.
Mitchell-Kernan, Claudia
    1969   Language Behavior in a Black Urban Community. (Working paper no. 23.)
            Berkeley: Language Behavior Research Laboratory.
    1972   "Signifying and Marking: Two Afro-American Speech Acts," pp. 161–179, in
            Gumperz and Hymes, eds.
Mitford, Nancy, ed.
    1956   Noblesse Oblige. London: Hamish Hamilton.
Morris, Charles W.
    1935   "Foundations of the Theory of Signs," in International Encyclopedia of Unified
            Science, vol. 2, no. 2. Chicago: University of Chicago Press.
    1964   Signification and Significance: A Study of the Relations of Signs and Values.
            Cambridge, Mass.: MIT Press.
Moscovici, Serge, ed.
    1972   The Psychosociology of Language. Chicago: Markham Publishing Co.
Mueller, Claus
    1970   "Notes on the Repression of Communicative Behavior," pp. 101–113, in Dreitzel,
            ed.
    1973   The Politics of Communication: A Study in the Political Sociology of Language,
            Socialization, and Legitimation. New York: Oxford University Press.
Nader, Laura
    1968   "A Note on Attitudes and the Use of Language," pp. 276–281, in Fishman, ed.
Nahirny, Vladimir C. and Joshua A. Fishman
    1965   "American Immigrant Groups: Ethnic Identification and the Problem of Genera-
            tions," Sociological Review 13:311–336.
Nash, Jeffrey E. and James M. Calonico
    1974   "Sociological Perspectives in Bernstein's Sociolinguistics," Sociological Quar-
            terly 15:81–92.

Nida, Eugene A.
    1975   *Language Structure and Translation.* Stanford: Stanford University Press.
O'Brien, Richard J., ed.
    1971   *Developments of the Sixties—Viewpoints for the Seventies.* Washington, D.C.:
            Georgetown University Press.
Oftedal, Magne
    1969   "What are Minorities?" pp. 16–25, in Holmestad and Lade, eds.
Ogden, C. K. and I. A. Richards
    1956   *The Meaning of Meaning: A Study of the Influence of Language upon Thought
            and of the Science of Symbolism.* New York: Harcourt, Brace.
Ohannessian, Sirarpe, Charles A. Ferguson, and Edgar C. Polomé, eds.
    1975   *Language Surveys in Developing Nations. Papers and Reports on Sociolinguistic
            Activities.* Arlington, Va.: Center for Applied Linguistics.
Oksaar, Els
    1972   "Bilingualism," *Current Trends in Linguistics* 9:476–511.
Oldfield, R. C. and J. C. Marshall, eds.
    1968   *Language: Selected Readings.* Harmondsworth: Penguin Books.
Omar, Asmah Haji
    1975   · "Supranational Standardization of Spelling Systems: The Case of Malaysia and
            Indonesia," *International Journal of the Sociology of Language* 5:77–92.
Opie, Jona and Peter Opie
    1959   *The Lore and Language of School Children.* London: Oxford University Press.
Ornstein, Jacob
    1977   Review of Sánchez-Marco, *Language* 53:949–952.
Padilla, Raymond V., ed.
    1979   *Bilingual Education and Public Policy in the United States.* (Ethnoperspectives in
            Bilingual Education, Research Series, v. 1). Ypsilanti, Mich.: Dept. of Foreign
            Languages and Bilingual Studies, Eastern Michigan University.
Pandit, Prabodh B.
    1975   "Linguistics and Sociology," pp. 171–179, in Bartsch and Vennemann, eds.
Partridge, Monica
    1972   *Serbo-Croat Practical Grammar and Reader.* Beograd: Izdavački Zavod.
Paulston, Christina B.
    1971   "On the Moral Dilemma of the Sociolinguist," *Language Learning* 21:175–181.
Peñalosa, Fernando
    1980   *Chicano Sociolinguistics: A Brief Introduction.* Rowley, Mass.: Newbury House.
Petrounias, Evangelos
    1970   "Modern Greek Diglossia and its Sociocultural Implications," *Linguistic Com-
            munications, Monash University* 2:117–157.
    1978   "The Modern Greek Language and Diglossia," pp. 193–220, in Vryonis, ed.
Piaget, Jean
    1923   *Le langage et la pensée chez l'enfant.* Neuchâtel: Delachau & Niestlé. (Various
            English translations available.)
Pool, Jonathan
    1972   "National Development and Language Diversity," vol. 2, pp. 213–230, in
            Fishman, ed.
    1976   "Impressions of Sociolinguistics in the Soviet Union," *Sociolinguistics News-
            letter* 7, no. 1:1–5.
Poole, Millicent E.
    1975   Review of Bernstein, ed., *Language in Society* 4:73–84.
Premack, David
    1970   "The Education of S*A*R*A*H: A Chimp Learns the Language," *Psychology
            Today* 4:54–58.

Premack, David
    1976   *Intelligence in Ape and Man.* New York: Halsted Press.
Pride, John B.
    1970   "Sociolinguistics," pp. 287–301, in Lyons, ed.
    1973   Review of Gumperz and Hymes, eds., *Language in Society* 2:245–263.
Pride, John B. and Janet Holmes, eds.
    1972   *Sociolinguistics.* Harmondsworth: Penguin Books.
Reinecke, John E.
    1964   "Trade Jargons and Creole Dialects as Marginal Languages," pp. 534–546, in
           Hymes, ed.
Rice, F. A., ed.
    1966   *Study of the Role of Second Languages in Asia, Africa and Latin America.*
           Washington, D.C.: Center for Applied Linguistics.
Robertson, Duncan M.
    1910   *A History of the French Academy, 1635–1910.* New York: G.W. Dillingham Co.
Robinson, William P.
    1972   *Language and Social Behavior.* Harmondsworth: Penguin Books.
Robinson, William P. and S. J. Rackstraw
    1972   *A Question of Answers.* 2 vols. London: Routledge & Kegan Paul.
Roeper, Thomas
    1975   Review of Dittmar 1973, *Language in Society* 4:341–345.
Rosenthal, Robert and Lenore Jacobson
    1968   *Pygmalion in the Classroom.* New York: Holt, Rinehart and Winston.
Ross, Alan S. C.
    1962   "U and non-U: An Essay in Sociological Linguistics," pp. 91–106, in Black, ed.
           Also in Mitford, ed.
Rubin, Joan
    1968   "Bilingual Usage in Paraguay," pp. 512–530, in Fishman, ed.
    1973a   "Introduction," pp. i–ix, in Rubin and Shuy, eds.
    1973b   "Language Planning: Discussion of Some Current Issues," pp. 1–10, in Rubin and
           Shuy, eds.
Rubin, Joan and Björn H. Jernudd, eds.
    1971   *Can Language be Planned?* Honolulu: University Press of Hawaii.
Rubin, Joan and Roger Shuy, eds.
    1973   *Language Planning: Current Issues and Research.* Washington, D.C.: George-
           town University Press.
Ruesch, Jurgen and Weldon Kees
    1956   *Nonverbal Communication.* Berkeley, Calif.: University of California Press.
Rumbaugh, Duane M., ed.
    1977   *Language Learning by a Chimpanzee: The LANA Project.* New York: Academic
           Press.
Sacks, Harvey
    1972   "On the Analyzability of Stories by Children," pp. 325–345, in Gumperz and
           Hymes, eds.
Sadler, Victor and Ulrich Lins
    1972   "Regardless of Frontiers: A Case Study in Linguistic Persecution," pp. 206–215,
           in Ghosh, ed.
Sadock, Jerrold M.
    1975   *Toward a Linguistic Theory of Speech Acts.* New York: Academic Press.
Samarin, William J.
    1968   "Lingua Francas of the World," pp. 660–672, in Fishman, ed.
    1971   "Salient and Substantive Pidginization," pp. 117–140, in Hymes, ed.
Sanches, Mary and Ben G. Blount, eds.
    1975   *Sociocultural Dimensions of Language Use.* New York: Academic Press.

Sankoff, Gillian
  1972   "Language Use In Multilingual Societies: Some Alternative Approaches," pp. 33–51, in Pride and Holmes, eds.
Sapir, Edward
  1912   "Language and Environment," *American Anthropologist* 44:226–242. Also in his *Selected Writings.*
  1915   "Abnormal Types of Speech in Nootka," Canada Dept. of Mines, Geological Survey, Memoirs: Anthropological Series No. 5. Also in his *Selected Writings.*
  1921   *Language.* New York: Harcourt Brace.
  1929   "Status of Linguistics as a Social Science," *Language* 5:207–214.
  1931a   "Communication," *Encyclopedia of the Social Sciences* 4:78–81. New York: Macmillan.
  1931b   "The Functions of an International Auxiliary Language," *Psyche* 11:4–15. Also in his *Selected Writings.*
  1951   *Selected Writings,* ed. D. G. Mandelbaum. Berkeley: University of California Press.
  1964   "Conceptual Categories in Primitive Languages," p. 128, in Hymes, ed. (Reprinted from *Science* 74:578.)
Sargent, Alice G.
  1977   *Beyond Sex Roles.* St. Paul: West Publishing Co.
Saussure, Ferdinand de
  1962   Cours de linguistique générale. Paris: Payot.
Sawyer, Janet
  1977   "The Implications of Passive and Covert Bilingualism for Bilingual Education," pp. 57–67, in Hoffer and Dubois, eds.
Schegloff, Emanuel
  1972a   "Notes on a Conversational Practice: Formulating Place," in Sudnow, ed., 1971, excerpts reprinted in Giglioli, ed.
  1972b   "Sequencing in Conversational Openings," pp. 346–380, in Gumperz and Hymes, eds.
Schegloff, Emanuel and Harvey Sacks
  1973   "Opening up Closings," *Semiotica* 8:289–327. Also in Turner, ed.
Schlauch, Margaret
  1956   *The Gift of Tongues.* New York: Dover.
Schlesinger, Hilde S.
  1978   "The Acquisition of Bimodal Language," pp. 57–93, in Schlesinger and Namir, eds.
Schlesinger, I. M. and Lila Namir, eds.
  1978   *Sign Language of the Deaf: Psychological, Linguistic and Sociological Perspectives.* New York: Academic Press.
Scotton, Carol Myers and William Ury
  1977   "Bilingual Strategies: The Social Functions of Code Switching," *International Journal of the Sociology of Language* 13:5–20.
Searle, John R.
  1969   *Speech Acts: An Essay in the Philosophy of Language.* New York: Cambridge University Press.
  1972   "What is a Speech Act?" pp. 136–156, in Giglioli, ed.
  1976   "A Classification of Illocutionary Acts," *Language in Society* 5:1–23.
Sebeok, Thomas A., ed.
  1960   *Style in Language.* Cambridge: MIT Press.
Serdyuchenko, G. P.
  1962   "The Eradication of Illiteracy and the Creation of New Written Languages in the U.S.S.R.," *International Journal of Adult and Youth Education* 14:23–29.

Sherzer, Joel
    1973   Review of Fillmore and Langendoen, eds. and O'Brien, ed., *Language in Society* 2:269–289.
Shuy, Roger W., ed.
    1971   *Sociolinguistics, a Crossdisciplinary Perspective*. Washington, D.C.: Center for Applied Linguistics.
    1973   *Sociolinguistics: Current Trends and Prospects*. Washington, D.C.: Georgetown University Press.
Shuy, Roger W. and Ralph Fasold
    1971   "Contemporary Emphases in Sociolinguistics," pp. 185–198, in O'Brien, ed. Also in Smith and Shuy, eds.
Shuy, Roger W., and Ralph Fasold, eds.
    1973   *Language Attitudes: Current Trends and Prospects*. Washington, D.C.: Georgetown University Press.
Sibayan, Bonifacio
    1974   "Language Policy: Language Engineering and Literacy in the Philippines," *Current Trends in Linguistics* 8:1038–1062.
Sjoberg, Andrée F.
    1964   "Writing, Speech and Society: Some Changing Interrelationships," pp. 892–898, in *Proceedings of the Ninth International Congress of Linguists*. The Hague: Mouton.
    1966   "Sociocultural and Linguistic Factors in the Development of Writing Systems for Preliterate Peoples," pp. 260–276, in Bright, ed.
Slama-Cazacu, Tatiana
    1972   "The Study of Child Language in Europe," in *Current Trends in Linguistics* 9:512–590.
Sledd, James
    1969   "Bi-Dialectalism: The Linguistics of White Supremacy," *English Journal* 58: 1307–1329.
    1972   "Doublespeak: Dialectology in the Service of Big Brother," *College English* 33:439–456.
Slobin, Dan I.
    1967   *Manual for the Cross-Cultural Study of Communicative Competence.*
    1971   *Psycholinguistics.* Glenview, Ill.: Scott, Foresman, and Co.
Smith, David M.
    1972   "Some Implications for the Social Status of Pidgin Langauges," pp. 47–56, in Smith and Shuy, eds.
    1973a   "Creolization and Language Ontogeny: A Preliminary Paradigm for Comparing Language Socialization and Language Acculturation," pp. 287–296, in Bailey and Shuy, eds.
    1973b   "Language, Speech and Ideology: A Conceptual Framework," pp. 92–112, in Shuy and Fasold, eds.
Smith, David M. and Roger W. Shuy, eds.
    1972   *Sociolinguistics in Cross-Cultural Analysis*. Washington, D.C.: Georgetown University Press.
Smith, Riley B. and Donald M. Lance
    1979   "Standard and Disparate Varieties of English in the United States: Educational and Sociopolitical Implications," *International Journal of the Sociology of Language* 21:127–140.
Spalatin, Christopher
    1970   "The Croatian Language," pp. 157–174, in Eterovich and Spalatin, eds.
Speier, Matthew
    1969   "Some Conversational Problems for Interactional Analysis," pp. 397–427, in Sudnow, ed.

1971   "The Everyday World of the Child," pp. 188–217, in Douglas, ed.
Spolsky, Bernard
1974   "Linguistics and the Language Barrier to Education," *Current Trends in Linguistics* 12:2027–2038.
Spradley, James P.
1972   *Culture and Cognition: Rules, Maps, and Plans.* San Francisco: Chandler Pub. Co.
Stam, James H.
1976   *Inquiries into the Origin of Language: The Fate of a Question.* New York: Harper & Row.
Steinberg, Danny D. and Leon A. Jakobovits, eds.
1971   *Semantics: An Interdisciplinary Reader in Philosophy, Linguistics and Psychology.* Cambridge: University Press.
Stewart, William A.
1968   "A Sociolinguistic Typology for Describing National Multilingualism," pp. 531–545, in Fishman, ed.
1969a   "On the Use of Negro Dialect in the Teaching of Reading," pp. 156–219, in Baratz and Shuy, eds.
1969b   "Sociopolitical Issues in the Linguistic Treatment of Negro Dialect," pp. 215–224, in Alatis, ed.
Stockwell, Robert P. and Ronald K. S. Macauley, eds.
1972   *Linguistic Change and Generative Theory.* Bloomington: Indiana University Press.
Stokoe, William C., Jr.
1972   *Semiotics and Human Sign Language.* The Hague: Mouton.
Stoller, Paul
1976   "The Language Planning Activities of the U.S. Office of Bilingual Education," *International Journal of the Sociology of Language* 11:45–60. (Also in *Linguistics* 189:45–60.)
Sturtevant, Edgar H.
1947   *An Introduction to Linguistic Science.* New Haven: Yale University Press.
Sudnow, David, ed.
1969   *Studies in Social Interaction.* New York: Free Press.
Swadesh, Morris
1972   *The Origin and Diversification of Language.* Chicago: Aldine.
Tervoort, Bernard T.
1978   "Bilingual Interference," pp. 169–240, in Schlesinger and Namir, eds.
Teschner, Richard V., Garland D. Bills, and Jerry R. Craddock, eds.
1975   *Spanish and English of United States Hispanos: A Critical, Annotated Linguistic Bibliography.* Arlington, Va.: Center for Applied Linguistics.
Thomas, William J.
1973   *Black Language in America.* Wichita: Wichita State University.
Traugott, Elizabeth C.
1975   Review of Labov 1972g, *Language in Society* 4:89–107.
Trager, George L.
1974   "Writing and Writing Systems," *Current Trends in Linguistics* 12:373–496.
Trudgill, Peter
1974a   *The Social Differentiation of English in Norwich.* London: Cambridge University Press.
1974b   *Sociolinguistics: An Introduction.* Baltimore: Penguin Books.
Turner, Jonathan
1974   *The Structure of Sociological Theory.* Homewood, Ill.: Dorsey Press.
Turner, Lorenzo D.
1949   *Africanisms in the Gullah Dialect.* Chicago: University of Chicago Press.

Turner, Roy
    1970   "Words, Utterances and Activities," pp. 165–175, in Douglas, ed. Also in Turner, ed.

Turner, Roy, ed.
    1974   *Ethnomethodology.* Harmondsworth: Penguin Books.

Ullman, Stephen
    1966   "Semantic Universals," pp. 217–262, in Greenberg, ed.

UNESCO
    1953   *Use of Vernacular Languages in Education.* Paris.

Valdés-Fallis, Guadalupe
    1978   "Code-Switching as a Deliberate Verbal Strategy: A Microanalysis of Direct and Indirect Requests among Bilingual Chicano Speakers." Paper presented at the National Conference on Chicano and Latino Discourse Behavior, Educational Testing Service, Princeton, N.J., April 17–19, 1978.

Van Den Broeck, Jef
    1977   "Class Differences in Syntactic Complexity in the Flemish Town of Maaseik," *Language in Society* 6:149–181.

Verdoodt, Albert
    1972   "The Differential Impact of Immigrant French Speakers on Indigenous German Speakers: A Case Study in the Light of Two Theories," vol. 2, pp. 377–385, in Fishman, ed. (Reprinted from *International Migration Review* 1971, 5:138–146.)

Vryonis, Speros, ed.
    1978   *The Past in Medieval and Modern Greek Culture.* (*Byzantina kai Metabyzantina,* vol. 1). Malibu, California: Undena Publications.

Vygotsky, Lev S.
    1962   *Thought and Language.* Ed. and tr. by E. Hanfmann and G. Vakar. Cambridge: MIT Press.

Wallerstein, Immanuel
    1974   *The Modern World System: Capitalist Agriculture and the Origins of the European World-Economy in the Sixteenth Century.* New York: Academic Press.
    1979   *The Capitalist World Economy.* Cambridge: Cambridge University Press.

Walum, Laurel Richardson
    1977   *The Dynamics of Sex and Gender: A Sociological Perspective.* Chicago: Rand McNally.

Waterhouse, Viola
    1949   "Learning a Second Language First," *International Journal of American Linguistics* 15:106–109.

Weil, Shalva
    1977   "Verbal Interaction Among the Bene Israel," *International Journal of the Sociology of Language* 13:71–85. (Also in *Linguistics* 193:71–85.)

Weinreich, Uriel
    1953a   *Languages in Contact: Findings and Problems.* New York: Linguistic Circle of New York. Reprinted by Mouton, The Hague, 1970.
    1953b   "The Russification of Soviet Minority Languages," *Problems of Communism* 2, no. 6:46–57.

Weinreich, Uriel, William Labov, and Marvin Herzog
    1968   "Empirical Foundations for a Theory of Languge Change," pp. 95–188, in Lehmann and Malkiel, eds.

Weir, Ruth
    1962   *Language in the Crib.* The Hague: Mouton.

Werner, Oswald *et al.*
    1974   "Some New Developments in Ethnosemantics," *Current Trends in Linguistics* 12:1477–1543.

West, Candace and Don H. Zimmerman
  1975   "Woman's Place in Conversation: Reflections on Adult-Child-Interaction." Paper presented to annual meeting of American Sociological Association.
Wheeler, Geoffrey
  1966   *The Peoples of Soviet Central Asia.* London: The Bodley Head.
Whitely, W. H.
  1971   "Introduction," pp. 1–23, in Whitely, ed.
Whitely, W. H., ed.
  1971   *Language Use and Social Change: Problems of Multilingualism with Special Reference to Eastern Africa.* London: Oxford University Press.
Whorf, Benjamin Lee
  1956   *Language, Thought and Reality: Selected Writings,* ed. J. B. Carroll. Cambridge, Mass.: MIT Press.
Williams, Frederick, ed.
  1970   *Language and Poverty: Perspectives on a Theme.* Chicago: Markham Publishing Co.
Wolfram, Walt
  1971   "Social Dialects from a Linguistic Perspective," pp. 86–135, in Shuy, ed.
  1972   "Overlapping Influence and Linguistic Assimilation in Second-Generation Puerto Rican English," pp. 15–46, in Smith and Shuy, eds.
  1973   "Objective and Subjective Parameters of Language Assimilation among Second Generation Puerto Ricans in East Harlem," pp. 148–173, in Shuy and Fasold, eds.
  1974a   *Sociolinguistic Aspects of Assimilation: Puerto Rican English in New York City.* Arlington, Va.: Center for Applied Linguistics.
  1974b   "The Relationship of White Southern Speech to Vernacular Black English," *Language* 50:498–527.
  1979   "Landmark Decision Affects Black English Speakers," *Linguistic Reporter* 22, no. 1:1, 5–6.
Wolfram, Walt and Ralph W. Fasold
  1974   *The Study of Social Dialects in American English.* Englewood Cliffs, N.J.: Prentice-Hall.
Wootton, Anthony J.
  1974   "Talk in the Homes of Young Children," *Sociology* 8:277–295.
  1975   *Dilemmas of Discourse: Controversies about the Sociological Interpretation of Language.* London: George Allen & Unwin.
Wright, Richard
  1975   Review of Burling 1973, and Labov 1972b, *Language in Society* 4:185–198.
Wurm, Stefan
  1960   "Preface" to Baskakov.
Zwicky, Arnold
  1971   "On Reported Speech," pp. 73–78, in Fillmore and Langendoen, eds.

Index

K

Kalmyk, 187
Karadžić, Vuk, 196
Karamanlis, Constantine, 188
Karanikolas, Alexandros, 188
Katharevousa, 115–116, 188
Kay, Paul, 55, 137
Kazakh, 186
Kees, Weldon, 18
Kelman, Herbert C., 200
Kent State University, 58
Kenya, 77, 84, 166
Kess, Joseph F., 15
Key, Mary Ritchie, 18, 71, 125, 127
Kikongo, 83
Kindergarten children, see Children,
    kindergarten
Kinesics, 18–19
Kinship terms, 56, 124
Kirghiz, 186
Kituba, 100
Kloss, Heinz, 167, 183, 184, 185
Koasati, 126
Kochman, Thomas, 139, 149
Kohn, Hans, 165, 167, 185
Koine, 86, 89, 100
Kolarz, Walter, 164, 166, 167
Koneski, Blaže, 196
Korais, Adamantios, 196
Koran, 115, 121, 192
Korean, 132
Krio, 87
Kurdish, 146
Kurds, 144, 177

L

Labov, William, 3, 8, 19, 22, 31, 32, 34,
    49, 58, 76, 97, 119, 120, 126, 136,
    142, 146, 153–154, 161, 190
La Guardia, Fiorello, 18
Lakoff, George, 24, 78
Lakoff, Robin, 70, 126–128, 130, 131
Lambert, Wallace E., 114, 120
Lambton, A. K. S., 132
Lames, 153, 156
Lana project, 15
Lance, Donald M., 160
Language, 12
    academies, 88, 190; acquisition, 31,
    40, 44–50, 113, 115; and age, 124–
    125; American Sign, see American
    Sign Language; attitudes, 33, 41,
    65, 119–122, 151, 153, 157–158,
161, 162, 196, 198; body, see Body
language; of children, see Children,
language; choice, 67; and cognition,
52–55; conflict, 199–200; "correct,"
21, 124, 192; and culture, 5, 26–27,
40, 53–55; death, 178; development,
181, 182; functions of, 37–38, 48,
83, 87, 160; of instruction, 190–191;
learning, second, 46, 113–115; loyalty, 173; maintenance, 156, 172,
173–178, 187; mixture, 156–158,
172; models of, 12–20; and occupations, 39, 98–99; origin of, 16–17;
phylogeny, 25–26; planning, 106,
194–199; policy, 175, 180–200;
"primitive," 26, 31–32; productivity
of, 16; and race, 26; repertoire, see
Linguistic repertoire; rights, 183–
184, 199; sexist, 14, 125–131; shift,
172, 173–178; study of, 21–22; suicide, 177; traditional transmission
of, 16; treatment, 194; typology, 26–
27; universals, see Universals, language; varieties, 33, 81–108
Languages
    African, 105; agglutinative, 26; arti-
ficial, 85; auxiliary, 100, 106; Baltic,
see Baltic languages; classical, 85,
189; contact, 100; diversification of,
180; ethnic, 83; European, 34, 53,
88, 100, 104, 132, 134, 182; flexional, 26; Germanic, see Germanic
languages; Indo-European, see Indo-
European languages; international,
83, 100; isolating, 26; national, 83,
88; nonstandard, 40, 189; official, 88,
112; regional, 83; secret, 49–50;
Semitic, see Semitic languages;
standard, 40, 84, 85, 87–91, 160–
161, 182, 195; teaching of, 192;
trade, 100; uniformation of, 180; vernacular, 28, 84, 85, 100, 189, 192;
written, 88
Langue and parole, 19–20
Latin, 25, 167
    alphabet, see Alphabet, Roman; as
classical language, 86, 116; as flexional language, 26; gender, 129;
grammar, 20; in Hungary, 185; as lingua franca, 100; medieval, 83, 118,
158; pig, see Pig Latin; study of, 192;
use of, 39, 83, 89, 96
Latin America, 2, 19, 84